10 0623710 6

WITHDRAWN

UNIVERSITY OF NOTTINGHAM

GEORGE GREEN LIBRARY OF
SCIENCE AND ENGINEERING

D1437368

CONTINUUM

Home Office building, London.
The coloured canopy sculpture
throws light across the building
and the street, which the locals
now call 'Rainbow Street'.

CONTINUUM

FARRELLS WORK OF THE
HONG KONG & LONDON OFFICES 2001–2011

University of Nottingham

UNIVERSITY OF NOTTINGHAM
GEORGE GREEN LIBRARY OF
SCIENCE AND ENGINEERING
WITHDRAWN
FROM THE LIBRARY

FROM THE CHAIR TO THE FAR HORIZON, FROM REGIONAL PLANNING TO DETAIL DESIGN

Published in 2012 by
Laurence King Publishing Ltd
361–363 City Road, London,
EC1V 1LR, United Kingdom
T +44 (0)20 7841 6900
F + 44 (0)20 7841 6910
enquiries@laurenceking.com
www.laurenceking.com

Text © 2012 Farrells
Terry Farrell and Partners have asserted their right under the Copyright,
Designs and Patents Act 1988 to be identified as the author of this work.

This book was produced by Laurence King Publishing Ltd, London

All rights reserved. No part of this publication may be reproduced
or transmitted in any form or by any means, electronic or mechanical,
including photocopying, recording or any information storage or
retrieval system, without permission from the publisher.

A catalogue record for this book is available from the British Library

ISBN: 978-1-85669-844-3

Design by Farrells

Printed in China

This page: The Deep, Hull.
Overlooking the Humber Estuary.

CONTENTS

THANKS

This book took two years to make: eighteen months to 'gestate' and then six months to bring it all together. Throughout this time, Terry Farrell was leading and driving the project and Emma Davies was coordinating and organising it. This is the fourth publication that Emma has done for us in eight years, and she has always been a model of efficiency, effectiveness and responsibility.

The project has involved many people in both Farrells offices, although Rebecca Holmes deserves particular mention for design coordination. All the partners – Gavin Erasmus, Stefan Krummeck and John Campbell in Hong Kong and Mike Stowell and John Letherland in London – have played their parts in leading the project. The contributions of the Hong Kong office were led, coordinated and written by Jo Farrell. Like Emma in London, Jo immersed herself enormously in this book; she was helped by Becky Lee and, of course, by Eugene Dreyer, who wrote the introductory essay 'Two Cultures: Two Cities'.

In the London office, Nigel Bidwell and Magnus Menzefricke-Koitz worked on the middle stages of the book, collecting projects and information, as well as taking the first steps in design coordination. Daniel Woolfson worked on the maps that appear at the beginning of each chapter and on the cover design. Emma also had help from Victoria Small and Susanne O'Donovan.

Externally, Chris Spurr did the initial design work on templates and layouts, but Vanessa Green at The Urban Ant pitched in most enthusiastically and professionally to help us over the line. The proofreading was by Dominique Shead.

Once again, our publishers, Laurence King, were very supportive and constructive, and special thanks are due to Philip Cooper for steering us through and making the book possible.

Of course, the real credit is due to the creative work that the book illustrates, and to the architects and planners, staff and collaborators, as well as the many clients, consultants and specialists that make these projects possible. Very many thanks indeed to all of them.

Opposite: KK100 tower in Shenzhen, recently completed, is the tallest building ever built by a British architect.

FOREWORD

This book broadly follows the format of the book we published 10 years ago in 2001, entitled *10 Years 10 Cities*. This also covers 10 years, 2001–2011, and in its character it continues our cultural lineage of an architecture that is founded on a broad picture view of urban planning and place-making. It is if anything more rooted and a more developed part of our DNA, and so the essential narrative of the book is based on explaining and illustrating this linkage as well, of course, as showing the work we have done on specific projects.

But there are differences: there has been an evolution in scale of projects to larger buildings and masterplanning from mega railway stations and super-high-rise towers to city-scale and even regional-scale masterplanning. This has given the book its title, *Continuum*, which, as the Introduction explains, expresses all the linkages of work range, specialisation range, geographic reach and the extension of collaborative working to much wider groups of architects, planners, artists, developers, and so on.

Also the arrangement of the contents can no longer fit into just 10 cities; indeed there are 21 cities and regions covered herein. There are three groupings of cities/regions, reflecting that, whereas 10 years ago the practice was led and centred on London and Hong Kong was a subsidiary office, now these two centres are each led by partners – whilst under the overall creative leadership of Terry Farrell to ensure cultural continuity and consistency – and have considerable independence of structure, scope and action.

So the first section is China where the lead is almost solely from Hong Kong, and the second section is the UK where in a similar way it is almost solely led from London. Then there is a section that was quite embryonic 10 years ago – that of the 'wider world', which has expanded considerably and where both London and Hong Kong share leadership on much of the work.

This expansion of geographic range and size and scope of project has been achieved whilst maintaining moderate staff sizes that are similar

in numbers to 10 years ago. And so we have maintained a dedication to 'hands-on' close working of partners and staff with clients and projects that places us, as before, somewhere between the studio and the more corporate practice – a combination that ensures, we believe, maximum creativity combined with the highest levels of craftsmanship and assured reliability in delivery.

Top: The dynamic new station platforms with sweeping roofs at Beijing South Station, inspired by the Temple of Heaven.

Above (circled) and Opposite: Rooftop aerofoil, Incheon International Airport.

INTRODUCTION

THE ARCHITECT / PLANNER AND THE CONTINUUM PHENOMENON

BY SIR TERRY FARRELL

The architect planner today is uniquely placed to make a significant creative contribution. As the ever-increasing world population becomes concentrated in urban areas – including the new cities of the emerging and newly industrialising countries – then the skills that the architect planner brings will be of enormous importance over the coming decades.

At the same time as specialisation is deepening and intensifying due to technology and human inventiveness, so too is the need for connectivity and for collaboration. Broad visionary disciplines will be brought together in the form of architect planners – hybrid creatives who will be required to crossover fields – and that very linkage, the very hybridity, will be a phenomenon that will be pivotal in making our world joined up, making the specialisations connect and work together.

The tensions behind this continuum have been very well expressed by my friend and client, the Darwinian biologist Matt Ridley (Chair, Centre for Life project, Newcastle): 'The essence of virtue is cooperation: pro-social rather than anti-social behaviour … growth comes about through people working for each other … millions of people you will never meet contributed to making for us each of the objects you use in your everyday life. Far from being a selfish creed, growth spreads collaboration.' And Ridley sets against this the other end of the continuum – specialisation will naturally deepen the more we polish our skills in cooperation: 'Self-sufficiency is poverty; prosperity is mutual exchange and specialisation, the more you specialise in doing one thing for strangers and they each specialise in doing one thing for you the better your productivity and the greater your standard of living.'

The architect planner is positioned to find ways of linking skills and knowhow in the key sector of the environmental challenges of the 21st century.

Seamlessness is the key to work in this field being meaningful but, in pursuit of this, size in itself is certainly not the only answer, a subject which we touch upon in the other introductory essay to this book.

It is not just the continuum between the generalist and the specialist, i.e. the process continuum, with which it is critical for architects and planners to concern themselves: there are several other continuums, including one of physical scale. 'Glocal' – meaning global to local (and presumably back again) – is a continuum of scale of place, a scale upon the physical surface of our world expressed in our geography, our societies and the human relationship with the natural environment. It's a continuum that goes all the way from house to hamlet, village to town, city to region and on to nations and continents and oceans, and, of course, like all continuums it flows just as well in reverse.

Above left: The self-ordering collective of a woodland, 2009. Edge trees grow lopsidedly and mid-woodland trees grow tall reaching for the light, but have spindly lower branches. A rich flora exists below, varying according to the position in the woodland. This is horticulture close to urbiculture.

Above right: Trees in their isolated state on grassland, 2009. How signature architects and their clients prefer to see their work and the city: stand-alone, but with no connectedness or rich undergrowth. There is a parallel in urban culture: separate grand architectural statements alone do not make for rich urbanism.

Opposite: The gentle curve of Peninsula Central building is rooted in the streetplan and follows the curve of the crescent of Greenwich itself.

I wrote about the connectedness of the physical environment in my recent book, *Shaping London*: 'But collectively each tree has adjusted its pure designed geometry of individual elements to its position in a higher layered ordering – edge trees grow lopsidedly, sideways; mid-woodland trees have to grow taller to get to the light and have magnificent crowns but spindlier under branches in the shadow below. Under the trees live plants and life generally in great variety within the woodland shelter, each different in growth and species according to where naturally yet opportunistically it sat within the larger plan. The whole thing is an entity. A "woodland" just like any village, town or city is in its own way an interactive, collective element' (see page 10).

I'm very mindful of the wonderful concluding parts of Darwin's *On the Origin of Species* where he wrote so eloquently about 'the tangled bank': 'It is interesting to contemplate a tangled bank, clothed with many plants of many kinds, with birds singing on the bushes, with various insects flitting about, and with worms crawling through the damp earth, and to reflect that these elaborately constructed forms, so different from each other, and dependent upon each other in so complex a manner, have all been produced by laws acting around us.' Our environment's interdependency is so well captured in Darwinian theory: everything relies and is connected to everything else, and yet each activity succeeds by its very increasing specialisation and diversity. The architect planner must see their role as not just being someone who sharpens specialist skills, but who brings a particular vision to the 'tangled bank' that is made up of our manmade urban environments.

For the last 50 years the roles of design and its alter ego, planning, have been fighting in opposition over territory that has desperately needed them to see themselves as linked – critically joined like twins. Our global environmental concerns are becoming increasingly clear. Energy conservation and production, pollution control, carbon emissions and global warming mean that the endeavours of the sole actor will be doomed to failure. One brilliant eco-house will not change anything if the rest of the world is hell-bent on going in the opposite direction. However, even though the designs of individual gadgets that make the electric car viable or the house more eco-friendly are each an intensely specialised endeavour, when repeated on a large scale they will collectively make the world work for the 21st-century human urban population.

Continuum and connectivity in the city

Farrells have been based for over 20 years in Hong Kong, China, and London, Europe, with each place offering us the opportunity to explore and react to the continuum. Our practice began in Greenwich with a ventilation building for the Blackwall Tunnel in 1963 (see page 16) and where recently we have created masterplan for the Greenwich Peninsula and designed the office building for London's transportation organisation, Transport for London. If you sit at a desk in that building, you are aware of the very gentle curve of the façade that follows the street pattern of the masterplan – it adds enormously to the quality of the workspace. It takes one away from the rectilinearity of so much modern space and yet the curve is not arbitrary: it is rooted in the streetplan and the curve of the crescent of Greenwich itself – a key to the masterplan (see page 19), because the crescent connects east to west across a narrow peninsula and arrives at each end at a right angle to the riverbank. The riverbank and the shape of the river here at this narrow peninsula are produced by the Thames and its estuary, so the workspace and the river are connected through the streetplan and masterplan.

The Thames is one of the great rivers of history – and on this stretch of the river from the Greenwich Naval Hospital to the Woolwich Arsenal to Chatham Docks an outward adventure began that was based upon exploration and led to the English language being given to the world. The adventure was also based on navigation: this was where the Greenwich Meridian Line – the zero from which all longitudes are measured – was set, running right through the Observatory and the Palace where Isaac Newton, the great scientist, contributed to our understanding of the globe, the stars, gravity and how to navigate the seas. Below this is the Naval Hospital, Britain's very own architectural ensemble to match Versailles in France or the Imperial City in Beijing. Here, Wren, Hawksmoor and Inigo Jones, three of our greatest architects, contributed to designing and building this monument which became the Royal Naval College. It is also where the explorers and navigators like Captain James Cook took their directions and set forth, along with the botanists and the explorers of

nature itself, whose findings helped Darwin and his contemporaries unlock so much of our understanding of life today. This link to nature has been a particular endeavour of our practice, borne out by our masterplans of Greenwich Peninsula and the Thames Estuary.

Understanding the continuum and having a big picture to connect everything up lies at the heart of the work of the architect planner and our whole practice both in the UK and China. Our masterplan in Greenwich is to some extent mirrored by our project in Shanghai – Chongming Island (see page 16) – where there are similar but different issues of environmental planning and where great regional thinking has been taking place. And, of course, there is the great connection of the Olympics in our work in East London and Beijing. In our Greenwich masterplan we helped to strategise the re-use of the Dome for sporting events, which will play a key role in London's Olympics, while in Beijing we were able to strategise a major new building at Beijing South Station (see page 8) in time for the 2008 games. This project initiated China's first high-speed rail line, and linked Beijing to Tianjin where Olympic events were held. The Olympics and the Beijing masterplan relate to China's new era of connectivity to the world, fostered through television, film and the internet – the immediacy of mass communication. The Olympics were a visual and design triumph, with stunning opening and closing events projected around the world.

The Beijing project takes all its cues from the city's great geometry, where there is a continuum of order from its heart to its extremities – from the Imperial Palace to gatehouses to ring roads, radiating like ripples from the very centre.

Beijing South Station is part of our practice's continuous work in transportation, particularly railways and railway lines. At the other end of China, down in the south on the Pearl River Delta, we have designed a station at Guangzhou (see page 15). These two stations are amongst the largest stations in the world. They are part of the revolution in China's rail which has made it, over the course of less than two decades, the world leader in high-speed rail, with more high-speed lines than all of the rest of the world put together.

Opposite: Natural history exhibition area, The Great North Museum, Newcastle.

There has been an extraordinary continuity between the British and Chinese in railway design. China is now emerging as the world leader and yet its first steps relied upon architects and engineers from Britain. The railway phenomenon is one that is very close to my heart, as I grew up in Newcastle where a century earlier George Stephenson had been experimenting with the detailed design of railway lines and sleepers, paving the way for the first passenger-carrying steam locomotives. I have seen the remnants of Stephenson's work at Killingsworth, near where I once lived. In the centre of Newcastle he built the railway engines themselves and developed the system of lines, sleepers and locomotion that in its main principles has hardly changed. My parents grew up in Manchester, where the very first railway station in the world was built in Liverpool Road, Manchester.

The first buildings that I ever designed, the ventilation shafts for the Blackwall Tunnel (see page 16) in Greenwich, are now historically listed. For over 40 years we have been involved in connectivity through transport, not only helping to masterplan the areas around Beijing South Station but also masterplanning the re-use of the Docks in London and, today, looking at cable car links across the Thames. Just as the first UK project was for transportation, so was our first project in China. It was Hong Kong's Peak tram (see page 16) and its visitor centre at the top that gave the incentive to begin our practice there. Our own office has its home in the office building on top of the Lower Peak Tram terminus.

Time continuums and conservation

We have seen several continuums between London and Hong Kong – spatial and place continuities, but also time continuums. It has been a considerable part of the work of this practice, and indeed any architect planner's work, to acknowledge that all our human settlements are based on an accumulated series of endeavours – the work of many hands over decades, centuries and often millennia beforehand. The shape and form of our places, as expressed in towns and cities, is a key

Above: Embankment Place, an office building using the air rights over Charing Cross Station, 1990.

Opposite: Guangzhou South Railway Station – approximately three times the size of London's Kings Cross and the largest single station in Asia.

Below: View of central
Hong Kong with Farrells
Peak Tower above.

Bottom left: Blackwall Tunnel
ventilation buildings, 1963.

Bottom right: Farrells
masterplan for Chong Ming
eco-island, Shanghai.

Opposite: The leafy suburb
of Petersham provided the

inspiration for the three
courtyard houses integrated
in their landscape.

component of our collective human culture. The
time continuum deserves enormous respect. The
Bauhaus revolution and early Modernism were part
of an era that tried to remake the world as though
history did not exist. The lesson of the second half
of the 20th century has been the realisation of just
how deep is our indebtedness to the past and that
to design afresh with no sense of the past is at
best a vacuous experiment and at worst a radically
destructive activity.

The continuity of past and present creates
the future. We need to study the continuum as
part of the design process: What made our towns
and cities? What psychology shaped our buildings,
our parliaments, opera houses, shops, and the very
idea of house and home? Learnt human experience
is ingrained in the world around us.

Just as the railways and indeed all human
engineering have progressed, building on the
shoulders of giants, so our urban environment
inevitably does the same. Work in this book includes
our conservation projects, from small ones such as
museums, restored houses and listed buildings –
putting back the best of our past and understanding
it to build on for the future – to our large-scale
masterplans, whether in the UK or indeed around
the world.

So much of our urban design, masterplanning
and regional planning work shown in this book are
the foundation for our architectural work, which
also looks to build a future based upon the past.
The Charing Cross railway and masterplan, the
TVam regeneration project, Comyn Ching in Covent
Garden, the Quayside in Newcastle and Brindley
Place in Birmingham have all built upon canals,
docks, street patterns and historic buildings, and
extrapolated from them their present identity.

As it is said, who that ignore history are
condemned to repeat it.

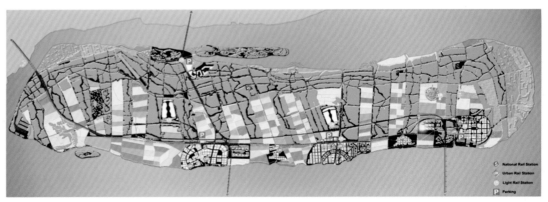

TWO CULTURES: TWO CITIES

BY EUGENE DREYER – URBAN PLANNING DIRECTOR, HONG KONG OFFICE

There are powerful links between Europe and China for our firm. The practice has a long record of infrastructure design, starting with the design of ventilation shafts for the Blackwall Tunnel, and there is a 40-year tradition of transportation, of tunnelling, of road and rail schemes, of connectivity. Railway stations appear repeatedly in this book – not just in China and the UK but in Australia, the Middle East, South Korea, Singapore, India and Africa – and we are now developing links in railways and planning in the USA and Brazil. Connectivity is the DNA that unifies all our architecture and urban design work.

It has been fundamental to our practice identity to be based in London and Hong Kong, in Europe and China. They are at opposite ends of the European and Asian landmass; each faces one of the two world oceans, the Atlantic and the Pacific. One contains one of the world's great estuaries; the other sits on arguably its greatest harbour. Each is based within one of the greatest cultures and civilisations in human history, China and Europe. We have been inspired by the fortuitousness of our geographic locations and the interest that took us to settle and develop our skills in these two cities. Rather than have multiple offices, we depend upon and indeed celebrate the focus that these two locations bring.

In many ways London and Hong Kong – each with roughly the same population – are mirror images of one another. Many years ago we did a drawing showing the two cities at the same scale. This turned out to be a real revelation for us about all kinds of fundamental issues relating to environment, city planning, place-making, urbanism, population density, infrastructure planning and transport design. We found that their metropolitan areas are similar in extent but that interestingly there is as much nature in Hong Kong as there is built-up area in London. Sixty percent of Hong Kong is designated Country Park (and 75% of its land is entirely undeveloped) – not something that is usually associated with one of the most intensive and vibrant cities in the world. So on the one hand you have a city in nature (Hong Kong) and, on the other, 'trapped countryside' or nature in the city (London).

The fact that Hong Kong is mountainous whereas London's topography is much more level accounts for many of the differences between the two cities.

Right: Diagrams show that Hong Kong city is dominated by mountains, whilst in London, green space is captured and disaggregated. The diagrams also show that Hong Kong occupies the edges, whilst London has grown from the centre.

Below: Greenwich Peninsula masterplan.

Opposite page: Guangzhou South Station masterplan.

 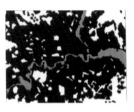  

In Hong Kong human settlement concentrated along the valley floors simply because it is easier to build there than on the side of a steep mountain. London had more room to spread out, and so it did; Hong Kong had to reclaim land from the sea to accommodate a growing population and to provide basic infrastructure such as its airport.

Nature accounts for many of the fundamental differences between the two cities, but history, culture and individual ways of doing things have played an important part as well. London has matured over two millennia, whereas Hong Kong emerged as a world metropolis in less than a century. London's forms and patterns are an expression of the pragmatic and sometimes idiosyncratic way in which its people have responded to constraint. Hong Kong has always been a place for bold infrastructure-led development and forward planning. Hong Kong uses planning rules more widely, though interestingly both cities have 'Haussmann-ised' the sky – London to protect views of St Paul's Cathedral, Hong Kong to protect views of its mountains. The major difference between the cities is that historically local people had more influence on development in London, though the public has become increasingly vocal about planning matters in Hong Kong over the last decade.

The opposites that these two great world cities represent have given the practice an considerable depth and breadth of knowledge and experience. London and Hong Kong have been laboratories for developing our approach to 21st-century urbanism. There has been an enormous knowledge transfer between the studios, ranging from the minimum track radius required for a high-speed train entering a station to the appropriate use of new environmental management technology within historic buildings.

Learning from such different places and projects has given the practice an considerable adaptability and the flexibility to work all over the world. It has provided us with the ability to work effectively at the micro as well as the macro scale and it has provided an understanding of rapid internationalisation, technological change and the environmental challenges that we now all face. These cities have also given us a wealth of insights into some key debates and have led us to challenge many of the preconceptions that are widely held in our profession, for example the idea that all tall buildings are

In both cities the practice has been responsible for many of the defining projects that have helped to set national and international agendas for architecture and planning.

In London our visionary project for the Thames Estuary on behalf of the government shows the interdependence between city-regions and the regional environment. We have proposed growth that is inspired by – and works in sympathy with – nature and natural order. We are advising London's Mayor on radical ideas to re-engineer and retrofit London's infrastructure in the interests of its continued status in an increasingly competitive world. This harnesses the latest environmental and energy technologies to transform London's use of natural resources. We are working on a significant new masterplan at Earl's Court, which has already won an international award. This will create one of the highest value destinations anywhere in the world by reinventing traditional London forms – the high street, the urban village – as the basis for successful 21st-century transformation. We have designed and built mix-use office buildings on the Greenwich Peninsula and at Regent's Place that apply the latest technology to create the most energy-efficient buildings in the city. We also have proposed small-scale interventions in central London to make the most of its Royal Parks, the public realm that sets it apart from other world cities.

In Hong Kong our Kowloon Station project – the most ambitious three-dimensional masterplan ever built and one of the world's finest transport interchanges – has formed the basis for a city quarter, more than twice the size of Canary Wharf, which will also include Hong Kong's new high-speed station. Next to Kowloon Station we are commissioned by the government to provide advice on the construction of its planned new cultural district on Victoria Harbour in collaboration with leading international architects and engineers. In Shenzhen, the Hong Kong studio has just completed the tallest building (KK100, see page 7) ever designed and built by a British architect. In Beijing we completed the city's new high-speed station in time for the 2008 Olympics. This has been voted by citizens – 3,500,000 in all – to be the city's finest new building in competition with the Bird's Nest amongst others. Guangzhou South Railway Station – the world's largest – will be completed shortly. At the other end of the scale we have undertaken intricate retrofit projects in complex city environments on behalf of Mass Transit Railway (MTR) to make Hong Kong's underground stations work more effectively and to allow disabled access.

Specialising in 'generalism'

Our experiences in London and Hong Kong have given us the confidence to promote ideas, visions and strategies on a broader stage. Throughout its history the practice has engaged in independent initiatives in the belief that architects and planners are uniquely placed to take a leading role in shaping the future of a rapidly changing and uncertain world. It has been extremely gratifying to see much of this work adopted as public policy.

The essence of these initiatives has been to bring a very wide range of people together. Some of our most ambitious and exciting work has involved scientists, engineers, economists, construction experts, developers, historians, artists, philosophers and cultural experts. These are critical times in world history. In the last 50 years its population has doubled, and by 2050 it is expected to reach 9 billion, mostly concentrated in cities. This will place immense pressure on finite resources, and the way in which our city-regions deal with this challenge will be fundamental to the future generations for whom we are planning now.

The skills that we as architects and planners bring will be of enormous significance. Global environmental concerns are becoming increasingly clear to us all; for us the focus must be on our ability to consider the big picture along with the detail. Neither one nor the other will make much of a difference by itself. To put it simply: one brilliant 'zero-carbon' building will achieve nothing if it is located in a place where people are dependent on car travel.

Visionary ideas mean nothing without the technology and specialist knowledge that can bring these to fruition. As specialisation deepens and intensifies due to technology and humanity's inventiveness, so also will the need for connectivity and collaboration, for broad visionary disciplines that connect specialist disciplines and make them work and interact locally as well as internationally. For 50 years or more architects and planners have been adversaries. What is desperately needed now is collaboration and connectivity. We need to look very carefully at how our resources can meet the demands of inevitable growth.

Tradition and modernity

The demands of the modern world have made us think very carefully about environmental resources as well as our existing assets – the infrastructure, buildings and utilities that make our cities work. We have always instinctively rejected the idea of renewal for its own sake. Re-use and retrofit have always formed a strong part of our portfolio.

Our conservation projects have ranged from small-scale redevelopments to large-scale masterplans all over the world. Whatever the scale, we always begin with what has made a place: what is its underlying landscape, its geography; what are the manmade interventions that have given a place its shape, whether it is a city such as Hong Kong, with its island, mountainous centre and harbour, or Delhi, with its great indigenous buildings like the Red Fort and later designs by Lutyens. Our approach is always inspired by the idea that historical continuity forms the basis of our plans for the future. Much of the urban design work shown in this book is the foundation for our architecture and appears here in ways that recognise the values of the past but express themselves in contemporary forms, technologies and materials.

Planning, leadership and collaboration

All our planning work merges and connects with public policy: much of our endeavour involves cities and urban areas, so part of our role is to advise local governments, mayors and central government on cities and city making. In Perth, Australia, and Auckland, New Zealand, we have been involved in concepts and visions for the future, while in Hong Kong our firm has done large-scale conceptual work on the waterfronts. As mentioned, we have now been appointed by the Hong Kong government to masterplan its greatest cultural and town planning enterprise yet – the cultural centre in Hong Kong.

In the UK, Sir Terry Farrell has been the Design Champion appointed to advise the political leaders of the great historic city of Edinburgh on its future, and particularly its new tramway system and the redevelopment of its old docks. In Newcastle he continues to advise the University and metropolitan enterprise company of Newcastle and Gateshead.

Our work on complex projects all over the world convinces us that collaboration and dialogue within our own professional community is the way forward rather than the inexorable growth of practices. The profession's diversity means that different practices

   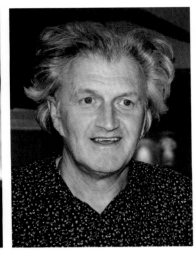 

and people bring different perspectives to the table. The wider the base of a project then the richer, the more useful and indeed the more genuinely creative the whole process becomes. We have never subscribed to the view that a practice can do everything for everyone. In fact, the corporate approach that goes with many very large practices does not nurture the creativity that is such an important part of our work.

An ever expanding world, with its information technology and communications revolution, means that professionals can transfer and apply their expertise more and more effectively. Each ambitious project needs its own creative community. Since we are involved heavily in strategic work it draws us into working with many different architects, designers and landscape architects in a way that individual 'design' architects, who are naturally introverted in their creative instincts, tend not to do.

Complex large-scale projects are built upon sharing – they have separate and competing components which are nevertheless joined in mutual interest. This is a phenomenon of creative activity in all different fields. Our international work reinforces this since we cannot deal with every local set of circumstances, nor can we get by with a cursory understanding of what makes a place tick, so we have collaborated with many practices in South Africa, the Middle East, USA, Singapore, China, South Korea, Australia, New Zealand and Portugal amongst others. We have also collaborated with a number of internationally recognised practices in the UK including Foster,

Rogers, Fuksas and Future Systems, and in the Far East, for example with Rem Koolhaas, Jean Nouvel and Mario Botta.

As an integral part of our working method we have always worked with a community of architects and planners – many of whom are former employees – who are embedded in the culture of what we do and with whom we work as if they are part of an internal team (though they work independently as well, which is of great value to us). We believe this adds immeasurably to the creativity of what we do, apart from being enormously enjoyable. This community has included some architects who we have worked with for many years, such as: Richard Portchmouth, Simon Hudspith, Gary Young, Toby Denham, Duncan Whatmore, Pankaj Patel, Steve Smith, Simon Sturgis and, more recently, John Thompson and Partners, Allies and Morrison Architects, Benoy, Chris Dyson Architects, Make, Kohn Pedersen Fox Associates, Paul Davis + Partners, John McAslan + Partners and Studio Egret West.

Over the years we have also worked with a great many specialists including landscape specialists such as Patel Taylor, Kim Wilkie, Camlin Lonsdale, Adrian Norman, Whitelaw Turkington, Gillespies, Grant Associates and Laurie Olin; artists including Julian Opie, Liam Gillick, Thomas Heatherwick, Anthony Gormley and Carmody Groake; energy specialists including Buro Happold, BioRegional and Beyond Green; writers including Colin Fournier and Tim Makover and economists and city thinkers such as Lord Stern, Bridget Rosewell, Tony Travers and Sir David King. They all bring a richness through collaborative working.

There are also the conventional consultants – far too many to name – from the fields of civil engineering, structural engineering, conservation and traffic planners who have been fundamental to our work. Our relationships are not always just project based, and we learn from their independence and their work for many other clients and architects.

The senior team within the practice is long established, and the practice's ethos has always been about continuity over time in working relationships both internally and externally. It has built intellectual depth, a sense of common endeavour and continuity of approach. The partners are: Mike Stowell and John Letherland in London, with Gavin Erasmus, Stefan Krummeck and John Campbell in Hong Kong. They are absolutely critical to our sense of being a unit and having our own cultural identity and of course work closely with senior partner and chairman, Sir Terry Farrell.

We are also proud of the quality of our young designers and the contribution they have made. Many of them go on to great things elsewhere. Current staff and all those involved in the projects, in both offices, are listed at the back of this book.

Top, left to right:
In addition to Terry Farrell, the above are the London and Hong Kong partners: Gavin Erasmus, Mike Stowell, Stefan Krummeck, John Letherland and John Campbell.

BEIJING

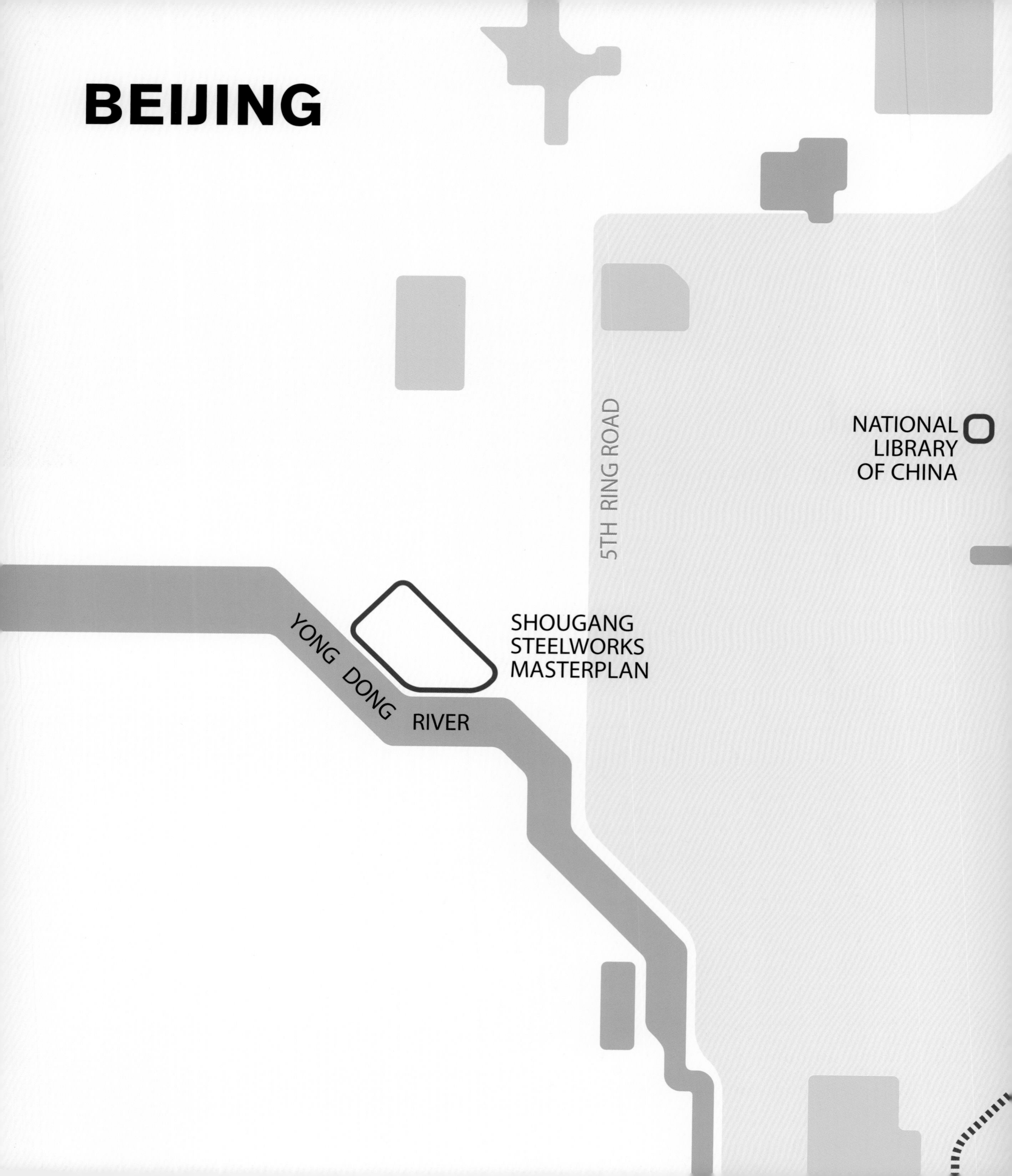

NATIONAL
LIBRARY
OF CHINA

5TH RING ROAD

SHOUGANG
STEELWORKS
MASTERPLAN

YONG DONG RIVER

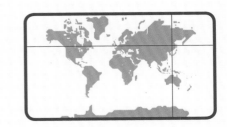

O OLYMPIC CULTURAL DISTRICT
MASTERPLAN

CHINA NATIONAL PETROLEUM
HEADQUARTERS
O

2ND RING ROAD

O BEIJING NATIONAL
ART GALLERY

Z15 TOWER
O CHAOYANG CBD

O
KAITER PLAZA

O NATIONAL OPERA
HOUSE

O
FINANCIAL
STREET

O BEIJING SOUTH STATION

BEIJING

Beijing is one of the world's oldest cities, planned as a series of cities within a city; its historic street patterns continue to influence the current urban morphology. Its rationale is the explicit order of systems and form where the micro and macro are one. Centred on the Forbidden City and Tiananmen Square, it is a rigorous metropolitan grid, with a series of carefully planned 'growth rings' expressed as a progression of ring roads.

Beijing had limited the height of new projects since 1974 when I.M. Pei urged authorities to protect the Forbidden City from encroachment by modern high-rises. With most of the land in Beijing being owned or controlled by the government, there has been a strict differentiation of districts through planning philosophy and policy. As a result of such a highly structured system Beijing's modern developments have largely occurred along its outer concentric ring roads, with the most

prestigious enterprises, such as China National Petroleum, positioning themselves along these arterial routes.

With the advent of hosting the 2008 Olympics, Beijing heavily invested in urban restructuring and development. Along with iconic stadia, a new Central Business District has been created and the implementation of new transportation and high-speed rail. Beijing South Station is one such core Olympic project that has generated prolific links to other cities and has enhanced the public realm for decades to come.

The new Chaoyang CBD has embraced the first super high-rises in Beijing; as an area destined for important socio-economic development it is a crucial piece in the contemporary Beijing plan. The 520m Z15 Tower epitomises modern, sustainable eco-living and working, which will advance Beijing's urban form into the next century.

Above: Cross-section through the foyer of Beijing National Opera House design proposal.

Top: The city of Beijing is laid out in ring roads emanating from the centre.

Opposite: The new Chaoyang CBD with six towers designed by Farrells. The Z15 Tower, at 520m high, will be China's tallest building.

Inset: Scheme shown within its urban context.

BEIJING SOUTH STATION

The city of Beijing with a current population of over 20 million people has five main railway stations located in the south, east, north, west and centre of the city. The reported number of domestic tourists in China in 2010 was 2.1 billion, many commuting by rail rather than air. Rail travel is the most popular mode of transport in China largely due to the average citizen's income level. For example, Beijing's set minimum wage of ¥1,160 ($177 USD) per month is roughly the same as a basic rail ticket to Shanghai. Over the Lunar New Year some 230 million people travel by train; many are migrant workers returning home for their annual leave.

Set on a 31-acre site, Beijing South Station is one of four key railway links for China's fast-growing high-speed intercity network. The station serves as a high-speed intercity rail link connecting Beijing with the Yangtze River Delta cities of Tianjin and Shanghai, with a catchment area of 270 million people. This multi-modal interchange facility acts as a 'Gateway to the City' for 285,000 passengers a day, with a predicted 105 million passengers annually by 2030.

Located on existing railway land, one of the main challenges was how the geometry of the station juxtaposes the diagonal fan of the railway tracks to Beijing's cardinal urban grid; an urban response was developed that unites them by connecting the building to two adjacent public parks. The scheme creates an urban link with the surrounding cityscape and acts as a connector by inserting a landscaped pedestrian spine in the formal north-south axis. Typically the tracks of a railway station fan will separate communities, but BSS provides a link that goes beneath the tracks, reconnecting the neighbourhoods and being a catalyst for new development in the area. In collaboration with the Third Railway Survey Design Institute (TSDI), Farrells focused on the potential of urban design to create an enduring building that would inform and become part of the city fabric.

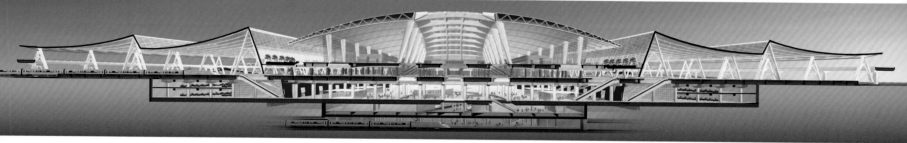

This grand station was designed as an architectural form and structure which is clear, simple and people-orientated. A key focus was to create efficient, convenient and direct passenger flow, with passengers boarding and alighting trains in the shortest distance and time possible. Accommodating five levels, 11 island platforms and two side platforms with 24 platform edges and numerous entrances, exits, waiting areas, interchange zones, etc, the station demanded a balanced and unifying form as an integral architectural solution to its complex functional and contextual requirements.

Incorporating traditional Chinese architectural motifs inspired by the Temple of Heaven, a low-rise roof is the most striking feature of the station's design. It is split into two crescent-shaped halves, which in turn are divided in two, with the central zone in-between defined by a dome-shaped roof. This sectional arrangement creates a maximum span of 70 metres. Its rigid frame includes tensile wire members to prevent uplift created by wind and can withstand heavy snow and sand storms.

The overall width and length of the platforms (the length being determined by the new intercity trains at 550m) directly affected the station size, and also the requirement and size of the roof to provide cover and protection to passengers. The central roof covers the entire Departures area, providing a fully enclosed environment that is air-conditioned using technology adopted from airport planning – air-binnacles –that cool only the lower 2.5m of the waiting concourses. Thus, reducing the amount of volume of air to be conditioned, and to a minimum temperature of 25°C, provides an energy-efficient solution.

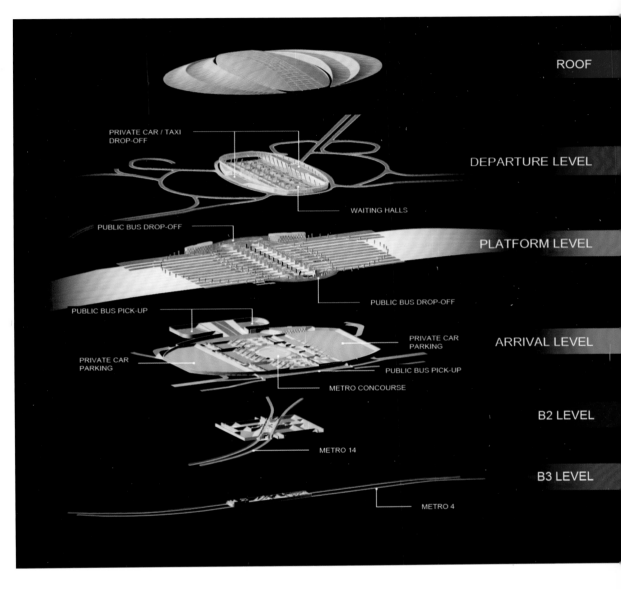

ROOF

DEPARTURE LEVEL

PRIVATE CAR / TAXI DROP-OFF

WAITING HALLS

PUBLIC BUS DROP-OFF

PLATFORM LEVEL

PUBLIC BUS DROP-OFF

PUBLIC BUS PICK-UP

PRIVATE CAR PARKING

ARRIVAL LEVEL

PRIVATE CAR PARKING

PUBLIC BUS PICK-UP

METRO CONCOURSE

B2 LEVEL

METRO 14

B3 LEVEL

METRO 4

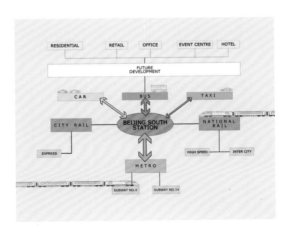

Opposite page
Top: Masterplan drawing showing roof plan of the station in the context of the surrounding area, vehicular links and landscaping.

Bottom: Cross-section through the station.

Above: Functional components of the station.

Far left: Functional strategy diagram.

Below: The station's low-rise roof incorporates traditional architectural motifs inspired by the Temple of Heaven.

Next page
Top: Beijing South Station is an integrated multi-modal transportation hub located on an existing railway fan, south of the Forbidden City.

Bottom: Natural light filters through the photovoltaic skylights illuminating the Departures Hall.

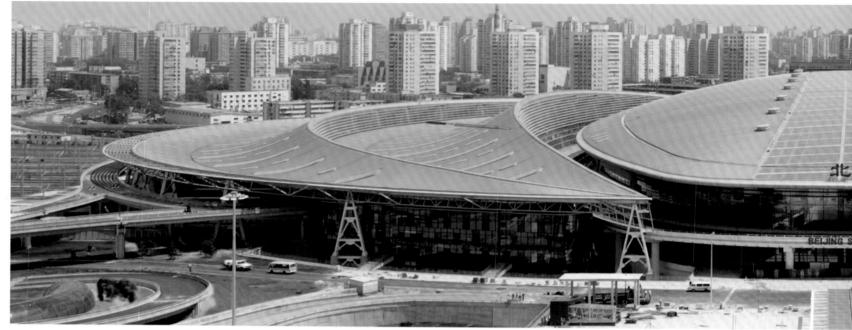

Although the outer canopy roofs are permeable to the open air for natural ventilation, the 350m-long, 190m-wide central roof is fully enclosed. A braced catenary system is used for the canopy roofs, which are supported by 60 raked columns around its perimeter and centre to create a sense of space. A 30,000m² skylight is designed to maximise natural light and provides a solution to energy conservation. Twenty-five percent of the skylight is made of high-solar-performance glass with a low-e coating; the remainder consists of thin-film, amorphous photovoltaic cells that have been laminated into glass to generate electricity for the basement car parking.

Everyone involved had an open and progressive attitude to reducing the on-going operational costs by the incorporation of sustainable technologies. This resulted in the adoption of several systems, namely photovoltaic cells, a combined heat and power system (CHP), a sewage source heat pump system, natural cross ventilation and reclamation of waste heat from urban discharge water. The environmental design of Beijing South Station was developed through innovative and cost-effective solutions to improve the energy utilisation ratio through dynamic thermal energy simulation using Integrated Environmental Simulation (IES) software, computational fluid dynamic (CFD) simulation and annual energy analysis.

The construction of the site was immense in size (1.5km long by 0.5km wide), and a 20m-deep excavation was required to accommodate the two metro lines. During the peak construction period the site contained over 10,000 workers per day and 22 cranes to deliver the station within only two and a half years. The ground-breaking ceremony was held on 24 December 2005, and the station opened for the Beijing Olympics on 8 August 2008.

Top: Platform Level showing the braced catenary system.

Bottom (from left to right): Low-level air-binnacles in the Departure Level concourse; metro concourse below the Arrivals Level; view of the station entrance (bus drop-off) from the Departures Hall; passenger drop-off is made easy by a perimeter ring road that maintains a smooth traffic flow.

CHINA NATIONAL PETROLEUM HEADQUARTERS

Beijing's Second Ring Road is roughly built on the site of the former city wall, with portions of the road named after former city gates, including Dongzhimen. The China National Petroleum Headquarters is located at the north-west corner of Beijing Dongzhimen bridge along the eastern part of the Second Ring Road, an iconic building that dominates the skyline.

China's largest oil and gas company, China National Petroleum, required a prestigious new headquarters building to complement its expansion. In collaboration with the Beijing Institute of Architectural Design, a conceptual approach for the complex was created, designing spacious, modern towers that reflect the company's status. The building's long and dominant façade in this prime location generates a powerful corporate image and has become a new landmark in Beijing with innovative and sustainable building design.

This 200,000m² headquarters houses commercial office space, and conference and catering facilities. Designed to accommodate both the company's oil and gas departments,

it is divided into two sub-departments, making it easy to allocate each branch of the company a defined space.

Located on a narrow east-west-oriented site, the development conforms to the capital height restriction of 90 metres. The main design focus was to increase the building's southern exposure in accordance with local custom, which was accomplished by clustering the building mass and breaking it into four 24-storey, L-shaped towers on a common base.

The elevations of the offices are composed of cubical forms rising from the podium. The building is essentially a stone construction, giving a sense of physical grounding that reflects the solid foundation of the company's identity. The exterior stone cladding fins generate a more slender visual proportion, whilst the various façades differ in their environmental response. For example, a glass, shield-like skin is suspended off the east façade, to protect the building from dust, wind and noise pollution and simultaneously creating a modern design statement.

To make the separate towers work as a unified whole, the design incorporated environmental, social, organisational and spatial elements; atriums with internal climate controls were conceived in each block. These are linked by internal streets running one level above ground from north to south, allowing the public to move easily from one block to another, and will connect to the proposed metro station at the south end of the development. The atriums attribute to the buildings optimum natural light and ventilation. CNP's sizeable basement accommodates common functions for all four towers including coffee shops, libraries and auditoriums.

The building's design and orientation makes full use of natural light and ventilation, reducing energy consumption. The innovative triple-skin curtain walling shields traffic noise and exhaust fumes from the busy main road to improve the internal environment. The application of advanced air-conditioning techniques have reduced operating costs, increased performance and made the building a pleasant environment in

Left: Roof plan in context.

Above: Beijing Planning Bureau city model showing

China National Petroleum Headquarters (circled) and top right of picture the Forbidden City's red roofs.

which to work. The building embodies the harmony between energy and the environment.

On two elevations fronting onto major roads triple glazing with a large cavity between the fixed outer double glazing and the inward opening single glazed full-height screens has been incorporated to minimise external noise penetration This system doubles up as a high-performance climate wall. Warm air in the cavity between the inner and outer glazing is extracted at high level back to a centralised heat exchanger; replenishing air is then introduced back into the cavity through the raised access floor.

A variety of different forms of climate wall systems were analysed at design stage and the finally selected system was one that sealed externally to deal with both the noise and effects of the regular sandstorms in the area.

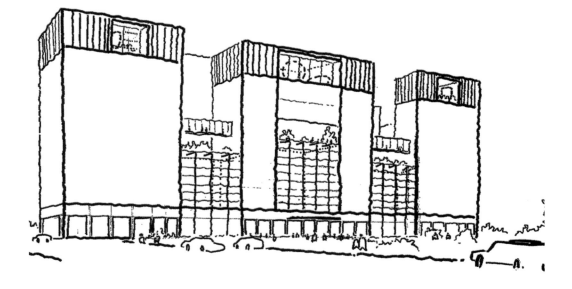

Top: An imposing view of the main façade of the building taken from the Second Ring Road.

Above: Concept sketch by Sir Terry Farrell.

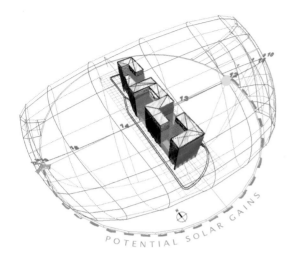

POTENTIAL SOLAR GAINS

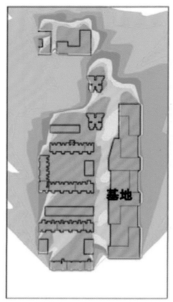

基地

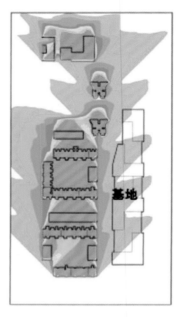

基地

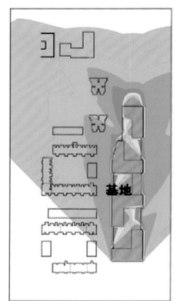

基地

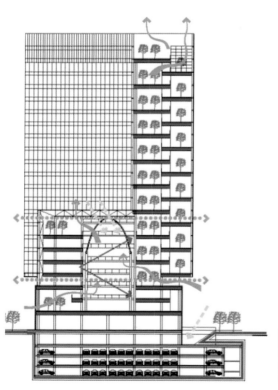

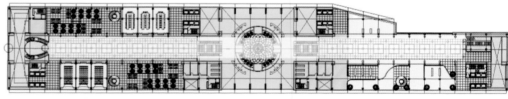

中国石油天然气集团公司总部   中国石油天然气股份有限公司

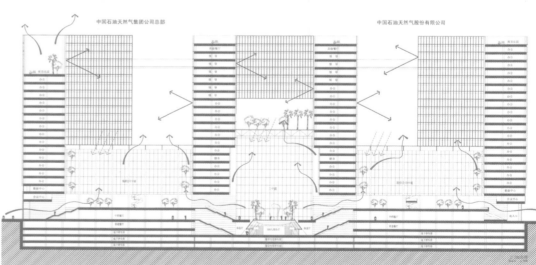

Top left: Environmental massing: potential solar gains.

Top right: Operating costs and energy consumption are lowered while human comfort is increased by creating a better environment.

Bottom left: Natural daylight and ventilation diagram, 'environmental response'.

Middle: Level 2 floor plan.

Bottom right: Cross-section illustrating how the great

atrium spaces allow for a generous flow of natural light and air between office areas and internal streets with full-height lobby spaces.

Opposite: The immense glazed entrance hall showing the elevated walkways between buildings.

This page: Detailed photos of the façade.

Opposite top: Main façade of the building taken from the Second Ring Road at night.

Opposite bottom: Atrium lobby details and façade detail of shadow patterns cast by the curtain wall sunshading vertical fins.

BEIJING NATIONAL ART GALLERY

Since 1962, the National Art Museum of China (NAMOC) has played a major role in expanding Chinese national arts, popularising and developing art education, and promoting cultural exchange. In 2002 a competition was held to expand the premises to include a National Art Gallery to accommodate the increased demand for cultural information and global exchange.

Located in the Dongcheng district of Beijing, the new National Art Gallery lies adjacent to the existing NAMOC, composing of an area 90m wide by 140m long. This phase II expansion needed to include nine different zones: exhibition/display, education/library, and research facilities, a shop and café, administration area, security, equipment/services, collection storage (for over 75,000 pieces) and underground parking. The gallery incorporates permanent and temporary display and exhibition zones, a special topic area and a Central Exhibition Hall. The new gallery design required accessibility for 20,000 daily / 6 million annual visitors alongside 200 full-time staff members.

This proposal was based on the harmonious integration of two concepts: first, an 'objet d'art' on a grand scale, inspired by the idea of a precious container full of treasured objects. Secondly, a 'city of water and ink', as in 'Chinese art', creating a space that combines the virtual and the real.

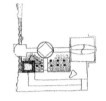

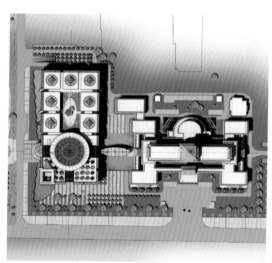

Above: Aerial perspective of the central gallery and roof pavilion.

Top right: Concept sketches.

Middle right: Masterplan of proposed expansion, incorporating links to existing parks and water features.

Bottom right: Cross-section through the galleries, café and education / lecture areas.

NATIONAL LIBRARY OF CHINA

The National Library of China, initially called Capital Library, was established in 1909. As a comprehensive research library, it functions as a National Repository / Bibliotheca (One Book) and (Three Centres) as a bibliographic centre, a national centre of library information networks, and a library research/development centre. It serves a multitude of users including government, research institutions, academia, and the general public.

The project brief required a multifunctional development to accommodate Phase II of the National Library of China. The Library has a rich collection of over 22 million volumes, and is open to the public 365 days a year.

The proposed design provides a comprehensive planning and forward-looking architectural solution to this civic and cultural building. With the large numbers of visitors anticipated, the new library is designed to facilitate easy orientation and movement. In section, the horizontal layering of the functions are simply arranged and expressed in order to separate public and private areas and routes. Reading rooms and public circulation are located above the garden, with private staff areas, book storage / archive, plant spaces and car parking beneath the garden.

The design required fulfillment of five main functions: bibliotheca, reading rooms, digital library, library operations and academic exchange. The functions needed to be accommodated in a rational and compact layout that ensured a smooth and convenient flow of readers, books and library staff.

The focus of the design is a formal and dignified impression expressed by a central high-rise bibliotheca surrounded by low-rise reading rooms. The new phase embraces the traditional courtyard garden, with flexible reading rooms on three levels overlooking the garden. The courtyard typology helps the two phases communicate in a common spatial language and at the same time creates a soft and approachable internal landscape for the users to enjoy.

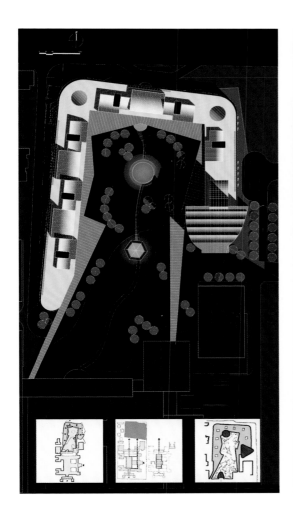

Above: Proposed masterplan layout of the National Library of China.

Above right: Aerial perspective of the National Library of China with traditional garden and pagoda.

HUAWEI SCIENCE PARK

Huawei Science Park is located in Haidian District, between the fifth and sixth ring roads, in an area traditionally associated with academia and research. The project site is part of a larger park context within the Beijing Environmental Protection Technology Park. A relatively flat greenfield area with man-made water features, the masterplan's three distinct zones were developed to provide a human scale environment that encourages interaction and fosters creativity.

The proposed masterplan for the telecommunications giant, incorporates an exhibition centre, club house, research and development facilities, galleries, gardens and administrative buildings.

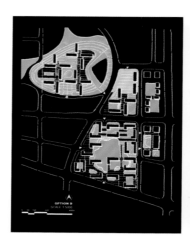

This image: Aerial perspective showing the canteen building, one of the foci of the entire project which has a pivotal role in the daily life of the development.

Top left to right: Greenery and water areas; land use; concept courtyards.

FINANCIAL STREET

This was an international competition submission for the planning and redesign of 103 hectares of land in central Beijing. The design incorporated a 780,000m² international banking headquarters and facilities over a 550,000m² site. The existing layout and buildings were systematically developed as financial offices with auxiliary living, business, entertainment and parking facilities.

The proposed masterplan is characterised by an undulating green landscape that forms a multi-level street, both above and below ground. The sky gardens and sky bridges create visual connections within this dense urban environment. The sloped park areas lead pedestrians to higher levels in order to aid the visual connections to parks and the skyline of the existing street.

To fully utilise land resources, the underground areas are constructed over four interconnecting floors, designed to link to the existing underground traffic system, subway station, and unite both sides of the street. The plan introduces integrated green links and public spaces which create a single organic underground space, providing a round-the-clock environment for shopping and entertainment.

Top: Bird's-eye view of Financial Street and the undulating landscape of the multi-layered street.

Bottom: Spatial concepts: establishing a direct physical connection to the underground network, and an elevated point of view, from which one can enjoy the panorama over the viaduct.

Right: Financial Street's proposed masterplan shows the density of the buildings and the multi-level street landscaping unifying the area.

CHAOYANG CBD: Z15 TOWER

In early 2011 there was fierce competitive bidding for land in the Chaoyang Central Business District, with more than 60 developers submitting a colossal 274 schemes for 12 of the 18 land plots available in Phase One. CITIC's team of Farrells, BIAD and ARUP submitted designs for eight plots and won five (six towers), each of which are now being implemented. The General Planner of China Academy of Urban Planning and Design, praised the success of this high-calibre joint venture, stating: 'Its greatest advantage is considering the overall urban spaces, architectural design and various engineering techniques in a unified manner to formulate a fully integrated urban design scheme in macro, meso and microscopic terms.'

Located in the east of Beijing at the heart of the new CBD extension, this 30-hectare masterplan was split into 22 land plots. Situated close to the new CCTV headquarters and China World Trade Center 3, the design incorporates 2,000,000m² of office space, a six-star hotel, luxury service apartments and high-end retail that connects to the existing metro station and adjacent shopping mall. The five plots / six towers winning schemes range from the city's tallest building at 123 storeys, 520m high (Z15), to twin towers at 42 storeys, 181.8m high (Z14).

The 300,000m² Z15 Tower includes Grade-A office space over 60 floors; 20 floors of serviced apartments; and a 300-key / 20-storey hotel, complete with state-of-the-art facilities. The tower's smooth vertical curve maximises the floor area at the top and provides structural stability at the base and it is designed to utilise the latest sustainable technology, materials and engineering concepts. The form of the building is inspired by the image of Zun (Chinese wine vessel), the texture of bamboo weaving and the Kongming lanterns. Different rhombic layers grow upwards from the bottom of the building, reflecting the delicacy and skillfulness of bamboo weaving and incorporating the freshness and beauty of flourishing lotus flowers.

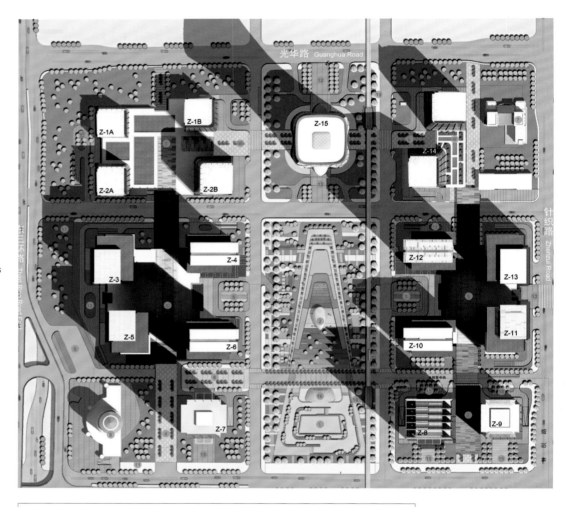

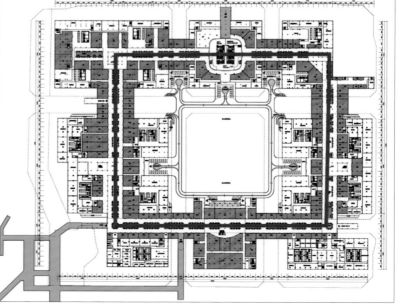

Top: Masterplan of the new area showing all 18 plots of land.

Bottom: Basement Level plan showing connectivity in red.

Below left: Z15 Tower in the context of the new CBD, showing the adjacent CCTV building and China WTC 3.

Opposite: Bird's-eye view of Z15 Tower. At 123 storeys high, this building forms part of a successful competition entry consisting of five land plots in the Chaoyang Central Business District.

CHAOYANG CBD

The most significant opportunities for setting an agenda for 21st-century urbanism within the new Central Business District are to redefine the way in which urban ecology works and to support changes to the way of life within Beijing, particularly in regard to encouraging a culture of walking and cycling. The vision for the development was to create a ground-based pedestrian network which encourages ground level activity, creating a sense of place.

At the centre of the site is a green spine designed to connect the CBD with other local centres. The perceived "greenness" of the place creates a sense of health and wellbeing essential to the success of the development. A key part of the approach was to regard the CBD as an important link in a network of green pedestrian-friendly routes and spaces linking the masterplan to the wider community.

The design of the 72-storey, 320m-high Z8 Tower was inspired by stacking ancient Chinese coins. As the office headquarters for a financial institution, the 184,664m^2 building acts as a gateway to the CBD.

Z11 Tower together with Z13 forms the eastern gateway to the CBD. This 53-storey-high office building offers a roof terrace sky garden with unprecedented views over the city.

Inspired by the Chinese ancient LuBan lock, Z12 Tower is designed as a sustainable live / work environment. The vision of Z12 Tower is designed to be the forerunner of green building design in Beijing.

Plot Z14 encompasses two towers that perform as a sculptured dancing couple, complimenting each other's form.

The top of the towers in the new CBD will glow at night, inspired by the Kongming lanterns in the sky, symbolising wealth and the energy of the city of the future.

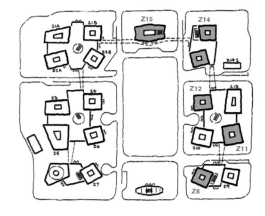

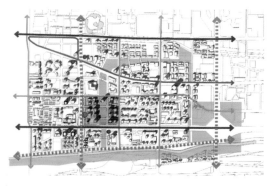

Z8

Z11

Z12

Z14

孔明灯
KONGMING LANTERN

Top: Plan of Chaoyang CBD with winning plots highlighted.

Middle: Context plan of Chaoyang CBD and main street axis.

Above left: Ancient Chinese LuBan lock inspiration for Z12.

Above right: Chaoyang CBD buildings lit up like Kongming lanterns.

OLYMPIC CULTURAL DISTRICT MASTERPLAN

Enriching the Beijing Cultural Olympics legacy, the 20-hectare Cultural District Masterplan was a collaboration with Tsinghua University who were responsible for the original landscaping of the Olympics including the Dragon Park that creates a setting for the new cultural quarter. Positioned on Beijing's grand axis, and centred on Tiananmen Square to the south, the cultural facilities celebrate China's past achievements as well as creating an environment for the production of new culture and art.

Eight crucial components make up the new District, including the Dragon Park, lake, collaborative public spaces, a Cultural Business zone, museums and galleries, floating pavilions and areas for temporary and permanent outdoor exhibitions and activities. The masterplan is a culturally rich destination that emphasises connectivity, the public realm, inspiration, education and enterprise.

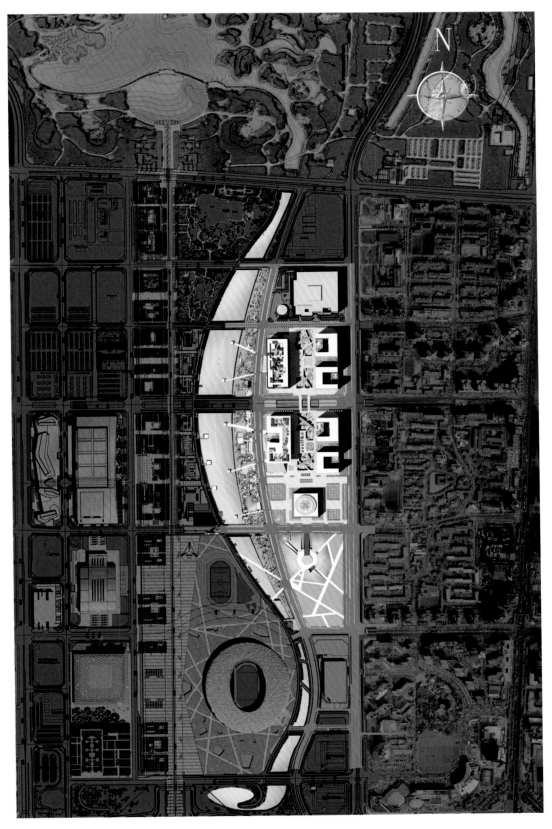

Top: Aerial perspective of the masterplan.

Right: Masterplan in the context of Beijing's Grand Axis.

Bottom: Conceptual sketch by David West.

KAITER PLAZA

Kaiter Plaza is located in Chaoyang District between the second and third ring roads in an area popular for tourists, shopping and office positioning. The new landmark headquarters building for the eminent international firm The Emperor Group stands on Jianguomen Outer Avenue, an extension of two of the most important city streets – East Chang'an Avenue and Jianguomen Outer Avenue.

The 27-storey, 120m-high office building, overlooks Beijing's Embassy District from the executive sky hall, towards its northern side. The west elevation has a glass façade hosting 10 two-storey-high sky gardens. This Grade-A office complex incorporates high-end retail, dinning and entertainment facilities.

From an urban planning point of view, the project will offer a unique spatial experience for the general public, promoting pedestrian flow into the development, which will benefit the commercial areas. It enhances the street elevation by creating a 'place' along the avenue, drawing pedestrians into its podium space. The open podium façade is designed to be permeable, creating a pleasurable street environment and a receptive building envelope.

The building has a unique overall identity. By utilising the concept of 'clustering', it comprises four individual areas with their own architectural expression: the people's city room, the plinth, the tower and the executive's sky hall.

Designed as a state-of-the-art office complex, it embraces new technology and sustainable living as befits the company's solid corporate image and multi-discipline interests. At night, the sky hall will become an urban beacon along this principal thoroughfare.

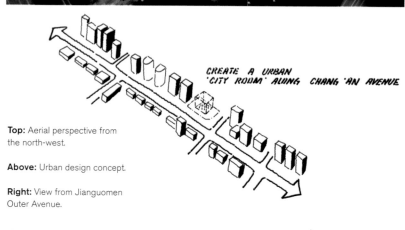

CREATE A URBAN 'CITY ROOM' ALONG CHANG'AN AVENUE

Top: Aerial perspective from the north-west.

Above: Urban design concept.

Right: View from Jianguomen Outer Avenue.

SHOUGANG STEELWORKS MASTERPLAN

Located in Shijingshan District, 20km from Tiananmen Square, the 8.79km² Shougang Industry Zone sits on the Yong Ding River. Shijingshan District, once considered a major polluting area in Beijing, aims to build itself into a Capital Recreation District (CRD), based on the highly successful Ruhr Museum complex in Germany. The Shougang Group, producers of iron and steel, closed its last furnace on this site on 31 December 2010.

This industrial zone previously occupied by Shougang will be developed into a cultural and creative industry centre. The proposed masterplan, developed with Beijing Institute of Architectural Design (BIAD), is divided into six districts: the Culture and Recreation District in the north, the Central Business Headquarters District, the Waterfront District along the river, the Business District in the middle, a high-end

service area in the east and a Mixed-use District in the south. There are eight nodes that connect the Districts, which include parks, business and community centres.

The Shougang masterplan utilises the Yong Ding River as a place for recreation and brings public spaces, commercial activities, business enterprises and culture / entertainment to this once heavily industrial and polluted area.

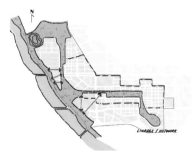

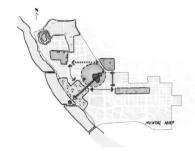

Top left: Shougang Marina.

Middle: Proposed landscaping.

Top right: Site connections.

Below: The proposed masterplan was developed together with the Beijing Institute of Architectural Design (BIAD).

SHIJIAZHUANG MASTERPLAN

Shijiazhuang is a provincial city of Heibei Province, 180 miles south-west of Beijing. The largest industrial city in the region, it has grown from a market town to become an important trading connection between main cities in China. In 1905, the Beijing-Wuhan railway reached Shijiazhuang, stimulating its trade and economy. The old city of Shijiazhuang, now home to 2.7 million residences, is upgrading its railway link and building a new train station to become part of the Jing Guang Railway, a high-speed railway network from Guangzhou to Beijing.

The new 11km Victory Avenue is located at the centre of the old city district alongside the railway and will stretch from Shi Tai Expressway to the new station. It will serve as the main access to the city on the north-south axis. The current area has various disconnected planning zones that include both residential and commercial areas.

Making use of the already established zoning characteristics, the plan is to build on the multi-centred identity and create a sense of arrival. The masterplan will shape the Avenue's undulating skyline with varied building heights, a landscaped spine and defining nodes. The design will transform Victory Avenue from a city barrier to a living, green connector.

The masterplan is based on ten principal design visions – The Legible City, Building on the Past to Create a Legacy for the Future, Rejoining the City, A New City Centre, Multi-centred Character, Shaping the Boulevard, Let Nature In, Create a Sense of Arrival, Pedestrian should be King and Defining a Sustainable Agenda.

The Avenue will include an environmental tram system, photovoltaic lighting, above-ground decks along the nodes, an underground shopping mall and a multi-level landscape.

This project is the first ever masterplanning design by a Hong Kong-based international firm, under Hong Kong Institute of Architects (HKIA) auspices, and appointed by local city government.

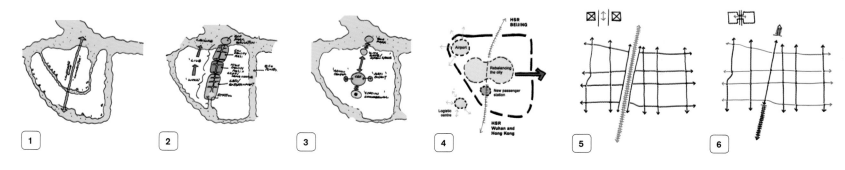

Top left to right:
Concept sketches
1. Green 'spine' through two landscapes.
2. Work / live zone.

3. Centres along the spine.
4. Building on the past to create a legacy for the future.
5 & 6. The opportunity to rejoin the city (2 towns vs. 1 city).

Bottom: Multi-level landscape spine – cross-section.

Oppposite page:
Top: Masterplan perspective.

Bottom from left to right:
Zoning and characteristics of nodes; five 'centres' concept; nodes and east-west connection and Gateway Square.

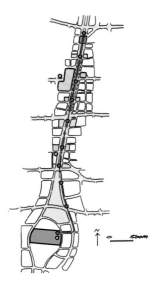

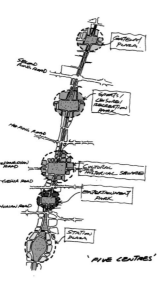

'FIVE CENTRES'

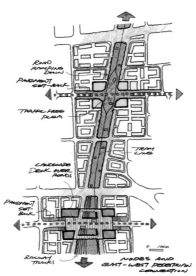

NODES AND EAST-WEST PEDESTRIAN CONNECTION

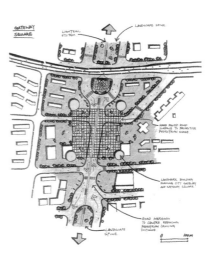

SHANGHAI

YANGTZE RIVER

WUXI TV
TOWER

HONG QIAO
STATION AND CBD
MASTERPLAN

HANGPU RIVER

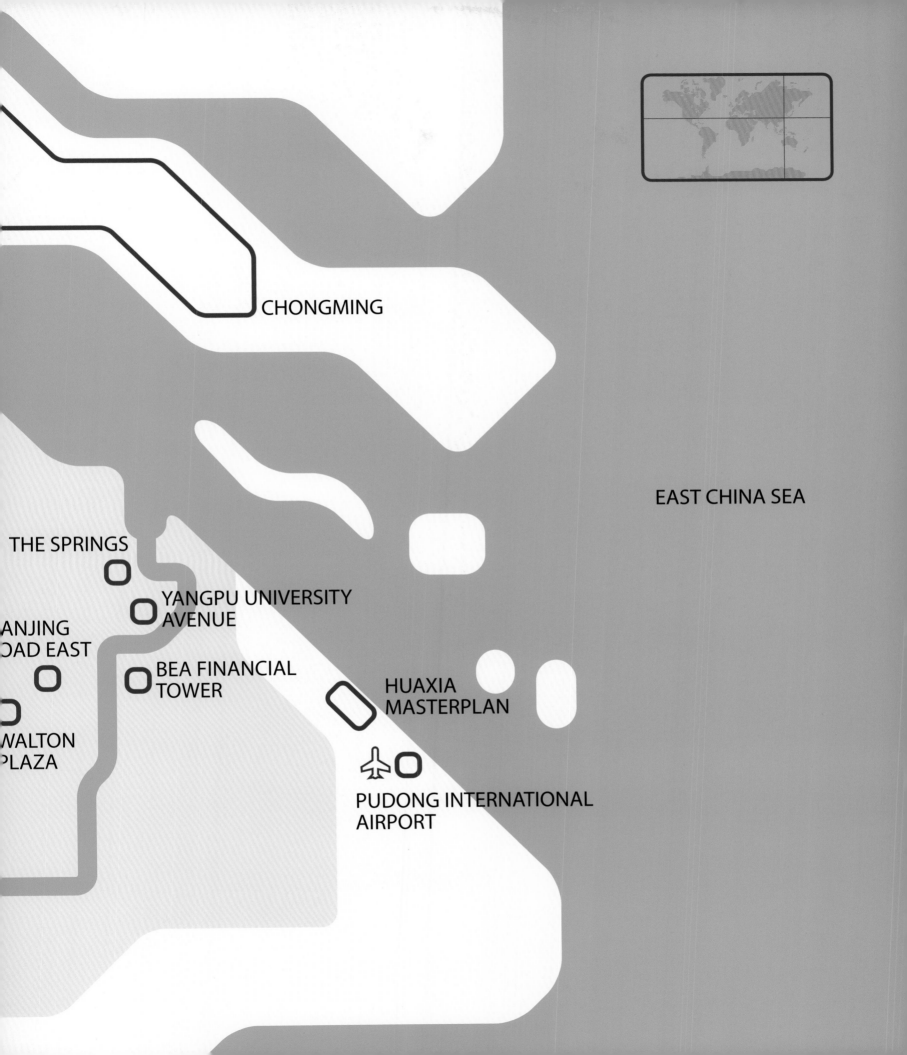

CHONGMING

THE SPRINGS

YANGPU UNIVERSITY
AVENUE

ANJING
OAD EAST

BEA FINANCIAL
TOWER

WALTON
PLAZA

HUAXIA
MASTERPLAN

PUDONG INTERNATIONAL
AIRPORT

EAST CHINA SEA

SHANGHAI AND THE YANGTZE RIVER DELTA

Shanghai was always China's most cosmopolitan and dynamic city and it is now a major international capital for finance, commerce, culture and fashion. It is a city that is larger than most regions and many countries in terms of its population – now approaching 20 million inhabitants – and the scale and speed of change in the city over the last two decades has been genuinely revolutionary.

Once a fishing village on the Yangtze, Shanghai was opened to foreign trade in the mid-19th century and by the 1930s it was firmly established as an international capital. Its growth has been such that its city planners are actively pursuing a decentralisation strategy that will see the emergence of four new metropolitan city centres in addition to that in Central Shanghai focused on the Bund and Pudong.

On 18 April 1990, the Chinese government implemented the development of the Pudong area into a Special Economic Zone. Located in the east of Shanghai, the Pudong New Area lies at the mid-point of China's coastline where the Yangtze River and the sea intersect, across the Huangpu River from downtown Shanghai. The Pudong has played a leading role in the transformation of Shanghai's economic growth. Divided into five districts, BEA Financial Tower is located in the Lujiazui commercial district of Pudong, Shanghai's CBD.

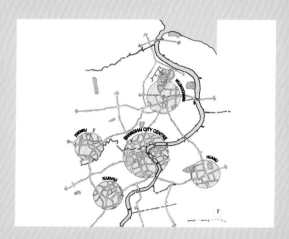

Above: The New Pudong District of Shanghai seen from the Bund. The BEA Financial Tower is set back from the waterfront with view corridors of the Huangpu River and the Bund.

Top: Sketch of Shanghai locale with the Huangpu River clearly seen. Shanghai's future planning proposes the shift from one city centre to a multi-centric structure.

Opposite: The BEA Financial Tower sits adjacent to prominent high-rises, most notably the Jin Mao Tower and the Shanghai World Financial Centre (at 492m, it is currently China's tallest building).

BEA FINANCIAL TOWER

With an ever changing skyline, the Pudong is seen as the commercial symbol of Shanghai. As a result, any new developments have to respond not only to market demand but are also required to contribute to the city's visual and spatial dynamism. Located in the Lujiazui commercial district of the Pudong, the design for the BEA Financial Tower combines elegant, contemporary aesthetics with a modern, technologically advanced building form. The striking development offers high efficency levels and responds to China's increasing concern for environmental protection.

Standing 198 metres tall, it consists of three underground levels, a 40-storey tower and a five-floor podium that includes restaurants and public facilities. The structure is layered into three principal forms: a central circulation and service core flanked by two floor plates, with the west wing of the building rising above the other two components. The creation of this stepped effect brings clarity and directness to the building's massing. Each element functions independently and is bound into a singular composition by complementary materials and modularity.

The design of the layered and stepped building mass created an opportunity to extend the nearby greenery and landscape into the interior. Sky gardens bring in abundant daylight, stunning views and natural ventilation.

The building's façades react differently to the environment through orientation, materials and technology within the building envelope. Each of the four façades have been designed to respond to the varying environmental conditions attributable to their orientation. This results in minimising both heat gain in the warmer weather and heat loss in the colder winter months, which contributes to the operational efficiency of the service installation. Glare is controlled through a combination of solar shading and individually operated blinds. On the elevations with high solar gain the percentage of glazing has been reduced and horizontal shading devices introduced. On the remaining elevations the percentage of glazing has been increased and vertical fins introduced to limit the glare from the low setting sun. High performance low-e-coated double-glazed units with a combination of body tint and reflective coatings along with high levels of insulation in spandrel areas were incorporated in the design.

Apart from low-level cladding the building envelope was constructed in factory-formed unitised metal and glass panels. These units were made continuous around each of the corners to ensure that the weather performance at the critical interface was not compromised. This led to some very complex double corner units incorporating different portions of the façade at a variety of angles to create the sloping geometry.

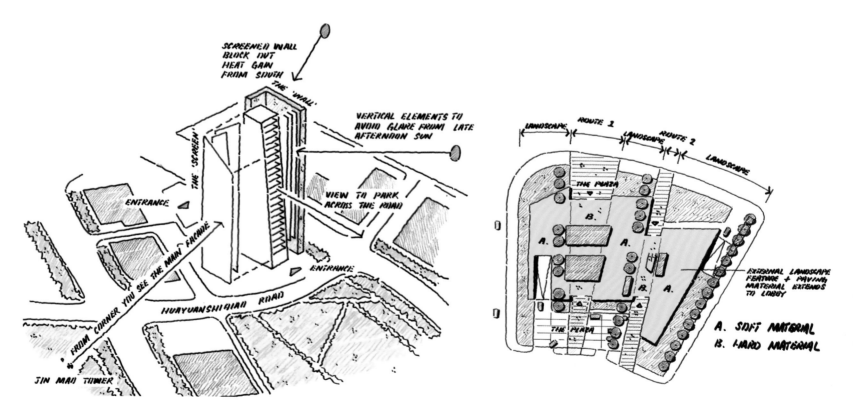

Above left: Sketch showing the treatment of the tower's response to environmental factors.

Above right: Landscaping plan.

Opposite: View from Huayuan Shiqiao Road.

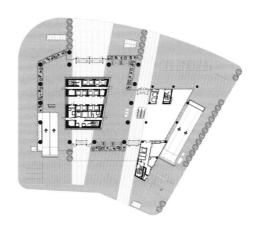

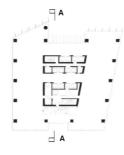

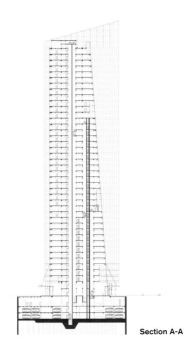

Section A-A

Opposite page

Top left: The grand entrance lobby is designed as a through link from the Northern Plaza to the Southern vehicle drop-off.

Bottom left: Detail of vertical glass fins that utilise surface frit to shade the interior.

Right: Each façade used different types of cladding in response to its orientation and specific environmental elements.

This page

Top: Ground floor plan.

Middle: Typical floor plan.

Above: Section A-A.

Right: The BEA Financial Tower, looking towards the Huangpu River. The stepped design of the building can clearly be seen.

WALTON PLAZA

Xuhui District was once the premier residential area of Shanghai. It became an industrial zone after the revolution and then evolved into a commercial zone in the 1990s. Today, Xuhui is famous for its handsome historic garden residences that give it grandeur and the recent invasion of retail malls. Located in the south-west of the city, it sits across the Huangpu River from the 2010 Expo site.

Walton Plaza, located in the Xuhui District of Puxi, is a landmark mixed-use office building that is sensitive to the surroundings and integrates harmoniously with its existing neighbourhood. By regenerating this old-town district into a high-end mixed-use office zone it has become a prime urban redevelopment model within the region.

The masterplan for the plaza focused on the positioning of a 40-storey, 80,000m² office tower, three high-rise buildings, four low-rise apartment blocks, a club house, and the landscape design. The massing and building location plan already existed, based on feng-shui principles and orientation.

While the office tower appears to be almost weightless, it is balanced by the scheme's residential blocks. To unify the site, the residential properties are arranged in two crescent shapes, which form an internal garden. Walton Plaza has a timeless yet modern feel and integrates a garden-style live/work area into the district. Farrells worked in collaboration with Chen Shi Min.

Right: The canopied front entrance.

Below: Early concept studies of Walton Plaza's main tower form.

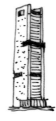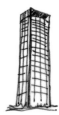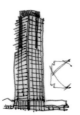

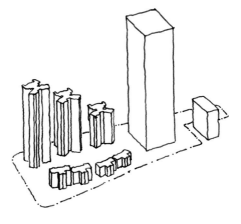

Top: Shanghai's drive towards high-density living.

Above: Walton Plaza massing.

Right: The central garden unifies the high- and low-rise buildings on the site.

HONG QIAO CBD MASTERPLAN

In 2008, the Yangtze River Delta Region was formally expanded from 16 major cities to include the entire region and to bring a smooth integration with Shanghai and the neighbouring Jiangsu and Zhejiang Provinces. Simultaneously the planned transportation network of the region included: 10 railway stations, 22 highways, 13 major airports, 11 ports and 9 bridges. To coincide with the Shanghai World Expo, the government's target was to build a 'Three Hours Transportation Circle'. to network the area on a large scale. With Shanghai being the centre of the Yangtze River Delta Region, the regional economy will increase with the integration and cluster effect among industries.

Hong Qiao CBD Masterplan is a multi-layered response that relates to its location, transportation structure, and commercial opportunities.

Our proposed masterplan transforms the district into a national arena that provides a business platform for leading innovators of science and technology. This three-million m² site also plans to incorporate hotels, retail and entertainment complexes into the Business District.

The green central connector links the transport interchange, business district and surrounding communities together. The plan creates a continuous landscape and ecological network, transforming the public realm through a bold green strategy. Waterways are incorporated, reinstating the canal landscape of Shanghai's past. Showcase avenues branch out from the transport hub, creating a sense of arrival with pedestrian routes connecting public squares and anchor buildings. A central high street is placed parallel to the station to establish a focus for retail shopping.

The masterplan grid allows for connectivity within the district, to the new Hong Qiao Railway Station and Shanghai city centre. A human-scale environment for live, work and play, it will be a business destination of the future without competing with the Pudong.

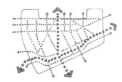

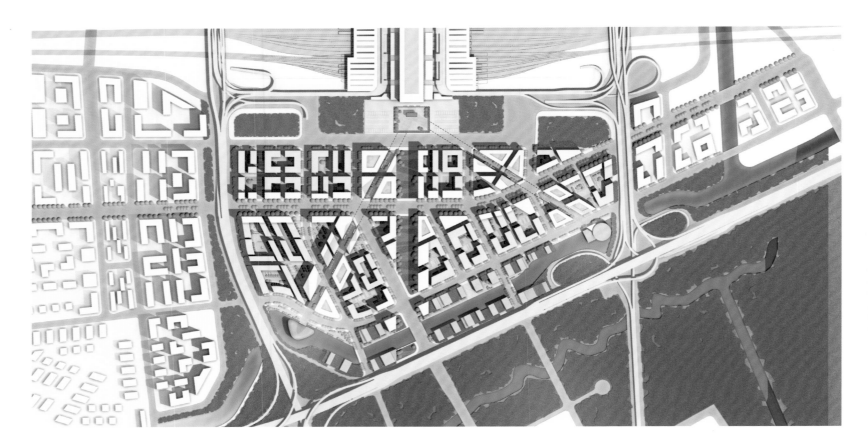

Above: Hong Qiao CBD masterplan.

Top (left to right):
Main axial diagram; proposed greenery system reinforces the axial plannning and design.

Middle (left to right):
Continuous landscape network; the diagram showing diversity within the urban grid to create zones of different character.

HONG QIAO STATION

One of Shanghai's four major railway stations, Hong Qiao Station is located in the Changning District close to the Shanghai Hongqiao International Airport. The station provides terminals for four high-speed lines, including trains between Beijing and Shanghai, Shanghai and Ningbo, and the Shanghai-Hangzhou maglev railway.

Our proposed design for Hong Qiao Station was driven by the 'station-as-airport' model, with arrivals and departures clearly separated, and acts

as a major transportation hub, connecting different modes of transport. Due to its huge scale, the proposal's architectural structure is elegant, strong, simple and streamlined, with a strong emphasis on efficiency and effortless passenger movement. The masterplan incorporates the railway station, transport interchange station and airport terminal as one entity. The railway station and airport terminal act as two anchors at either end, and are connected by pedestrian bridges and a landscape corridor.

This design prioritises passenger requirements and flow. Platforms are column-free to ensure unimpeded sight lines and structural columns in the halls are kept to a minimum to prevent obstruction. Inspired by the shape of a butterfly, the building symbolises contemporary flight, using design and technology to create a modern integrated transport hub.

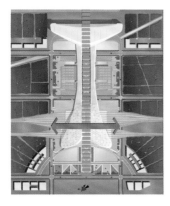
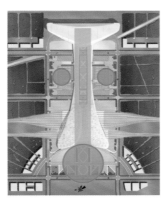
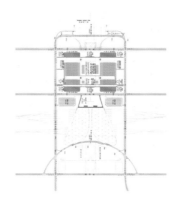
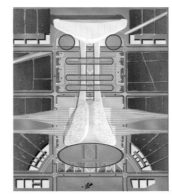

Left (left to right): Main axial diagram; proposed greenery system reinforces the axial planning and design; functional diagram showing mode of transport on ground floor; diagram showing water feature system.

Below left: Aerial perspective of the masterplan.

Below: Axonometric demonstrating the functional relations between the different levels of the station.

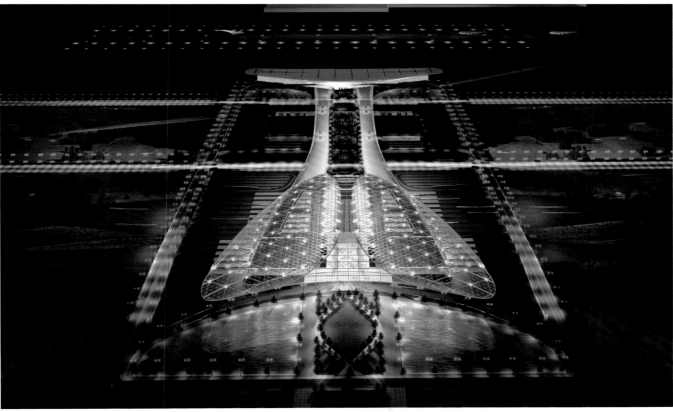

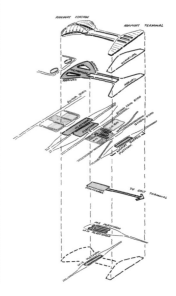

YANGPU UNIVERSITY AVENUE

Yangpu is located in the north-east of the city, bordering the Huangpu River and only 4km from the Bund. Situated within the Yangpu District are two of the most prestigious universities, Fudan and Tongji Universities, the Jiangwan Stadium (built in 1935 – shown right in purple) and the largest concentration of research centres in China. The Knowledge and Innovation Community (KIC) masterplan was jointly developed by the Yangpu government and Shui On Land with the participation of the world's leading architects, designers and planners. Farrells designed the residential live/work space in red (sector 6-6).

The idea behind KIC was to create a community for students, technological innovation and entrepreneurial spirit that allowed for greater interaction between home, study and work. This courtyard of buildings consists of a 16-storey high-rise residential tower and 12 continuous low-rise residential blocks from four to eight storeys high and a landscape garden shared by all residents. These residential blocks along University Avenue step gently down and up to allow southern sunlight exposure to all units. The variety of unit types and sizes with working spaces provide a diversity of housing choices and flexibility for the university community.

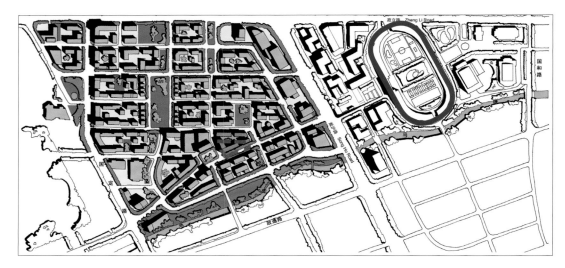

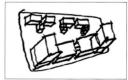 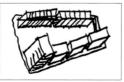 

Above: KIC masterplan with Farrells University Avenue housing highlighted in red, landscaping in green, Huangpu River in blue.

Middle: Courtyard housing studies sketches.

Below left: View of the courtyard area.

Below right: Yangpu housing along University Avenue.

NANJING ROAD EAST

In 2002, the Shanghai municipal government announced plans to redevelop both banks of Huangpu River and develop Nanjing Road – Shanghai's largest shopping street. Aiming to strengthen the city's profile and culture through the preservation of historic buildings and new landscape features.

The proposed new masterplan was for the redevelopment of 11 colonial-style buildings built in the early 1900s, where the old Central Market used to stand. The design revitalised these colonial buildings for contemporary commercial purposes while keeping their original style. The scheme would give the buildings a new lease of life, striking a balance between preservation of their historical value and their modern function as high-end retail and fine dining.

The first stage was a heritage assessment that determined which elements to retain and which to add. Various properties are in poor condition with significantly altered façades and modifications, which have been badly carried out. The proposal endeavoured to restore and integrate old with new without losing the original character. To unify the disparate buildings, it was proposed that the site be reworked into a galleria with intersecting streets covered by a glass cruciform canopy. The site entrances are redefined to draw people into its new, more animated centre.

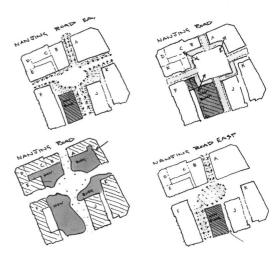

Left: A modern canopy sitting betwen the historic buildings is part of the proposed revitalisation of 179 Nanjing Road East.

Top: Preliminary concept studies of massing options.

Middle: Model showing how the glass canopy unifies the site.

Bottom: Intersection of Nanjing Road East and Sichuan Zhong Road.

HUAXIA MASTERPLAN

Thirty-two km from central Shanghai, on the banks of the Yangtze River, the Pudong Huaxia Masterplan is a unique development designed as a resort destination. Incorporating a new central lagoon surrounded by cultural, retail, and community facilities, it will provide an oasis away from the metropolis.

Farrells proposed Huaxia Resort will be the key cultural tourism district of the Pudong New Area. The 6.6km² district is located to the south-east of the Pudong, near the airport. The eastern side of the development will accommodate the seaside resort zone. A natural scenic spot, the harbour will be developed to celebrate its seashore, fresh air and sea vistas.

Its proximity to both river and sea has inspired the theme of water throughout the landscaping and parks. This is predominantly expressed in the gently curving waterfront promenade that embraces the lagoon, providing expansive views from every vantage point. A variety of green parks are interspersed throughout and include wide, tree-lined boulevards creating an elegant sense of place. The inland, narrower streets provide a village-like intimacy, and add to the relaxing ambience away from city life.

The distinctive free-flowing canopies are designed to create a comfortable micro-climate beneath, cooling during the summer, warming in the winter and providing shelter from the rain. These semi-enclosed areas use passive environmental strategies to temper the climate.

The flowing organic forms create a warm and welcoming embrace. Like the undulating sand patterns on the seashore, there's a sense of natural beauty. This relaxing haven for residents and tourists is also a bustling 24-hour environment without the chaos of the city and a vibrant destination for international visitors.

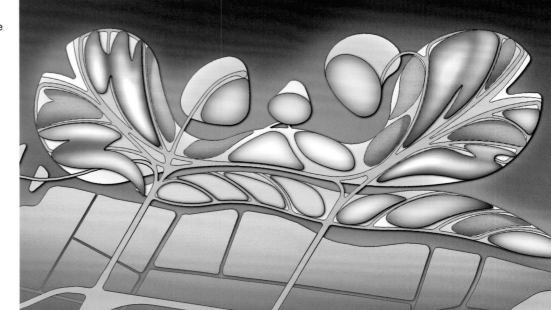

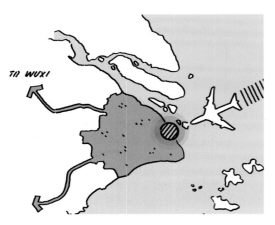

Left: Gateway to the world: Huaxia's proximity to Pudong International airport.

Top: Masterplan aerial perspective.

Middle: Huaxia Resort Coastal Dunes masterplan.

Bottom row (left to right): Figure ground plan; waterway and traffic network plans.

THE SPRINGS

Shanghai's success as a commercial hub in Asia has resulted in an increasingly congested city centre. In 2007, the Shanghai Planning Bureau announced that the city's future planning would shift from one city centre to a multi-centric structure.

The Springs masterplan is a prominent site within one of these new centres, located to the north of Shanghai's historic core near the confluence of the Huangpu and Yangtze rivers. It forms part of Jiangwan New Town, where much of the infrastructure has already been built – a unique area situated on a former military air-base within one of the last remaining natural Shanghai wetlands. In a city which has expanded rapidly over the past two decades, it represents a rare haven of tranquillity characterised by a network of canals and estuary landscapes.

The vision for The Springs is to create a vibrant, urban place within a garden setting, inspired by Shanghai's great streets, lanes, courtyards, public squares and parks. The masterplan creates an interconnected and varied sequence of spaces, including fine garden squares, a metropolitan square, and a magnificent galleria. Connected to Puxi in the city centre by metro, the high level of public transport accessibility provides The Springs with the opportunity to create a sustainable and integrated transport-orientated development.

Right: The Springs masterplan. **Below (left to right):** Concept masterplan sketch; Springs living; model of site.

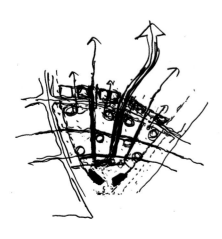

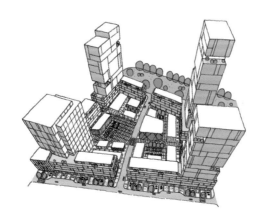

NINGBO EASTERN NEW TOWN

With its close proximity to Shanghai and Hangzhou, and as one of the economic development centres of the Yangtze River Delta, Ningbo has a strong manufacturing sector for export and is one of the greenest cities in China. Located in the heart of the newly developed Eastern New Town, this mixed-use development incorporates sky gardens, sunken plazas, two office buildings, three residential towers, a 350m-long retail street and a business hotel.

The 40,660m^2 site is composed of three street blocks with an above-ground GFA of 175,000m^2. An urban route connects this new Urban Mixed-use District with Ningbo CBD to its west and the Government Administrative District to the east. The western end will host outdoor cafés and restaurants, whilst the eastern end has a public square with high-end retail. Nodes are created at each end forming gateways to the project site. It allows people to interact horizontally and vertically by utilising sky gardens, sunken plazas, raised podiums, high-level bridges and roof terraces. These activate the site at all levels: physically, visually, public, semi-public and private.

The Sunken Plaza will link to the underground metro station below the office tower and serve as the main entrance to the project by public transportation. An underground link is also proposed here for connection to the Art and Culture District across the main city axis.

Residential buildings are located along the northern end. The 680 apartments are designed with maximum flexibility, and have views of the Art and Culture District towards the south. Residential sky gardens open up view corridors and act as natural breezeways. Luxury apartments have outdoor terraces, a private pool and gardens, achieving the idea of a house in the sky. The 120-room business hotel is strategically located near the retail area, close to the office building and the Government District.

The two landmark office buildings at 152m and 76m, following predetermined height restrictions, anchor the corners of the project. They are designed with a central core arrangement for maximum efficiency and flexibility.

Top: Aerial perspective of Ningbo Eastern New Town.

Bottom: Ningbo Eastern New Town urban street masterplan incorporates links to the metro and neighbouring districts..

Opposite: The 350m urban street integrates vertical and horizontal interaction through sunken plazas and sky bridges.

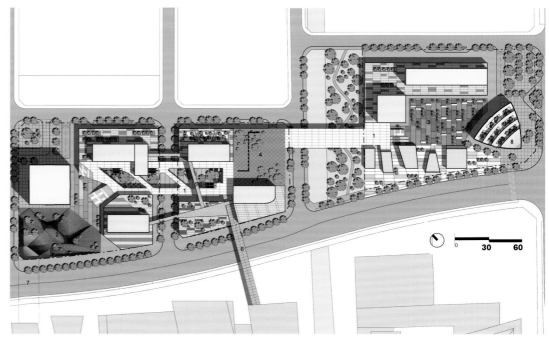

PUDONG INTERNATIONAL AIRPORT

Serving as the gateway to this key city, the Pudong International Airport is designed to reflect Shanghai's position on the world stage. Located approximately 30 kilometres (19 miles) east of the city centre, it occupies a 40km² site adjacent to the coastline on the eastern edge of the Pudong.

Shanghai Pudong International Airport initially opened in October 1999 and design proposals for Phase Two were requested in early 2004. It required that the airport be fully integrated between Terminals One, Two, and the satellites, as one single operational entity.

This Phase Two design proposal was built upon the intent of the initial masterplan, embracing the original infrastructure to bring about a world-class international hub. A joint competition bid with Integrated Design Associates Ltd. (IDA), it introduces primarily Terminal Two and an expansion to international and domestic passengers. The Airport Plaza is the centre of the arrival hub, which lets passengers access all modes of transit and connects the two terminals. The design of the Plaza roof acts as a unifier to integrate all facilities.

Key elements of the proposal design drew upon China's rich heritage combined with state-of-the-art technology to create an energy-efficient, sustainable Terminal in a contemporary dynamic structure. The design provides simple movement orientation; passengers require only one level change on arrivals or departures to maximise convenience and comfort. The Terminal has three primary levels: Departures Level at the top; Arrivals at Level 2; and a baggage handling area, functional rooms and car parks on Level 1.

Shanghai Pudong International Airport is currently the third biggest passenger terminal (in China) and cargo terminal (globally).

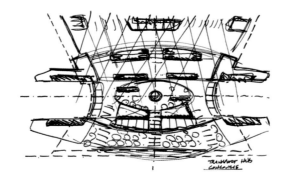
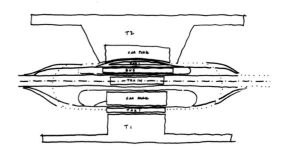

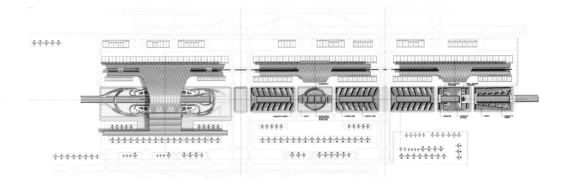

Above: The Airport Plaza.

Top right: Concept studies of transport interchange.

Middle: Terminal Two building and landscape plan.

Bottom: Aerial perspective of proposed airport.

WUXI TV TOWER

A monument to the past, present and future, this 240m tower points skywards from Wuxi's geographical centre. The proposed design and masterplan was developed to enhance the natural profile of the land form whilst promoting the definition of space. The geometry of the three transport links – road, cable car and tram – that converge at the tower's base inform the fluid lines of the tower. The result is a smooth transition between the urban city, natural landscape and the vertical form. Once at the summit, visitors can access a wide range of activities and experiences, from the cultural Wuxi history walk to 360° panoramic views from the Observation Pod's sky decks and restaurants located at 100m above ground level.

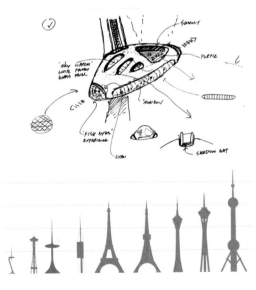

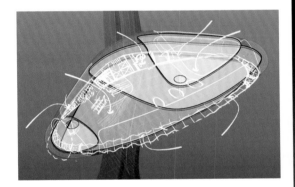

Top: Floor levels study, viewing deck and vista arrangement.

Middle: Concept sketch of the Observation Pod.

Bottom: Wuxi TV Tower height comparisons.

Right: Wuxi TV Tower at night with the backdrop of the city.

GUANGZHOU

GUANGZHOU
DAILY NEWS

GUANGZHOU SOUTH
RAILWAY STATION

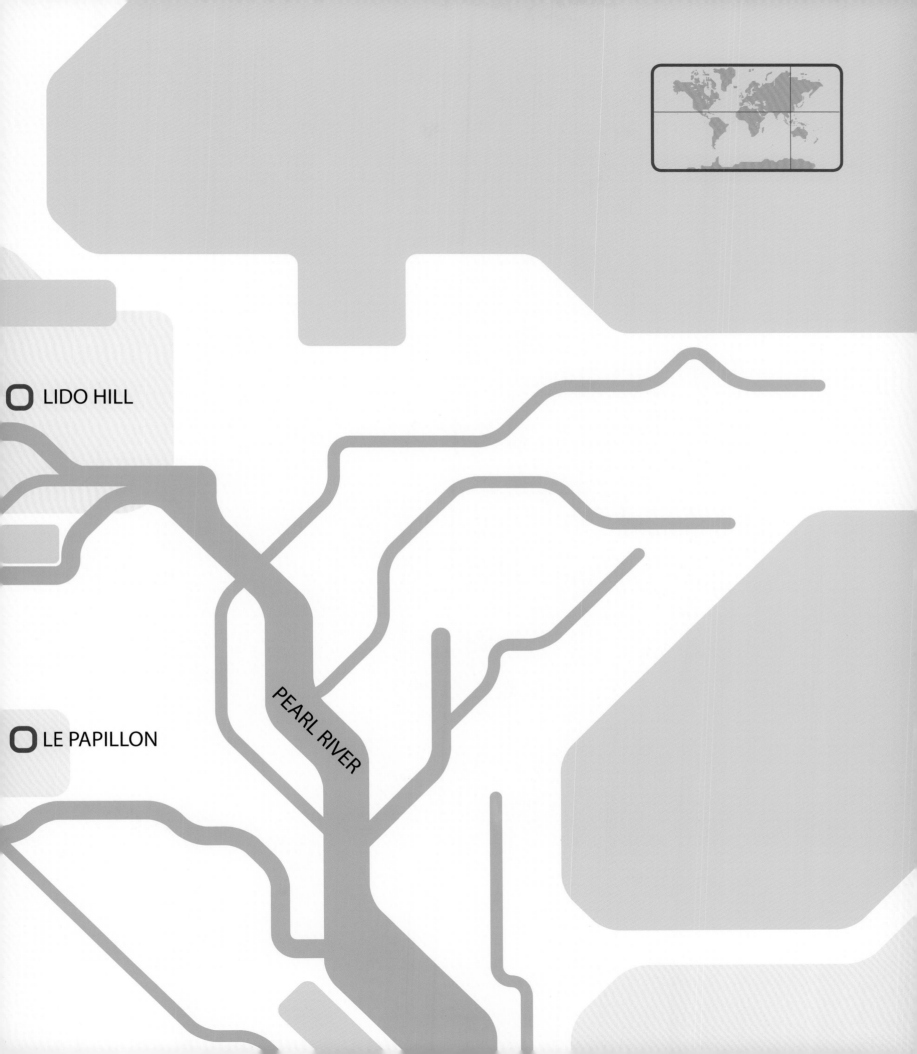

LIDO HILL

LE PAPILLON

PEARL RIVER

GUANGZHOU

According to the 2010 National Population Census of China, within Guangdong's 179,812.7km² Province there are currently 104.3 million residents. Guangdong is divided into nine major, cities including Guangzhou and Shenzhen. It has also recorded a GDP of ¥4.55 trillion yuan ($58.6 billion USD) in 2010, ranking top in China and higher than Hong Kong, Singapore and Taiwan, since 1998.

At the head of the Pearl River Delta, Guangzhou dominates southern China and provides the country's main outlet via the Pearl River Delta to the South China Sea. Along with Shanghai and China's other great cities, it is effectively a city state with a total of 24 million inhabitants within the urban agglomeration.

Guangzhou has a lengthy history as China's main commercial and trading centre with its close proximity to the sea. Foreign traders have utilised its location since the Tang Dynasty, with Arab,

Persian and Indian merchants, the formation of the East India Trading Company in 1699, through the Opium Wars to the establishment of the Treaty of Nanjing (1842) whereby Guangzhou officially became a treaty port. Deng Xiaoping's economic reform policies of the 1970s and '80s made Guangzhou one of the first Chinese cities selected for open market reform.

Since the 1980s the Province of Guangdong has become a heavily industrialised region that has attracted a glut of transient migrants looking for work. This has resulted in an urban form that is much more responsive and organic than Beijing's, although the grid remains the main ordering device. It has created huge economic growth for Guangzhou and a need to develop the city's infrastructure.

Guangzhou had three main passenger railway stations: Guangzhou East, North and Guangzhou

(central) Railway Stations are located in the city's Tianhe, Huadu and Yuexiu districts. These stations have been brutally overloaded and unable to meet growing demands from commuting passengers. The solution was to build a new transportation hub that would accommodate the proposed high-speed rail corridor from Beijing to Guangzhou and a link to Shenzhen and Hong Kong.

In March of 2004, Farrells were invited to collaborate in a rigorous three-month design study proposal for the new Guangzhou Station for the Ministry of Rail in an international competition. Submitted in the June, the shortlisted teams went through several stages to redefine, adjust and develop the project, whereby Farrells won the competition to design and construct the masterplan and building. Guangzhou South Railway Station opened to the public in January 2010.

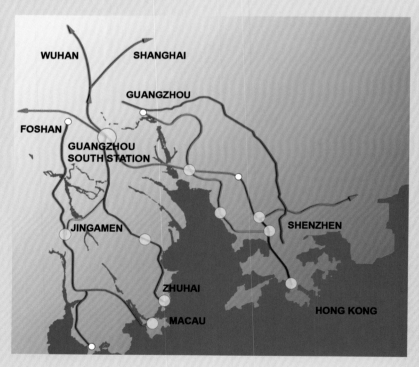

Above: Map of Guangzhou South Railway Station and Pearl River Delta links.

Right: Farrells' Guangzhou Daily News Building – proposed scheme.

GUANGZHOU SOUTH RAILWAY STATION

Located at the heart of the Pearl River Delta, 17km from Guangzhou city centre, this comprehensive transportation hub serves a catchment area of over 300 million people. It is part of China's new high-speed rail network that incorporates four new major transportation interchanges, including Guangzhou South Railway Station and Beijing South Station (see Beijing chapter). As a world-class railway station it helps connect the cities of Beijing–Wuhan–Shanghai–Guangzhou–Hong Kong. The station was designed in collaboration with the Fourth Railway Survey and Design Institute (FSDI) and the Beijing Institute of Architectural Design (BIAD).

When Farrells started work on the station in collaboration with the Fourth Railway Survey and Design Institute (FSDI) and the Beijing Institute of Architectural Design (BIAD) its huge size and remote location of the project were questionable until it became apparent that rather than the existing patronage dictating its form, the idea was to create a catalyst for future growth.

Guangzhou South Railway Station officially resides in Shibi Village, Panyu District. The decision to create a new transportation hub to link Mainland China to Panyu 番禺区 was because of its close proximity to the south of downtown Guangzhou. Designed as a key interchange station, it contains the most metro connections in Guangzhou (metro lines 2 and 7), a terminus for the new Express Rail Link (Guangzhou–Shenzhen–Hong Kong), Guangzhou–Zhuhai Intercity Mass Rapid Transit, and Guangzhou Railway and Wugang Passenger Lines.

Passengers arriving at Guangzhou South Railway Station from around the country can efficiently interchange to other major cities in the Pearl River Delta by using the advanced network available. The Guandong provincial government has stated that this new railway station will help fortify Guangdong's status as a logistics centre and contribute to the Province's sustainable economic growth.

Railway stations do not come much larger than this. At 590 metres long and 350 metres wide, it is approximately three times the size of London's King's Cross and is the largest single railway station in Asia, as well as one of the biggest in the world.

Two landscaped urban plazas constitute the main east and west entrances to the station while tree-filled spines add a welcome splash of green to the Arrival and Departure halls. Other environmentally friendly features include: natural ventilation and lighting to avoid excessive air conditioning, photovoltaic cells – which harness solar energy and convert it into electricity – and an open plan station arrangement to assist with natural light and generous view corridors. By centering the columns between the tracks, large column-free open platforms enhance the distribution with convenient and efficient passenger flows, within the shortest distance and time possible.

The station is arranged over six floors, with voids for lifts and escalators. An elevated concourse on the uppermost level is dedicated to departures. Below this concourse lie the 28 platforms for high-speed,

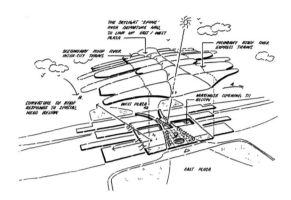

Above: Guangzhou South Railway Station from the east.

Top: The station's roof responds to various factors such as weather conditions, light and spatial needs.

Center: Aerial view of Guangzhou South Railway Station during construction.

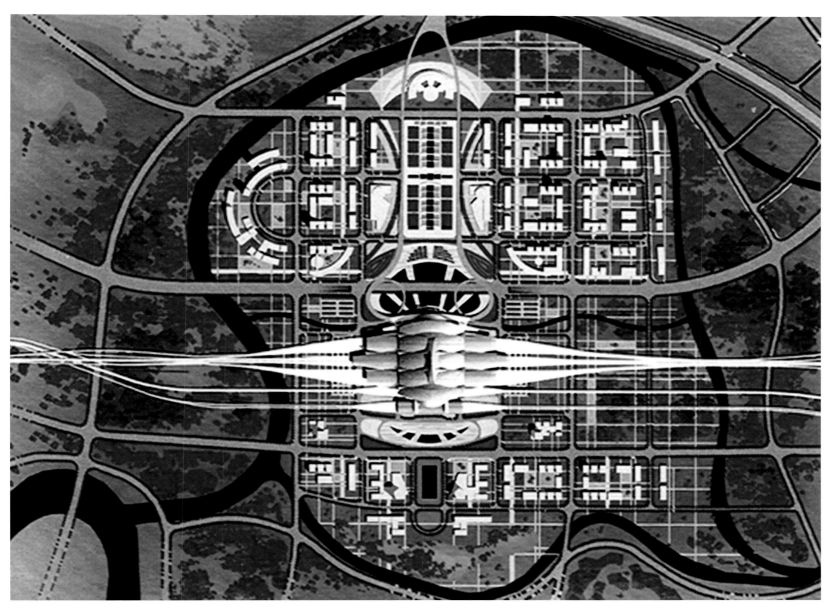

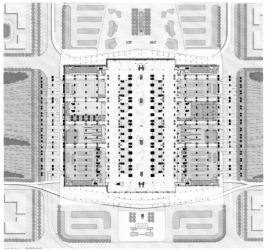

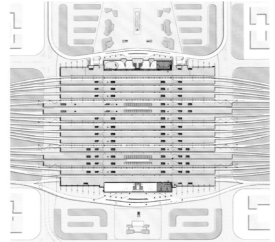

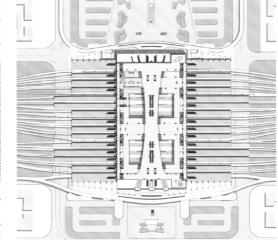

Opposite: Guangzhou South Railway Station Departures Level concourse.

Top: Masterplan (winning competition entry).

Bottom left to right:
Arrivals Level in context; Platform Level; Departures Level.

long-haul trains, uniquely elevated to prevent damage to ecologically sensitive wetlands below.

Beneath the platforms at ground level, city and station meet. Arriving passengers can make their connections easily from here to other modes of transport including the metro and underground railway networks, which take up the station's three subterranean levels.

The station planning arrangement is well executed, especially given the various modes of transfer required. A strategic model using horizontal separation has been adopted to improve passenger flow and create convenient and efficient passenger interchanges whilst preventing cross-over and mixing of different flows of passengers.

The roof shape was inspired by banana leaves, incorporating longitudinal skylights that provide the station's highest level (Departures) with maximum daylight. Lower down, it partially covers the open-sided platforms to promote the circulation of fresh air. Skylights are positioned between the railway tracks so natural light can filter down to the ground-level concourse. The roof is designed to protect the station from the wind and prevent uplift from the trains passing through.

Bisecting the roof is a central spine that joins the station's east and west ends. It is at its widest near the entrances but narrows towards the centre reflecting passenger flows. Its complex curved form responds to the circulation route below and acts as a route finder. A canopy at either end terminates the spine but continues its geometry and construction, and provides shelter to the drop-off areas. The roof unifies all the platforms, and its in-built flexibility allows for potential new platforms and station expansion.

The design of Guangzhou South Railway Station strikes a relaxed balance between function and formal expression. This is achieved through the concise articulation of its organised structure, which simultaneously endows the station with a unique identity. The station is generating a new urban area, and is a significant factor in the rapid development of the regional economy.

Top: Functional diagram of the multi-modal transportation hub.

Bottom left: Exterior of the station allows for clear pedestrian flows to neighbouring areas.

Bottom right: A station guard salutes the Guangzhou high-speed train as it departs.

Opposite page
Top: Departures Hall. The use of 68m spans creates column-free waiting rooms.

Bottom: Details of the Departures Hall.

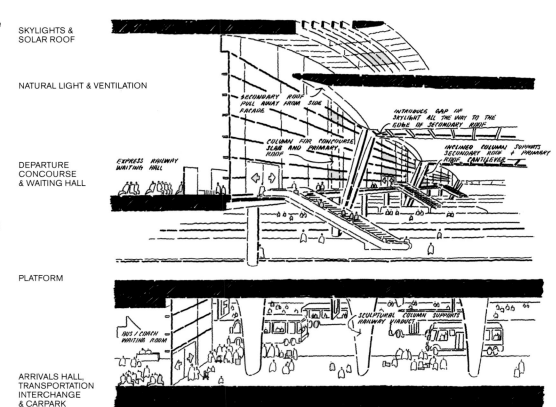

SKYLIGHTS & SOLAR ROOF

NATURAL LIGHT & VENTILATION

DEPARTURE CONCOURSE & WAITING HALL

PLATFORM

ARRIVALS HALL, TRANSPORTATION INTERCHANGE & CARPARK

车次	终到站	开点	检票
Train	To	Departs	Check
G1100	武　汉	18:32	A6
G1103	武　汉	18:48	A6
D7653	珠海北	19:00	A22
G6064	长沙南	19:00	A8
G1102	武　汉	19:18	A6

票口区域候车检票

Top: Departures Platform 2 and 3.

Bottom left: Arrivals level platform

Bottom right: The elevated viaduct structure forms the primary support to the rail tracks and platforms, as well as the columns for the roof structure.

LIDO HILL

Located to the north-east of Guangzhou city, Lido Hill is close to Tianhe Commercial District and local universities. A green-field site previously used for agriculture, it is now an up-and-coming residential area. A distinctive profile on the skyline helps create a unique identity for the project: a residential community with a club house, outdoor swimming pool and private internal courtyards. The landscaping incorporates green contoured steps moving south to north and envelopes the roof tops.

Right: Aerial perspective of Lido Hill, from the north-east.

LE PAPILLON

Overlooking Lianhu Harbour, the site is located near metro 4 and is 23km from Guangzhou South Station. This is a comprehensive new township development for residential, commercial, office, and hotel accommodation. Consisting of 11 residential blocks arranged in three radial strips, it accommodates over 357 apartments. The towers' curved shapes reflect the organic theme, and they align to form a variety of central open spaces. Double-height sky gardens were added to open up view corridors and act as natural breezeways to the river.

Left: Street view of the completed residential towers along Shilian Road.

Above: Le Papillion – aerial perspective of the masterplan model. The inspiration for the massing was the geometric shape and colourful markings of a butterfly.

SHENZHEN

○ TCL HIGH-TECH
INDUSTRIAL PARK

NOBLE TOWER ○

PEARL ISLAND ▢

NANSHAN
BUSINESS AND
CULTURAL
DISTRICT

○

SHENZHEN BAY

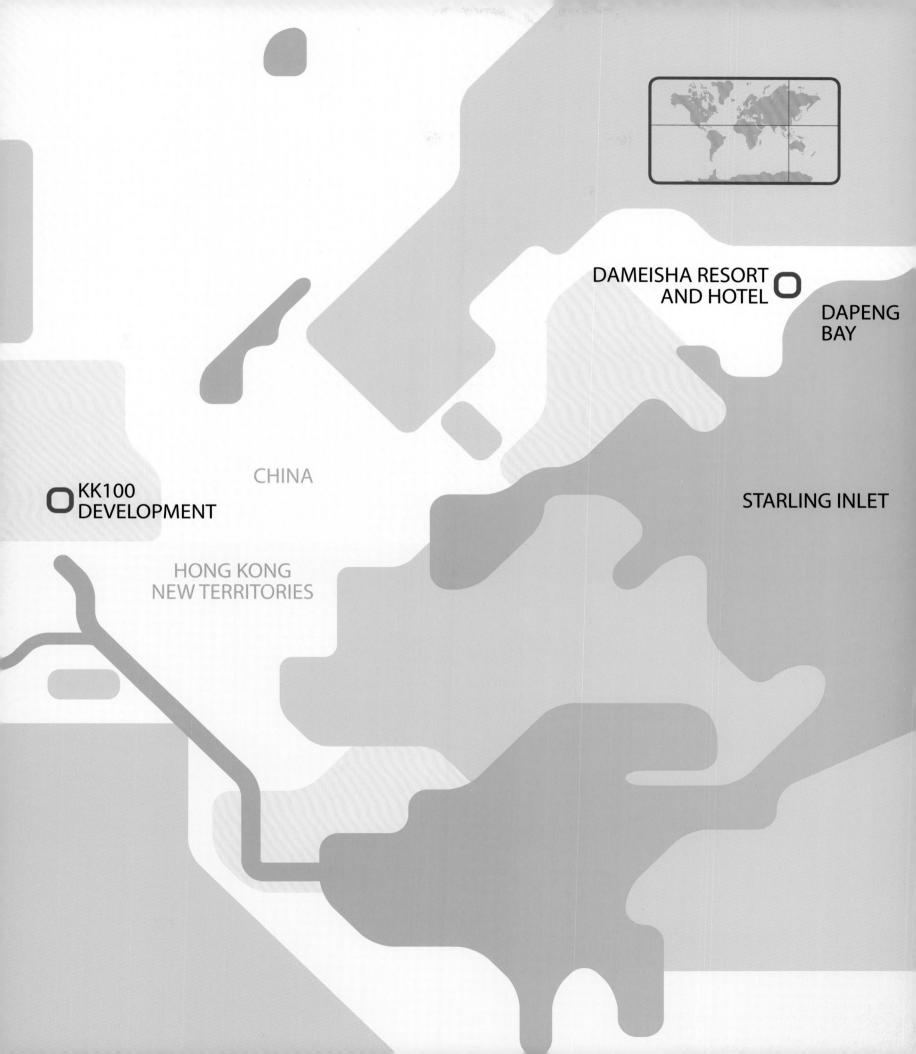

DAMEISHA RESORT AND HOTEL

DAPENG BAY

STARLING INLET

CHINA

KK100 DEVELOPMENT

HONG KONG
NEW TERRITORIES

SHENZHEN

Shenzhen was a fishing village of approximately 20,000 inhabitants in the 1970s. It was characterised by the paddy fields and fish farms which can still be seen in the area today. After 1979 when it was declared a Special Economic Zone, the city grew explosively and it is now approaching a population of 8 million. Shenzhen, along with Guangzhou, is a pivotal city in the Pearl River Delta and borders Hong Kong to the south.

Since the 1990s Shenzhen has seen unparalleled rapid urbanisation and foreign investment. The State Council approved the Shenzhen Comprehensive Plan (1996 – 2010) whereby it envisaged that Shenzhen will evolve into a modern, international city with a strong identity and image. The strategic objectives were to develop Shenzhen into a regional economic centre, garden city and world-class metropolis.

New high-profile projects such as KK100 Tower, the ninth tallest building in the world, has put Shenzhen firmly on the map as a modern metropolis.

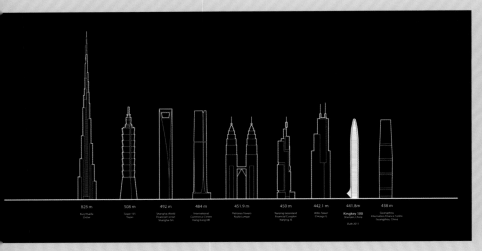

Top left: Height comparisons of the world's tallest building. KK100 is the ninth tallest.

Top right: Aerial view of Pearl Island model.

Above: Shenzhen's skyline with rice paddies in the foreground.

Opposite: Construction of KK100 Development is nearing completion; the tower was topped out in May 2011.

Inset: Paddy fields on the edge of Shenzhen. Photo taken by Terry Farrell in 1964 from the Chinese border in Hong Kong.

DAMEISHA RESORT & HOTEL

Twenty-five km from Shenzhen city centre, on the eastern coastline, the five-star Sheraton Dameisha resort sits on a secluded 2.5km stretch of white sandy beach. This six-hectare site faces Dapeng Bay and the ocean and has a magnificent mountain range framing the development from behind. Located on the largest and closest public beach to Shenzhen, it uniquely offers guests the luxury of being able to walk from their hotel room through the lobby and garden and directly onto the sand.

Dameisha beach is a tourist destination for locals and Hong Kong visitors to relax and enjoy the 1,800m coastline, an oasis from the busy city. Host to international events, including the 2011 Universiade Volleyball games, Dameisha is one of the most popular attractions in the region. The Sheraton Dameisha Resort was the first five-star facility in the region to offer luxurious accommodation, a private beach and a marina.

The topography of the beach allowed the hotel and private villas to be arranged along the site's east-west axis, taking full advantage of the sea views and southerly aspect. The plan was drawn up to create a symbiotic relationship between itself and the surrounding landscape. Next to a wetlands park, the resort's lagoon-style swimming pool and loosely ordered landscaping embraces its natural environment.

The Dameisha Resort is a 386-key hotel with two two-storey private villas with their own indoor and outdoor pools, a library, dining areas and conference facilities. The planning of the hotel is based on a single-loaded, single-aspect building approach. The constraints of the site's boundaries, set-backs and height limits meant that a straight building mass with single aspects was too long for the site and therefore favoured a curved plan layout. Maximising the beach frontage, this sinuous, angle-free form guarantees that all rooms have ocean views and avoids a long, straight corridor thanks to the curvelinear flow. This unconventional curved-radial arrangement is extremely complex and posed a major design challenge. The site-planning geometry of a single-loaded aspect building form makes the layout of the hotel guest rooms more difficult than a typical double-loaded arrangement because the rooms are a mix of concave and convex form.

Like most landmark structures, the hotel went through several design options. The first was a conventional star shape with a centrally located core, double-loaded corridor and dual aspect, which meant that public circulation and fire escape routes were efficient but the overall layout was lacking, particularly in terms of ensuring sea views for each room. Borrowing from the hotel's ocean surrounds, the second scheme evolved from a sail concept. Its shape was reminiscent of a series of waves or yacht sails with a section of the building curved like a billowing sail. The third concept adopted the form of a breaking wave but was discarded as the issue of tsunamis was too sensitive. The fourth concept combined the ideas of the billowing sail and waves to create a plan form reminiscent of the ocean, a sine curve and the mountains' silhouette. This approved design evolved from the abstract 'aura' concept – that of creating a sense of place and a building with a distinct spirit and good energy.

The elevation and massing of the building are a creative response to the pragmatic and practical considerations of the client's requirements and are designed as two separate building forms – a free-flowing podium base containing semi-public functions (the conference centre, restaurants and a health and fitness club) and an elevated tower sitting above the podium. This is conceived as a long, serpentine plan form housing the private and quiet zones required for the guest rooms.

Based on the motif of a traditional Chinese dragon, the head, body and tail of this undulating shape have each been assigned various functions. The head at the western end of the building is lifted to make it more prominent and suitably prestigious to contain all the presidential and executive suites. The body accommodates the hotel's more standard rooms, while the tail angles downwards to house executive rooms with outdoor garden terraces.

The hotel experience begins at the entry to the site along a single-lane road lined with palm trees. The atrium lobby entrance comprises a dome supported by the circulation core and the base with a width of 50m and a height of 35m. Although the geometry of the structure is asymmetric, it is based on a geodesic dome that allows a self-supporting structure without the need for columns. This grand spatial volume adds to the expansive ocean views beyond and the feeling of being somewhere unique.

Below left: Map showing site in relation to Hong Kong.

Below: The Sheraton Dameisha Hotel and villas site plan.

Opposite page
Top: View of the Sheraton Dameisha Hotel from Dapeng Bay.

Bottom: Each room has a balcony with open vistas to the sea.

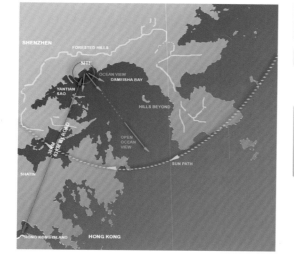

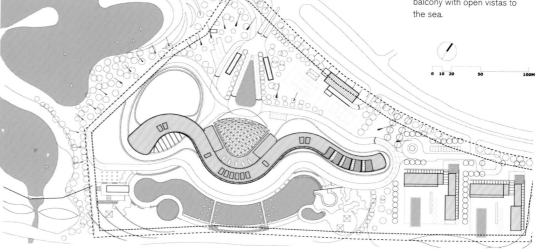

Left: Detail of the hotel's curved façade.

Above: The hotel's private villas.

Opposite page
Top: The hotel's unusual shape is based on the motif of a traditional Chinese dragon.

Bottom left: The private villas boast secluded indoor and outdoor areas to relax.

Bottom right: View from one of the resort's outdoor pools.

KK100 TOWER DEVELOPMENT

This 3.6-hectare site housed the old dwellings of Caiwuwei Village, an area known for its bad environment, insufficient transportation infrastructure and degraded buildings. The developer took the initiative to form a company with the villagers (a Joint Development Initiative), Caiwuwei Co. Ltd., for a new model for the district that would benefit everyone. The existing buildings were mainly run-down housing with with inadequate living conditions the old residences were replaced with new resettlement housing on the same site. Seven towers of the development are for reprovision of the residential and commercial space of the villagers, and three of the seven are housing for the villages to rent out. The new development has created an area that provides a higher quality of life for the original residents. It provides them with their own space and a rental apartment for them to obtain rental income. This Joint Development Initiative takes up a large amount of the site and therefore to be financially viable for the developer the most effective solution was to build a mixed-use high-rise tower and retail podium to offset the costs. Planning work was initiated by Shenzhen government in 2002 with the goal of redeveloping the area into Shenzhen's main Financial District.

The winner of an in an international competition, Shenzhen's KK100 Development was commissioned on the strength of its superior design and masterplan. Located in Shenzhen's Luohu District where 74% of the city's banking institutions now reside, it has spectacular panoramic views over the city and, on a clear day, Hong Kong on the horizon. This 441.8m-high, 100-storey tower is currently the tallest building in Shenzhen, the third tallest in China and the world's eighth highest mixed-use building.

The tower has a striking, gently curving profile. The fluid shape and reflective skin is an allusion to a spring or a fountain, which reflects the wealth and prosperity springing from the economic success of Shenzhen. It also reflects the unprecedented economic growth currently being experienced in China and the identity, stability and stature of the developer, The Kingkey Group.

In addition to its aesthetics, the tower's elegant form is married with a rational and pragmatic footprint, which allows for high-efficiency levels and an optimal operation of its components. Its orientation maximises the park and city views; its cladding is a sophisticated environmental skin that allows the tower to maintain an optimum interior environment while minimising potential solar heat gain; and the modular approach of the system ensures that it is cost-effective.

The tower is linked to a podium containing a vast shopping mall, containing high-end retail, flagship stores, and Shenzhen's first IMAX theatre. KK100 Mall connects directly to Shenzhen metro line at below ground level, providing direct links to the city centre. It incorporates extremely versatile spaces and its combined use of human-scale volumes, landscaping and natural light from the podium roof results in a living and working environment of the highest quality.

KK100 Tower has a mixed-use arrangement, with floors divided into three major functions. Levels 4 to 72 incorporate 173,000m² of Grade-A office space, with seven trading floors distributed evenly throughout the office section. Levels 75 to 95 accommodate the five-star St Regis Hotel (opening November 2011), complete with 250 rooms and executive suites, state-of-the-art conference and business facilities and a fitness centre. Crowning the top of the building is a breathtaking Sky Garden with panoramic city views, in which the hotel's range of fine-dining options will be located. Hotel guests will arrive at the Sky Garden Hotel Lobby on the 94th Floor, to check-in or to use the restaurants, bars and enjoy the panoramic viewing areas. Below the hotel reception is a 16-storey atrium with scenic lifts for access to guest rooms located between levels 77 and 90.

Existing site of Caiwuwei Village

The tower's curve gives a dimensional difference between adjacent floors, while an ample floor-to-floor height of four metres allows daylight to penetrate deep into the floor plates. The perimeter column arrangement provides an unobstructed working environment on each level and views towards Lizhi and Renmin Park as well as the city. Lifts, E & M openings and service rooms lie within a rectangular central core. This allows for multi-tenancy opportunities by providing access corridors leading to escape stairs on each of its four sides.

The tower has eight lift zones, four below and four above the Sky Lobby, which helps to reduce the footprint of the core by stacking the lift shafts. This in turn provides more space for upper floor executive offices with the expansion of the floor plates. Six double-decker shuttle lifts accessed at B1 and Ground Level alight at the Sky Lobby levels 39 and 40.

Emphasis on sustainability was intrinsic in the tower's design. Major green proposals included an environmentally friendly built form and envelope design; energy-saving building-services systems; a free-cooling system; and advanced building energy and environmental simulations.

However, it was not just the tower – the scope for the masterplan was larger than that, with the whole area being redeveloped. KK100 Development has already uplifted the surrounding neighbourhood by stimulating economic growth and it will become a landmark in its own right.

Opposite page:
Top right: View of the site prior to construction.

Bottom right: The site area with its 'nail house', whose owners held out for some time against the development.

Bottom left: Masterplan.

Bottom right: Aerial perspective of KK100 Development.

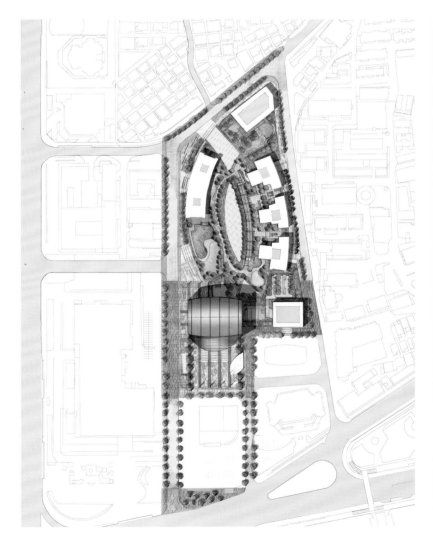

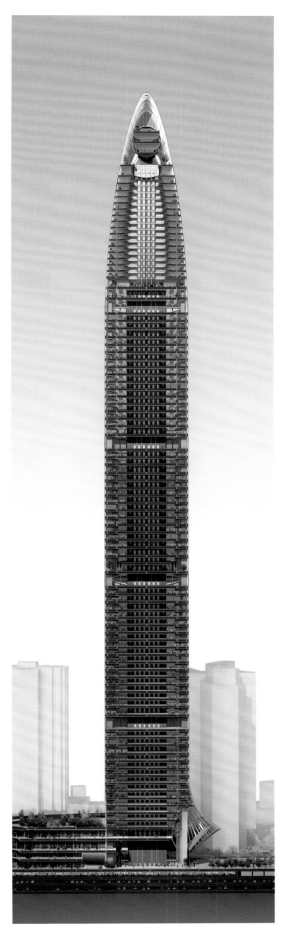

Opposite page
Top left: South elevation detail of Sky Garden façade.

Top right: View across Shenzhen from the 100th Floor facing north.

Bottom left: Detail of entrance canopy underside.

Bottom right: Detail of entrance canopy curve.

Far left: Cross-section showing 100 storeys.

Left: View of the almost completed tower, 2011.

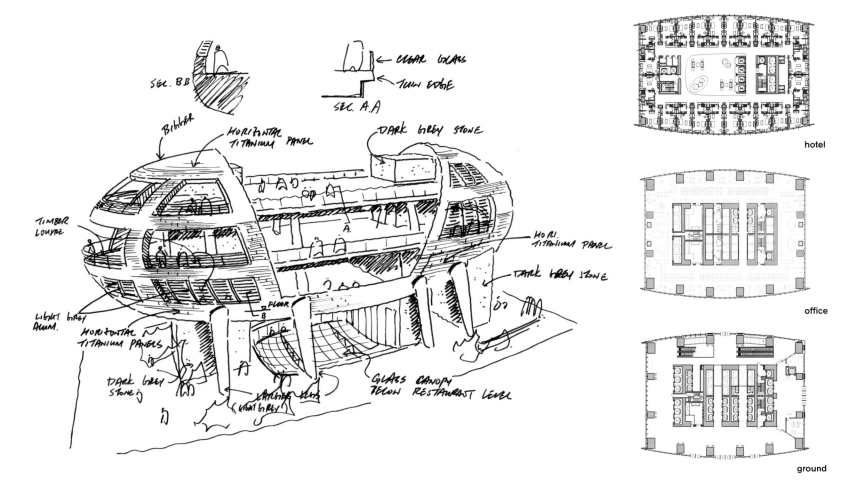

SEC. B.B

CLEAR GLASS
TURN EDGE
SEC. A.A

BIBLER
HORIZONTAL TITANIUM PANEL
DARK GREY STONE
TIMBER LOUVRE
HORI. TITANIUM PANEL
DARK GREY STONE
LIGHT GREY ALUM.
HORIZONTAL TITANIUM PANELS
FLOOR B
DARK GREY STONE
LIGHT GREY
GLASS CANOPY BELOW RESTAURANT LEVEL

hotel

office

ground

Top left: A conceptual cross-section of the hotel lobby and Sky Gardens.

Left: The towers' crowning pod features a rooftop garden terrace and restaurants.

Top: Floor plans (top to bottom): the hotel, typical office floor and the ground floor.

Above: Magnificent panoramic views of Shenzhen and beyond can be seen from the Sky Lobby.

Above: The entrance to KK Mall with residential towers above.

Top right: The podium skylight above KK Mall and the private residential gardens can be clearly seen from KK100 Tower.

Middle right: Through the skylight can be seen the residential towers and landscaping above.

Bottom right: Inside the Mall, abundant daylight filters from the podium skylight.

NOBLE TOWER

Strategically located in the city's Central Business District, Noble Tower rises 190 metres into the Shenzhen skies, between civic buildings to the west and residential neighbourhoods to the east.

To enhance the building's elevations according to predefined architectural plans, the design creates a unique 40-storey building that gives a distinct identity and stature by means of a minimalist but striking scheme. The tower houses 70,000m² of prime office space and executive suites at the top with panoramic views over downtown Shenzhen. The design also included the façade and cladding of the tower's low-rise annex building for commercial use.

A vertical-order, curtain-wall treatment was applied to the tower, which incorporated a glass lookalike spandrel panel to give uniformity of external appearance. The continuation of the vertical mullions reinforced the exterior's elongated effect and resulted in a slim, rhythmic tower. The insertion of a 200mm, transom upstand above the floor level in each typical office storey, provided a workspace adjacent to the window workspace with unobstructed views.

Recessed rectangles at the top of the building enabled glass shafts to run skywards from the ground and further lengthen the whole tower. These recessed panels act as a dramatic architectural feature and, as well as creating a glittering effect through the interplay of the glass shafts and rooftop lighting, they echo the ground-floor portal entrance.

Patterns made by the outdoor water features and landscaping are mirrored by the lobby's interior. Designed with a pale, bright palette, it accentuates the openness and fluidity of the entrance.

Left: Noble Tower lit up on the 30th Anniversary of Shenzhen SAR, August 2010

Above: Detailed facade studies show ceramic fritting and spandrel panels.

Opposite page
Top left: Detail of the exterior's vertical mullions.

Top right: The lobby entrance echoes the outdoor environment.

Bottom left: Entrance canopy.

Bottom right: Initial concept sketches for the building's façade.

TCL HIGH-TECH INDUSTRIAL PARK

Located 20km from Shenzhen along the Pearl River, Shekou sits at the tip of Nantou Peninsula. In 1979, prior to SEZ, it became Shekou Industrial Zone developed solely by China Merchants of Hong Kong. In the '80s it was developed as an expatriate zone for the major oil companies chasing oil in the South China Sea. A ferry ride from Shenzhen, Shekou is an expanding industrial area.

The architecutre and masterplan for TCL (one of the world's largest consumer electronic producers) consists mainly of research and development, and production buildings. The high-

tech industrial park is divided into four different zones: the Headquarters Base, comprising research, development and production facilities; the Comprehensive Business Development Zone for offices, exhibition, recreation and hosting visiting experts; the Living Facilities Zone for housing senior and production staff; and the CEO clubhouse for senior officials.

The Intergraded Business Display Zone, CEO clubhouses, service apartments and staff dormitory are situated along the east of the main road and enjoy views of the landscaped hills. The

R&D clusters have unobstructed view corridors west to east across the site, like the stretching 'Green Fingers' across the site. Internal courtyards are added within each R&D cluster acting as a central focal point and a place to relax.

The project also includes a 200-key business hotel, a 30-key boutique hotel, an exhibition centre, serviced apartments, staff dormitories and supporting commercial developments.

TCL High-Tech Industrial Park Phase One has recently been completed.

Left: Masterplan of TCL High-Tech Industrial Park and concept sketch of the Green Fingers.

Above: Study model of the high-tech clusters and Business Hotel tower.

NANSHAN BUSINESS & CULTURAL DISTRICT

Designed as an iconic gateway to the new Nanshan Business and Cultural District, this 25,727m² site is positioned on reclaimed land, upon an existing green-field plot. Located an hour's drive from Hong Kong just over the Guangdong border, the site overlooks Shenzhen Bay and can be easily reached by the Hong Kong—Shenzhen Western Corridor Bridge or the Shenzhen metro Line 2.

The design has evolved by reinforcing environmental considerations, such as: orientation, climate, preferential views, open spaces, efficiency and commercial building arrangement. The elevated Central Plaza to the north-west of the site is formed by the tower and apartment building, and is connected at ground level by a grand public staircase which flows to an elevated walkway. The apartment and banqueting hall buildings encircle an intimate garden space screened by planting from the Central Plaza.

Our proposed 308m tower consists of 68,000m² of Grade-A office space, a 49,000m² five-star luxury hotel, and 44,000m² of serviced apartments. Crowning the tower is an exclusive private members' VIP Club. The project also includes a 100m apartment tower and a three-storey, low-rise banquet hall with function suites to accommodate 600 guests.

The floor plate alters dramatically as the tower rises, transforming from a square footplate at the base to a dynamic diamond shape at the crown, oriented along the base diagonal. From floor-to-floor this is a subtle almost imperceptible geometrical transformation. Across the entire height of the building an apparent rotation with a dramatic tapering effect results in an elegant tower that addresses views to the surrounding area.

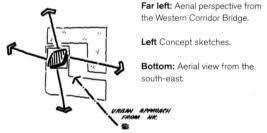

Far left: Aerial perspective from the Western Corridor Bridge.

Left Concept sketches.

Bottom: Aerial view from the south-east.

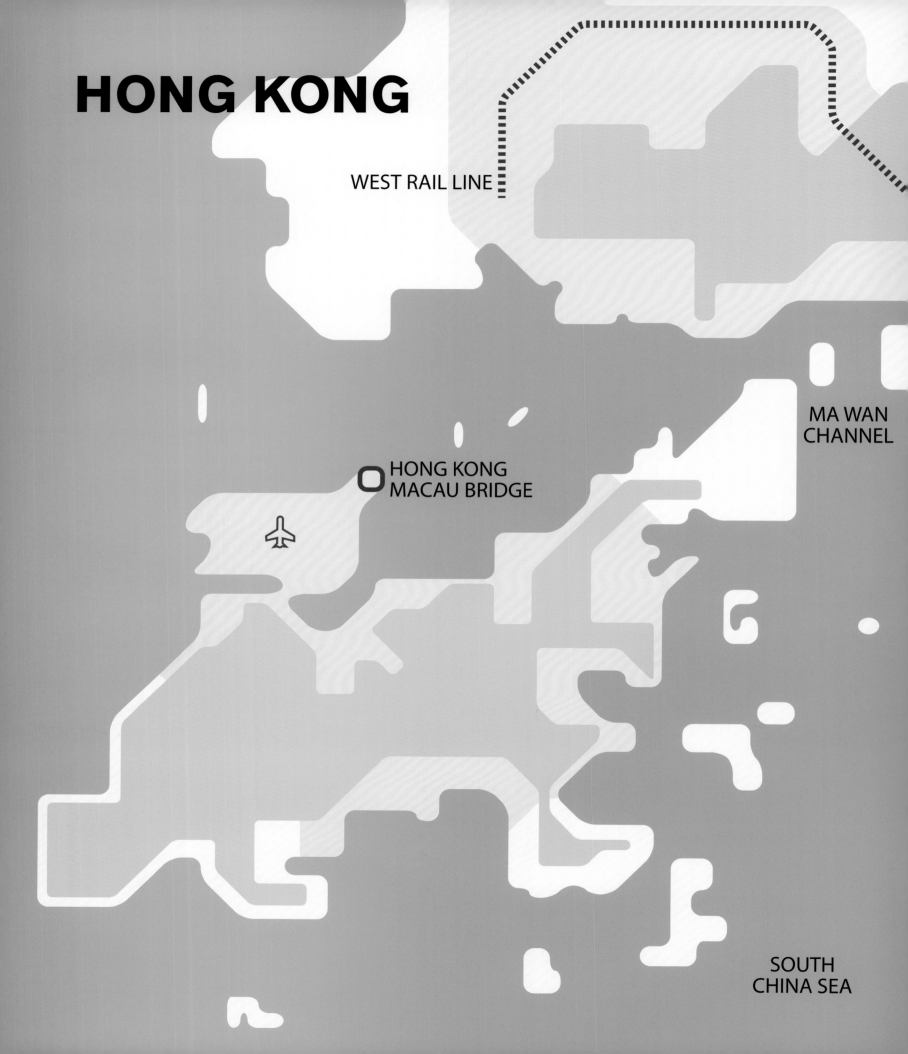

HONG KONG

WEST RAIL LINE

MA WAN
CHANNEL

HONG KONG
MACAU BRIDGE

SOUTH
CHINA SEA

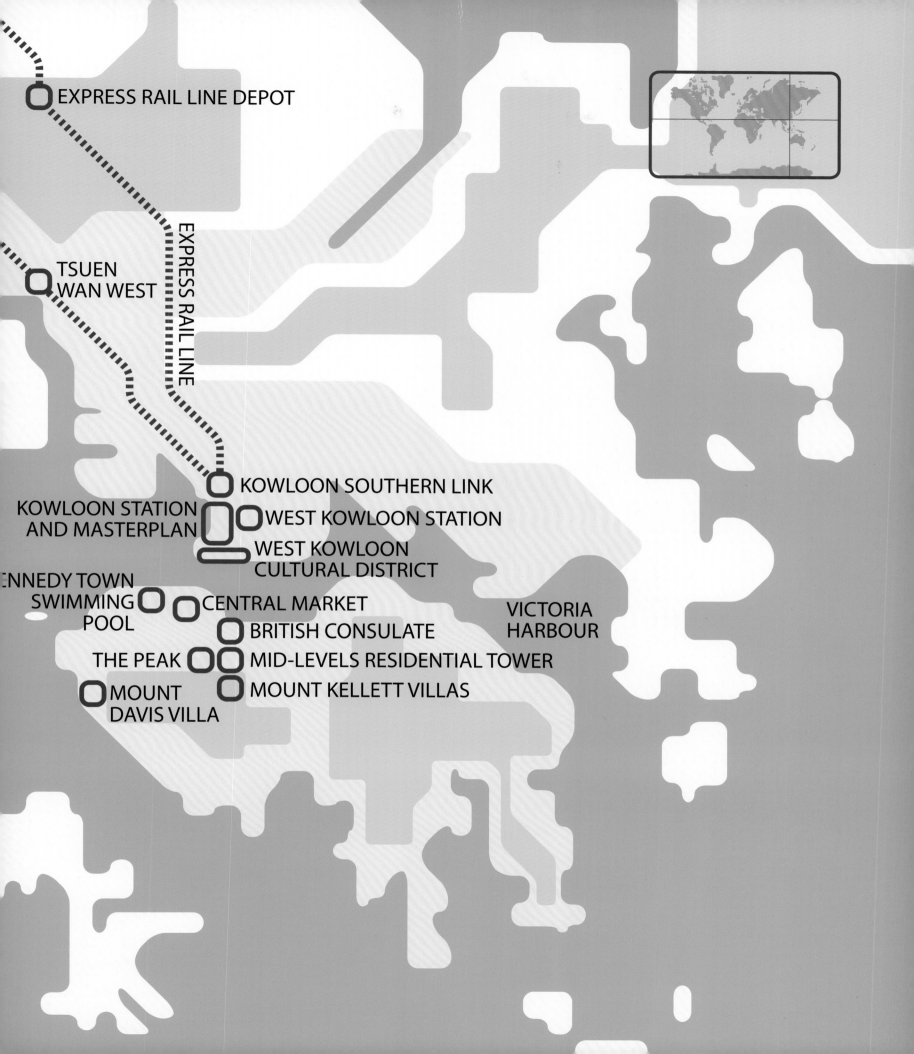

EXPRESS RAIL LINE DEPOT

TSUEN
WAN WEST

EXPRESS RAIL LINE

KOWLOON SOUTHERN LINK

KOWLOON STATION
AND MASTERPLAN

WEST KOWLOON STATION

WEST KOWLOON
CULTURAL DISTRICT

ENNEDY TOWN
SWIMMING
POOL

CENTRAL MARKET

BRITISH CONSULATE

VICTORIA
HARBOUR

THE PEAK

MID-LEVELS RESIDENTIAL TOWER

MOUNT
DAVIS VILLA

MOUNT KELLETT VILLAS

HONG KONG

Hong Kong is famous for its skyline. It is one of the densest cities in the world. But in contrast to western cities, towers do not merely sprout up in selected parts of the centre; these have proliferated in all urban areas. Many form part of mixed-use development integrated with multi-modal transport infrastructure.

Due to the city's topography this dense urban fabric is aligned along the waterfront and on the valley floors. When available land became saturated with development, parts of the harbour were reclaimed to provide for taller, more modern buildings along with new infrastructure. This was repeated several times on both sides of the harbour until the people of Hong Kong became wary of reducing the harbour's size any further.

The linear city which developed along the waterfront has given Hong Kong phenomenal advantages. Not only are dense city centres more productive and efficient, they also have unprecedented benefits for public transport and infrastructure. Metro systems were integrated with these linear settlements, and an extremely efficient system with excellent coverage led to very low car ownership. Hong Kong became the city with the lowest transport carbon footprint worldwide.

When we first arrived in Hong Kong 20 years ago, we were fortunate to be involved in shaping and defining one of the last – and arguably the most significant – reclamation project on Victoria Harbour, the West Kowloon District.

Above: View from Farrells' Kowloon Ventilation Building – designed to ventilate Kowloon Station rail lines – across Victoria Harbour to the Peak Tower, Hong Kong's number one tourist destination.

Top right: The Peak Tower.

Bottom right: An earlier study of Kowloon Point by Farrells examined the feasibility of carrying out harbour reclamation on the western side of the Kowloon Peninsula in the 1990s.

Top: Hong Kong's skyline in 1964, photos taken by Sir Terry Farrell during his first visit to the region.

Above: Hong Kong's ever expanding skyline and high-rises in 2011.

Far left: The British Consulate building in Hong Kong.

Left: 3D concept drawing showing a cross-section of Kowloon Station development facing south towards Victoria Harbour and Hong Kong Island.

Airport Express and Tung Chung Lines
West Rail and KSL to East Rail
Tsuen Wan Line
Kwun Tong Line

Our journey started with winning the design competition for Kowloon Station Development, where 11 million square feet of mixed-use development was integrated with the multi-modal station which provides, amongst other resources, a fast rail link to the airport.

The peninsula didn't exist when the design process started. In the early 1990s Hong Kong's planners were wedded to the idea of separating transport and people vertically. An elevated pedestrian network – characteristic of Hong Kong's financial centre today – would connect one urban hub to the next in new urban areas. Development would be inward-looking with public open space provided on podiums 20 metres above ground.

Kowloon Development had to follow these principles. In fact a whole new city district called Kowloon Point was envisaged following this model, eventually connecting to Tsim Sha Tsui. Whilst Kowloon Station Development went ahead rapidly to allow the airport railway link to become operational by 1997, the Kowloon Point masterplan came to a grinding halt following public objections to further reclamation.

West Kowloon Peninsula was designated as a major transportation hub and a further metro link connecting East Rail and West Rail along with a cross-border facility (later reconfigured to incorporate the high-speed rail) followed, both designed by Farrells. Further mixed-use development was to be planned above these rail facilities and we won the bid to design this toward the end of the millennium. However, sentiment in Hong Kong now vigorously opposed reclamation and inward-looking development. It was recognised that the intensity and vibrancy of Hong Kong's street life helps to set it apart.

The final chapter in our role of shaping Hong Kong's harbour is our appointment as development planner for the West Kowloon Cultural District. Two kilometres of waterfront at the peninsula's southern edge will become a pedestrian-friendly cultural district of international significance. An underground network of vehicular routes will allow Hong Kong to reclaim its harbour as a public, accessible urban quarter for the first time in more than a generation.

Top left: Satellite photo of Hong Kong.

Bottom: Study model of the Kowloon Point development.

Top right: Hong Kong mass transit railway lines superimposed on Victoria Harbour.

KOWLOON STATION DEVELOPMENT

Kowloon Station Development is a masterplan for the development over and around Kowloon Station; the detailed integration of the property development with the complex design of the new underground stations, and the optimisation of the property development into seven independent and sequentially phased development packages.

One of the world's largest station infrastructure developments, it grosses over one million metres of mixed-used space above and around the station, and has created a new city in the West Kowloon reclamation area. The masterplan development includes hotel, office, retail and residential accommodation all organised around a central public square (Union Square) with easy access to the station below. The masterplan provides a focus for the development of a new district on the reclaimed land of West Kowloon and is the foundation for pioneering new projects, including: Landmark Tower, the original proposed tower design by Farrells for a 110-storey prominent landmark at the entrance to Hong Kong's harbour; the 118-storey International Conference Centre (ICC), completed in 2011; and the West Kowloon Cultural District, one of the most ambitious cultural ventures that covers 40 hectares of land that embraces Kowloon Station Development.

Top: View from Hong Kong Island overlooking Victoria Harbour and Kowloon Station Development.

Below and bottom: The human-scale pedestrian area of the first development package of Kowloon Station; cross-section.

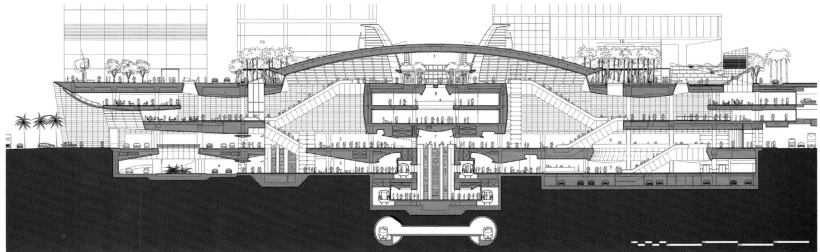

EXPRESS RAIL LINE (XRL)

The design of all the above-ground structures associated with the southern section of the rail link from Hong Kong to China's new national high-speed rail network at Guangzhou. When completed in 2015 the tunnel, running below Kowloon and the North West New Territories, will be among the longest rail tunnels in the world. The contract is divided into two sections for the southern section; the project involves the design of a number of ventilation buildings. A major challenge has been to develop a system-wide language for the buildings, which sit on a

variety of sites ranging from constricted, complex urban settings to sensitive rural sites in the New Territories. The northern section of the project involves the design of large scale maintenance/stabling facilities, an Emergency Rescue Station, two ventilation buildings and an Emergency Access Point. The rural settings of all these sites has meant that particular attention has been paid to blending these utilitarian structures into their surroundings in a sensitive yet economical and efficient manner, by utilising vertical planting and green roofs.

In addition to our current involvement in XRL, Farrells were also a part of the team for the earlier West Kowloon Station design proposal. The key to our station's design was its pivotal role as a transportation hub and the consequent need to integrate bus, car, ship and airport express train services as efficiently as possible to avoid congestion and maximise passenger convenience. Provision was made within the station's structure for potential property development, including a podium level containing retail areas, car parking, residential towers and clubhouse facilities.

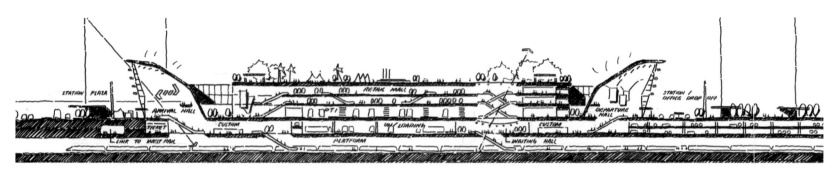

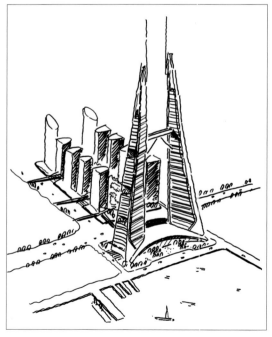

Top: Sectional concept sketch of the terminal.

Left: Perspective view of our proposed design for the station entrance.

Above: Conceptual sketch of the gateway towers proposed for the XRL terminal in West Kowloon.

Top: Perspective renderings of the Ventilation Buildings for the XRL.

Above: Aerial perspective of the Kam Tin Valley storage and maintenance facilities, where great attention was paid to greenery.

WEST KOWLOON CULTURAL DISTRICT

The West Kowloon Cultural District is one of the world's most ambitious cultural projects, proposing to offer 17 new world-class performing arts venues, a new cutting-edge museum of visual arts and an exhibition centre as well as spaces to live, work and play, set in 40 hectares of prime land on the northern shore of the breathtaking Victoria Harbour.

Since 2009, as part of a multi-disciplinary team, we have been actively involved in developing for the WKCD Authority a development plan as well

as detailed architectural briefs for each individual cultural venue, in close consultation with the public and the arts community.

The project requires delivery of an implementable, community-responsive detailed masterplan based on the winning concept of Foster+Partners' City Park. The detailed Development Plan is due to go through to planning application by the end of 2011 after a last round of public consultation in the summer of 2011.

The masterplan will ensure that WKCD becomes a vibrant new quarter in Hong Kong where the public realm takes centre stage and creates an environment conducive to creativity and the enjoyment of arts and culture by all.

Below: Farrells' conceptual masterplan model.

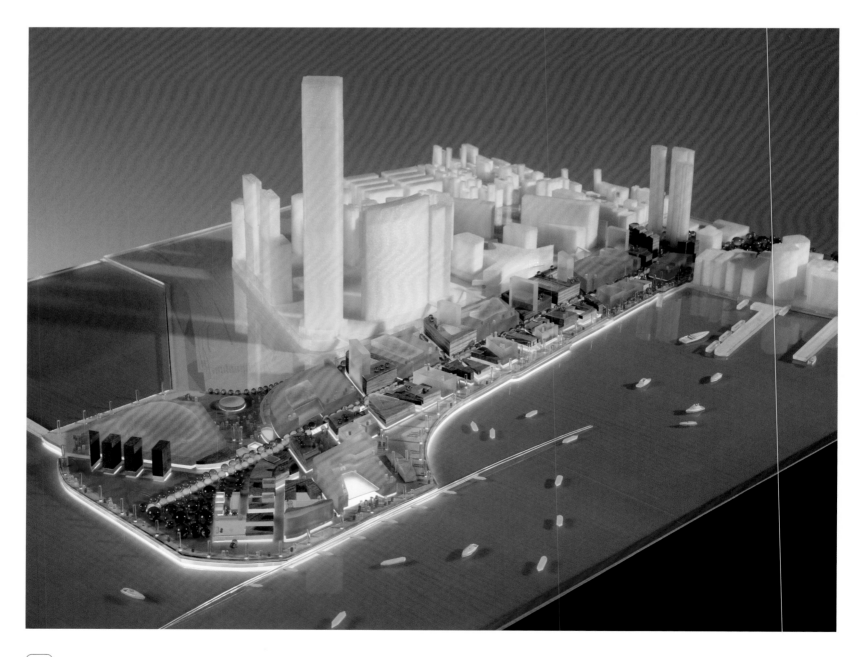

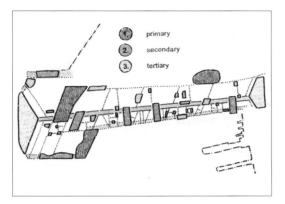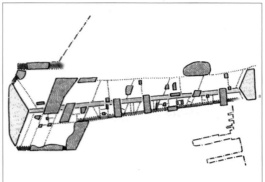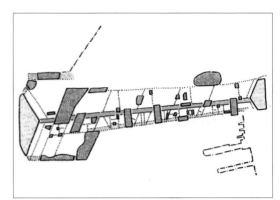

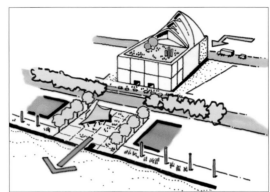

- 1. primary
- 2. secondary
- 3. tertiary

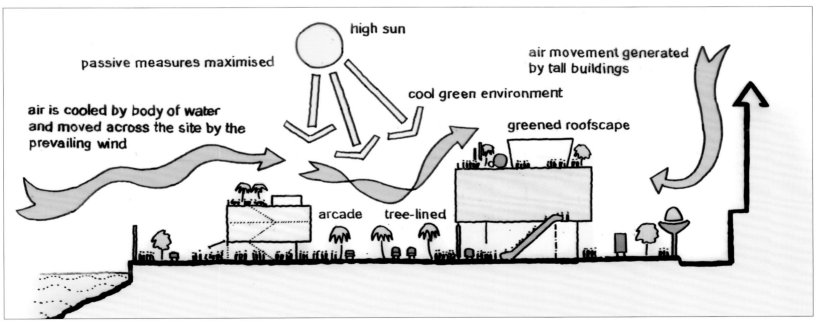

high sun

passive measures maximised

air movement generated
by tall buildings

cool green environment

air is cooled by body of water
and moved across the site by the
prevailing wind

greened roofscape

arcade   tree-lined

Top row: Plan analysis for zoning, waterfront promenade and the central boulevard.

Middle left: Hong Kong's urban developments.

Middle centre and right: Study sketches on the treatment approach of the waterfront – hard edge design for public plaza and events, and soft edge zone for beach and waterfront activities.

Above: Cross-section study of the masterplan and its environmental features.

KOWLOON SOUTHERN LINK

The government's Railway Development Strategy 2000 identified the Kowloon Southern Link as an extension of West Rail. It would connect Nam Cheong Station with East Tsim Sha Tsui Station to form a major link in Hong Kong's railway network.

The Kowloon-Canton Railway Corporation (KCRC) initiated a preliminary project feasibility study for the railway under an engineering-led consultancy to investigate its engineering and operational viability. The detailed research included the identification of any railway-related property development potential along the railway alignment.

Farrells acted as architectural sub-consultants for the planning and architecture of West Kowloon Station and Canton Road Station, two stations along the Kowloon Southern Link, as part of the overall feasibility study and government proposal. West Kowloon Station would be a below-grade, cut-and-cover construction on a green site, whilst Canton Road Station was envisaged as a bored-tunnel proposal under a busy city road. The concourse of Canton Road Station would be built beneath an existing park and involve the resumed use of existing buildings.

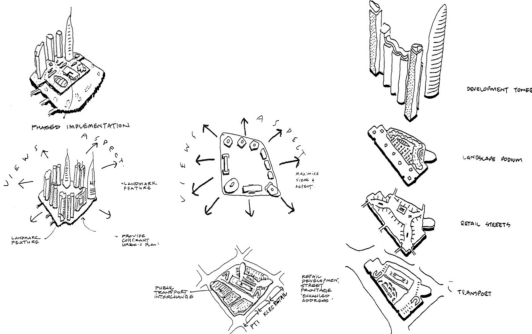

Above: Conceptual sketch of the development and its strategic location in the West Kowloon area.

Top: Study model of the scheme.

Above: Analytical sketches of the view aspect, phased implementation and layers of functional arrangement.

CENTRAL MARKET DEVELOPMENT

Central Market was the first 'wet market' selling fresh produce in Hong Kong. Opened in 1939 it is one of two Bauhaus-influenced markets in the city. The Market closed its doors in March 2003. In 2011, the Hong Kong government requested proposal submissions to sensitively redevelop the site.

Farrells design concept and subsequent architectural and functional involvment is inspired by the purity and linear characteristics of the original building design. This is expressed by restoration of the building façade and through the design of the interior spaces which retain their market street perspectives. By mirroring the external glazing style within the atrium and open courtyard whilst restoring existing features, the design preserves the buildings character and uniqueness. These horizontal window openings run the full-length of the markets' façade and immerse the internal corridors with abundant daylight.

Our philosophy has been to restrain over-zealous creative aspirations and allow the vision and simplicity of design produced by the original architects to speak for itself. Instead of imposing a new overbearing design, our intent is to respect and complement rather than detract from the original design intent.

The design's response to the general public's aspirations for Central Market delivers a contemporary and relevant public space whilst safeguarding the heritage of the original building. The introduction of new as well as original functions such as the market on the second floor is based on a conservation approach. The existing building was designed as a public space and therefore is very versatile and can be adapted easily for public use such as restaurants, exhibition and performance space with minimal intervention.

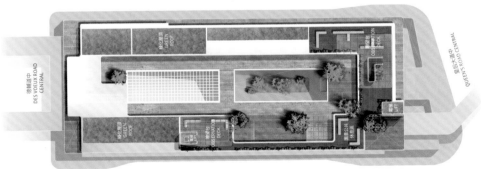

Top: Aerial night perspective from Queens Road Central.

Right: Roof plan of revitalised Central Market.

KENNEDY TOWN SWIMMING POOL

This is a new swimming pool complex designed to enrich the local community by providing a public facility that is easily accessible and complementary to existing public amenities. The pool will contribute to the character of Kennedy Town, which is currently defined by the historic tram line that terminates in the heart of the community. The design brief was for an iconic structure, housing both indoor and outdoor swimming pools, Jacuzzis, changing facilities and associated management and plant rooms. Some of the key design considerations include the building's transparency, response to existing view corridors, sensitivity to adjacent residential towers, the relationship to Victoria Harbour and an environmentally sustainable design solution.

Occupying a 0.8 hectare site, the construction of the new pool will be completed in two phases. The first phase—an outdoor lap pool and a leisure pool—has been completed and was opened to the public in May 2011. The second phase is scheduled to open in 2016 and will provide a multi-purpose pool, teaching pool and a Jacuzzi.

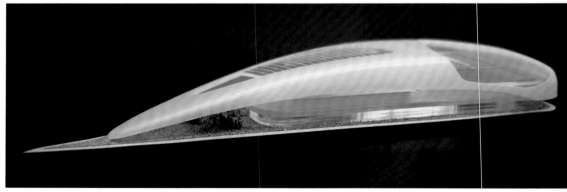

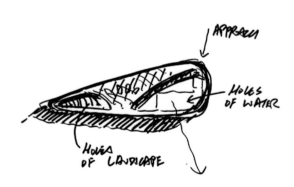

Above: Conceptual sketch.

Top right: Perspective view of the Victoria Harbour looking out from the upper balcony of the pool building.

Middle: Study model of the pool building.

Bottom left: Aerial photograph of completed Phase One.

Bottom right: Kennedy Town Pool from Shing Sai Road.

MOUNT KELLETT VILLAS

Located on Hong Kong's prestigious Peak, the Mount Kellett villas command 180° views south over the Lamma Channel. In the 1860s the area was known for its summer sojourn bungalows away from the blistering heat of Central Hong Kong and became an increasingly fashionable address to fair-weathered ex-patriots after 1888 when the Peak Tram opened.

Due for completion in early 2012, the 2,325m² site accommodates three detatched luxury residences ranging from 360 – 400m². Each villa has of a two-storey residence with a flat roof over a carpark. The design created long rectangular building forms to maximise panoramic sea views and elevated the villas to allow for larger garden terraces and living spaces that flow directly into the garden, blurring the distinction between the indoors and the outdoors.

Above: Study model of the villas.

Above right: Perspective drawing of one of the villas.

Below: Ocean side (south-west) elevation.

MID-LEVELS RESIDENTIAL TOWER

Desirable residential addresses abound in Hong Kong Island's Mid-levels district but those boasting progressive green features are decidedly thin on the ground. Farrells worked on the redevelopment design for one such tower situated above a three-building complex.

Our design received Building Department planning approval, conforming to local planning regulations without typifying the standard Hong Kong housing block. Keeping the same allowable building area, the plan was for the tower to be rebuilt at a greater height, to allow one rather than two flats per floor and has been divided into three residential zones. Apartment size and desirability, increase towards the top and a stunning duplex with its own private roof garden crowns the block.

The key concept was the creation of two curved façades that responded to orientation and views. The tower's sail-like shape also reduces the wind load. To maximise the panoramic vista of Victoria Harbour, the north curve of each flat incorporates sky balconies and floor-to-ceiling glazing fronts the main living area; the bedrooms by the south curve face the mountainside and allow for a greater depth of privacy and shade.

Although the complex has top-of-the-range recreational and car-parking facilities, what sets it apart from the rest is its environmental agenda, which features an impressive list of hi-tech green facilities. These include an elegant wind turbine on top of the building, which becomes a city landmark in its own right, solar panelling, grey-water collection tanks (for flushing and irrigation purposes), energy-efficient lighting and water-conserving plumbing fixtures. Photovoltaic cells convert the sun's energy into instant electricity while other systems recover and recycle heat from showers, sinks and dehumidifiers.

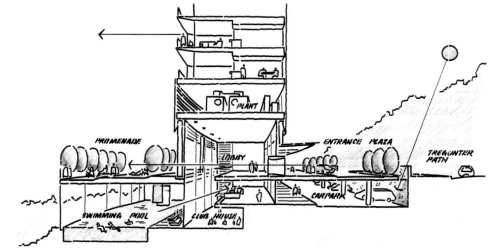

Top left: Site model showing the tower in context.

Top right: Study model of the tower.

Middle: Sectional sketch showing the green design of the tower.

Bottom left and right: Apartment plans vary and increase in size towards the top.

MOUNT DAVIS VILLA

Located 70m above sea level, Mount Davis Villa is a highly sophisticated and imaginative solution to a demanding but special site. It combines thoughtful and appropriate planning, high-tech structure and servicing, natural materials and elegant detailing to create an aesthetically pleasing house of great comfort. An impressive house on every level, it works as a family home and as an example of innovative thinking. The design employs green ideas ranging from construction methods and system designs to the choice of materials.

Inspired by a Malaysian long house, the entry level has a single living area with a kitchen at its eastern end. Beyond the kitchen lie a partially covered lap pool and a games room, above which the maid's quarters are positioned. The second level is dedicated to the family's sleeping arrangements – master bedroom, children's bedrooms and two bathrooms. All have the same views and each room leads onto a terrace, created by 'cutting a slot' in the roof.

Air-conditioning is powered by solar energy using an absorption-chiller system and is delivered through floor-to-ceiling vents. The system can be reversed to heat the house and swimming pools as necessary. There is also an integrated grey-water system, which collects, treats and purifies rainwater for lavatories and garden watering.

Left: Solar collectors power the air conditioning system and 'slots' in the roof ensure each room has its own balcony.

Below left: Elevation showing under-house garage.

Below centre: Cross-section drawing through the dining room and bedrooms.

Below right: The infinity lap pool, overlooking the Lamma Channel.

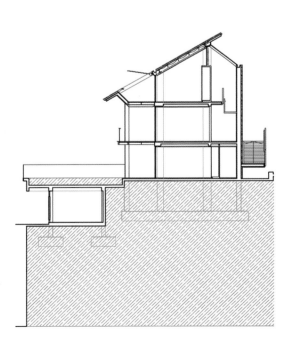

HONG KONG MACAU BRIDGE

In 2002 the Hong Kong government and Guangdong (China) local authorities conducted a study of cross-border traffic and transport linkage. As a result, it was decided to open a new border crossing that would connect Hong Kong, Macau and Zhuhai, Guangdong Province, in the Pearl River Delta. This series of bridges (including the world's longest bridge) and tunnels is currently under construction with a completion date of 2016.

In 2011, Farrells submitted a joint bid with Arup for the Passenger Clearance Building, which will house a customs and immigration checkpoint for cross-border traffic. The Hong Kong Boundary Crossing Facilities are situated at the northeastern edge of the Hong Kong International Airport island.

Farrells' proposed vision was a 'garden island' that would be both a healthy, pleasant and sustainable environment and an unforgettable icon with a strong identity from a masterplanning and architectural perspective. The island uses both passive and active measures of sustainability, applying the latest in green technology and extensive soft landscaping.

The masterplan draws inspiration from the Chinese saying 'like a fish to water', which symbolises the strength of cooperation. The sharing of space among passengers, traffic and nature, through convenient pedestrian circulation,

an effective road network and abundant greenery, establishes a balanced and vibrant environment.

The Passenger Clearance Building appears to 'float' above the surrounding landscape, bringing harmony between the built environment and nature. Inspired by the contradictory idea of the airport being both the point of departure and arrival, the building also symbolises the merging and unifying of China, Macao and Hong Kong. The architectonic is inspired by the Chinese character 互, in which the top and bottom strokes represent two people, and the middle interlocking shape symbolises the action of shaking hands. The two interlocking shapes of the building embrace the open-air, landscaped courtyard at the center, representing harmony between humankind and nature.

The Passenger Clearance Building is designed to provide passengers with convenient access to different modes of transport. The close proximity of the Hong Kong–Shenzhen Western Express Line railway station allows a direct passenger link to the arrivals hall for inbound passengers. For outbound passengers, platform-to-platform interchange is provided between the Western Express Line and Hong Kong International Airport's automated people-mover extension. The design can also accommodate a future Tung Chung Mass Transit Railway line extension.

Inbound and outbound passengers will arrive at the grand arrival/departures hall, designed to echo the sense of being at a gateway. The interior is designed to be flooded with natural daylight through solar-powered skylights. The formation of the skylights reflects the functions and needs of different zones, acting as a way-finding system to guide passengers through the building. Outside the staff offices are two internal feature walls designed as backdrops that represent China and its two special administrative regions, Hong Kong and Macao. Contemporary signage is superimposed onto these feature walls as another orientation device.

A simple and rational layout provides single-direction passenger flow. With the majority of people either arriving or departing, special consideration was given to assisting those with luggage, the elderly and the disabled.

The design proposes weather-protected drop-off areas along the curb in front of the upper level of the Passenger Clearance Building. Both inbound and outbound commuters enjoy same level access into the arrivals and departure halls respectively, and gently progress downwards across the halls. After passing through immigration and customs zones, passengers arrive at the drop-off area and will be directed to the bus and coach pick-up bays.

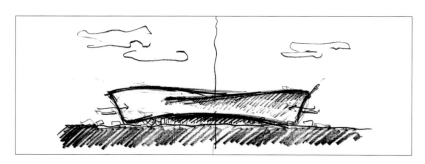

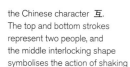

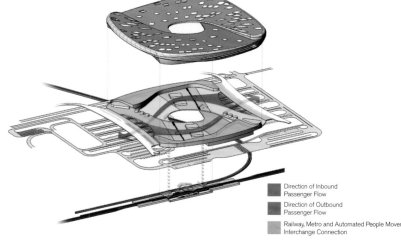

Direction of Inbound Passenger Flow

Direction of Outbound Passenger Flow

Railway, Metro and Automated People Mover Interchange Connection

Top left: Concept sketch of the interlocking building form.

Above: The interlocking building form is inspired by

the Chinese character 互. The top and bottom strokes represent two people, and the middle interlocking shape symbolises the action of shaking

hands. The two forms embrace the open-air, landscaped courtyard at the centre, which symbolises harmony between mankind and nature.

Above: Passenger flow diagram showing the barrier-free design approach and the segregation of the inbound and outbound

traffic and interchange connections.

Opposite: Aerial rendering of the masterplan and the Passenger

Clearance Building; approaching view of the facility; interior view of the immigration hall.

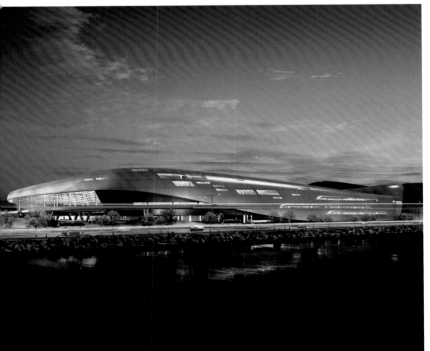

TSUEN WAN WEST STATION

Tsuen Wan West MTR Station consists of four tracks servicing two island platforms and a large passenger-transport interchange (PTI). Its concourse is situated below ground level in the middle of the station, but strategically placed entrances allow for integration with the PTI and future property development, as well as serving the nearby public ferry pier, the vehicle drop-off area and public open space next to the station. It has been built with high passenger capacity in mind, with a peak of 33 trains an hour in each direction and 36,000 passengers at rush hours anticipated for 2016.

Provision has been made for future property development above and around the station, including a PTI at ground level and up to six levels of podium development. Ten residential blocks, each about 35 to 45 storeys high, will lie on either side of the station to reduce strain on its columns and foundations.

The development has been thoughtfully integrated with the railway to permit construction phasing and staged development. Connections between the station and the development sites have been maximised, while the ground floor is primarily open space to separate the new promenade from the site of the PTI. For operational reasons, the first level of the podium structure and the ground-level PTI areas have been roofed over to allow future construction to proceed without any impact on the operation of the railway and other transport facilities.

Right: Cross-section through the station.

Below: Sketch of the internal spaces and the station's potential to connect to future property developments.

Below right: Axonometric of the station.

Bottom: The station within its urban context.

Opposite: The station's clear planning allows for easy passenger circulation.

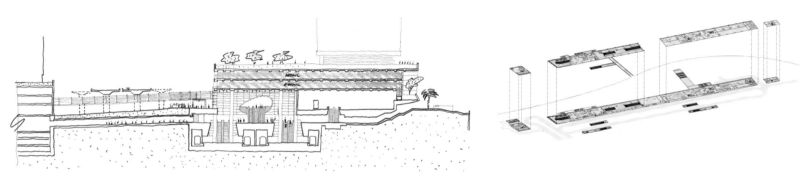

LONDON

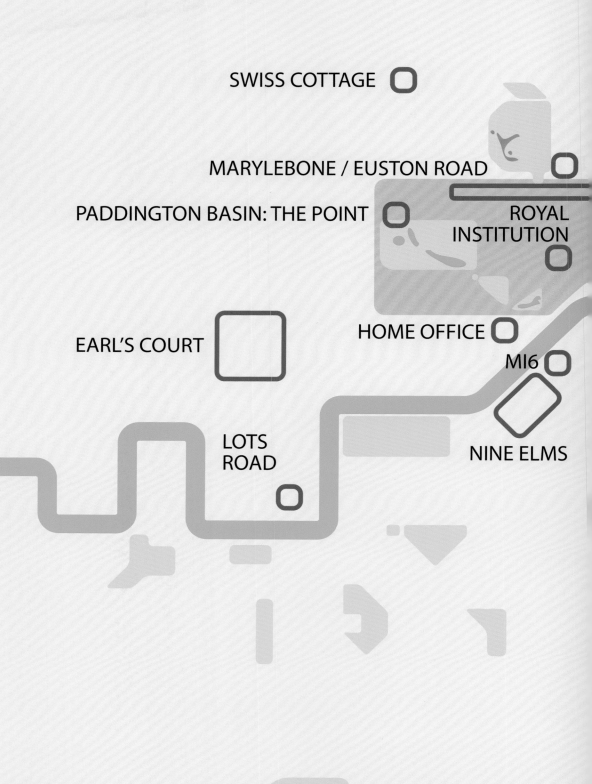

SWISS COTTAGE

MARYLEBONE / EUSTON ROAD

PADDINGTON BASIN: THE POINT

ROYAL INSTITUTION

EARL'S COURT

HOME OFFICE

MI6

LOTS ROAD

NINE ELMS

PETERSHAM

REGENT'S PLACE

◯ BISHOPSGATE

◯ EMBANKMENT PLACE

◯ FOUNDER'S
PLACE

THE THAMES

LONDON

Providing inspiration as a laboratory for urbanism throughout the life of the practice, London – the world's first metropolis – has matured over more than two millennia to become one of the world's greatest and most liveable cities. A key to understanding London is to see it as a collection of intensely characterful and distinctive places. In his book *Shaping London*, Sir Terry Farrell points out that it is 'a natural city, collectively planned over time, built by many hands working with natural forms, with no grand overarching, superimposed design hand or ordering plans, or geometries.' It has a multi-centric character as a result, incorporating two 'cities' – the economic powerhouse know simply as the 'City' worldwide, and Westminster, the UK's famous heart of government – along with innumerable 'urban

villages', many of which have acquired international reputations in their own right for arts and science, culture, media, education, or simply urbanity. A list of some of these makes the point – Soho, Shoreditch, Camden, Brixton, Mayfair, Hoxton, Chelsea, Marylebone, Bloomsbury, Greenwich are all names redolent with meaning and association.

To the outsider London can appear both enigmatic and chaotic, a city that is the antithesis of its consciously planned European or North American counterpart. But the city has an underlying order which, over time, has emerged in response to its subtle topography, to nature, to a complex pattern of public and private land ownership (itself a product of natural form) and the diverse culture of its people. The most obvious example of this is the way in which

London has responded, whether obviously or subtly, to the course of the River Thames. This has influenced the location of urban villages and centres, the alignment of high streets, the configuration of central London's wonderful Royal Parks, even the alignment of London's roads, railways and canals.

The quality of life that London offers has generated enormous wealth. It is at the heart of an economic 'super-region', the Greater South-east, the most important economic entity in Europe. So its future success influences and is influenced by what happens in this wider region.

Over the last decade the practice has been involved in projects and initiatives which are intended to transform the potential of the Thames Estuary to the east of the metropolis, so that this makes a full

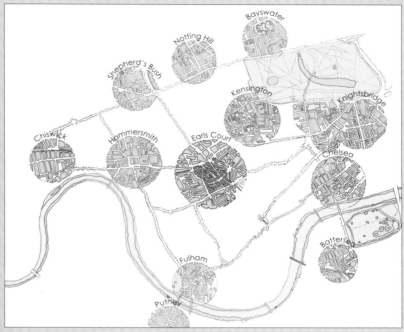

contribution to the region as its 'engine room for the 21st century' as well as a place that people want to live and invest in. What happens to the west in the Thames Valley is equally important.

The Thames Valley already enjoys an exceptional quality of life. This is reflected in its high values and the expense of living and working there. But it cannot be seen as something which will remain static simply because it is successful. It is under intense growth pressure. The Thames Valley needs to adapt just as the Thames Estuary will. Here the emphasis must lie on growth that has a minimum impact on energy consumption and the environment. Places that are identified as areas for growth – Oxford, Bicester, Reading – need to grow in ways which build on the spirit of place that underpins their success.

Above: The River Thames at night with the north bank's distinctive silhouette and the illuminated Embankment Place.

Inset: MI6, Vauxhall Cross.

Top right: London's urban villages.

Above right: London's lost rivers.

Right: *Architectural Review* – Terry Farrell's Manifesto for London 2007.

Far right: *Shaping London* 2010

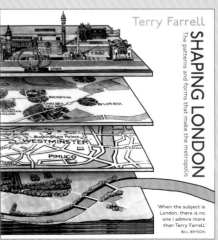

MARYLEBONE – EUSTON ROAD

The Marylebone-Euston Road is a key east-west artery in London. It has the potential to be transformed into one of London's greatest assets with street life, attractive landscaping, major squares and green spaces. Our studies have focused on major transport infrastructure, interchanges, pedestrian flows, commercial addresses, office precincts and landscape improvement. Much of its enormous potential stems from the close proximity of a number of mainline stations; it is a significant arrival/departure point for mainland travel as well as having direct access to Europe via the Eurostar at Kings Cross St Pancras.

Our intellectual framework has acted as a catalyst for change. Central to proposals is the need to shift the perception of this area as an urban motorway serving through traffic to a distinctive 'place'. We have actively helped initiate a number of key public realm projects. One significant part of the masterplan is a detailed design study of the Euston Road underpass, which aims to create a place which is a pedestrian-friendly connection between Fitzrovia and areas to the north.

Marylebone-Euston Road is one of London's great assets. It has the history, scale and critical mass to be transformed and our vision allows for a real improvement in the heart of London, whereby communities and places are linked together to greatly improve the public realm. It is London's best-connected street, and it could become a celebrated and liveable part of London.

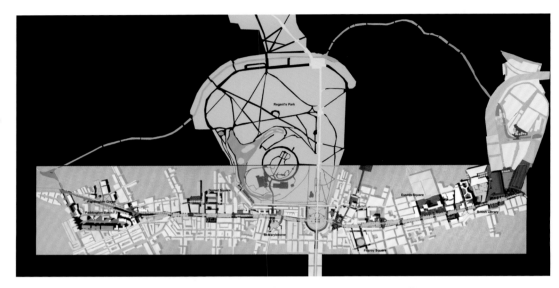

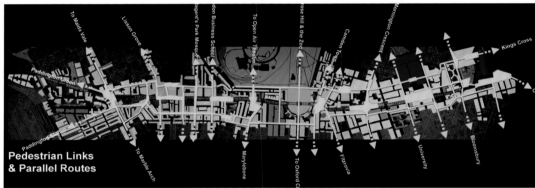

Pedestrian Links & Parallel Routes

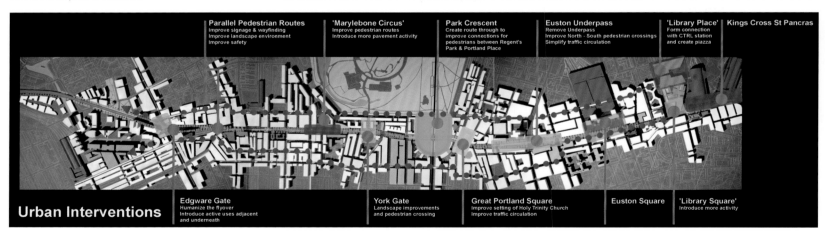

Parallel Pedestrian Routes	'Marylebone Circus'	Park Crescent	Euston Underpass	'Library Place'	Kings Cross St Pancras
Improve signage & wayfinding Improve landscape environment Improve safety	Improve pedestrian routes Introduce more pavement activity	Create route through to improve connections for pedestrians between Regent's Park & Portland Place	Remove Underpass Improve North - South pedestrian crossings Simplify traffic circulation	Form connection with CTRL station and create piazza	

Urban Interventions

Edgware Gate	York Gate	Great Portland Square	Euston Square	'Library Square'
Humanize the flyover Introduce active uses adjacent and underneath	Landscape improvements and pedestrian crossing	Improve setting of Holy Trinity Church Improve traffic circulation		Introduce more activity

Above: Plan of Marylebone-Euston Road showing urban interventions.

Top: The Marylebone - Euston Road can be improved incrementally; a series of projects were identified and a number are underway or implemented.

Centre: Plan showing pedestrian links and parallel routes that would take the priority away from the Marylebone-Euston Road.

Right: Euston Circus today.

Far right: Farrells' proposal to integrate pedestrians and traffic will bring a huge improvement to the pedestrian movement across Euston Road.

REGENT'S PLACE

The Regent's Place masterplan and completed commercial mixed-use development represent the culmination of several years of planning, consultation, development and construction, successfully enhancing and transforming the urban fabric of a key area of the West End of London bordering the Euston Road and Regent's Park.

Before the masterplan, Regent's Place was a disconnected commercial enclave. The brief demanded that it become a diverse community: a place to live, work and play, and an integrated part of the West End of London. This was achieved by creating high-quality spaces and places between the buildings, and a network of new streets enabling and encouraging linkages to the surrounding area, including a new north-south pedestrian route through the masterplan, animated by a new Arts Centre and linking to Fitzrovia via a new at-grade pedestrian crossing over the Euston Road. The most radical intervention was the creation of Triton Street, a completely new east-west route through Regent's Place, forming an important pedestrian link between Regent's Park and Drummond Street, only one block north of the Euston Road yet protected from traffic noise and pollution.

The Regent's Place mixed-use development is comprised of two commercial office buildings (366,000 ft² Grade-A office space) sited at the gateway to the new Triton Street, a residential building on Osnaburgh Street comprised of 154 apartments with a 20-storey tower with views over Regent's Park and private landscaped gardens, (92 social rented), a community theatre (New Diorama Arts Centre), 7,940 ft² of A3 retail space, external landscaping and public works of art, and active, open and safe streets. The residential component of the scheme has been designed as a model of high-density urban living to complement the existing uses of Regent's Place – leisure and commerce.

The development completes the Euston Road frontage and creates a strong corner with Osnaburgh Street. Corners curve in reference to the oval form of the tube station opposite. The 10 Triton Street frontage on Osnaburgh Street pulls back from the boundary to provide an appropriate space and setting for the adjacent Holy Trinity Church. The building maintains the scale of the Euston Road frontage without overpowering or dominating the church. This set-back allows a clear view of 20 Triton Street beyond and signals the opening to the new east-west route. The end façade of 10 Triton

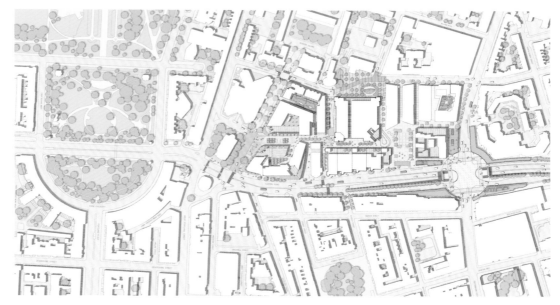

Top: The masterplan vision for the Regent's Place estate and Euston Circus.

Above: Aerial photograph showing the finished development. The permeability and greener landscape can clearly be seen.

Street curves into an open courtyard providing light to this and the neighbouring building. 20 Triton Street responds contextually to each frontage and orientation, creating internal atria allowing natural light deep into each floorplate.

The landscaping flows through and around the base of the buildings with a strong granite base. A soft undulating landscape feature wraps around the corner of the building on the Euston Road, both drawing people to the entrance and protecting the internal users from the direct view of the passing traffic. Tall trees and low shrubs are used to break up the public realm and provide seating and interest.

As part of Farrells' wider strategic vision for the Euston-Marylebone Road, the masterplan creates high quality spaces and places between the buildings, and a network of new streets enabling and encouraging linkages to the surrounding area.

Below: The curved frontages of the commercial buildings respect and reinforce the setting of Holy Trinity Church.

Bottom row: Care has been taken in the design of the buildings and their landscape settings to nurture a variety of street activities.

Opposite: The angled façade of 10 Triton Street allows 20 Triton Street to have a presence on Marylebone-Euston Road and encourages people to wander into the street network behind.

Left: View from 20 Triton Street: a curved landscape base encourages pedestrian movement and provides privacy.

Below: The illuminated façade of 10 Triton Street.

Bottom left: 20 Triton Street with sandstone piers and expressed bay features.

Bottom right: Roof terraces have been seized as opportunities for biodiversity and water retention.

Opposite: 10 Triton Street reception with a vacuum-formed reception desk.

Opposite: Internal residential courtyard.

Inset: Site plan, ground level.

This page: The residential tower enjoys excellent views over Regent's Park and its neighbouring streets.

THE POINT

The Point was the first building completed at Paddington Basin as part of Farrells' 1996 masterplan. It comprises 222,000 sq. ft. of office space over 10 storeys in a wedge shape, marking the gateway to Paddington Basin. On the western edge of the waterfront adjacent to Paddington Station, this flagship high-end office building has set a high standard for the whole of the development.

The building was designed with two main entrances to accommodate different tenancy options, with a central bank with eight lifts, two of which are feature lifts within a glass atrium. The building also comprises a car lift and lorry lift housed in a separate pavilion, providing access to a loading bay/car park plant space basement.

The massing is a response to the site – essentially triangular, with two curved sides to the north and south and two towers, with a recessed entry between, to the east. The ground and lower ground levels have full-height glazing, recessed behind a strong colonnade of polished concrete columns.

The two curved façades above this, from levels one to six, comprise full-height glazing behind a frame of expressed vertical metal fins, creating a strong vertical rhythm. These fins create an impression of solidity when seen from an oblique angle, whilst providing good views of the Basin for the occupants. Between these fins on the south side is a system of timber brise-soleil, providing effective solar control to the office space, while giving the exterior a strong identity.

On the north side the fins hold a 'light-shelf, reflecting light into the office space while maintaining the external expression of the south side. The upper three floors are a 'smooth skin' climate façade in contrast to the more modelled lower floors. The east elevation is a simple composition of two towers, of the same glazing system, addressing the adjacent plaza.

There was a separate commission to design the fit-out for the tenant – an international telecommunications company, whose central thesis and subsequent brief was the sharing of information. The core concept for this was a volcano: the lower ground floor is the 'magma chamber' of ideas, and the atrium is the vertical focus of communication and activity, with ideas fountaining out into the wider world.

The regeneration of Paddington Basin has resulted in the emergence of a vibrant new quarter close to the City and West End and just 15 minutes from Heathrow Airport, via the Heathrow Express, which runs from Paddington Station. Improvements to the canal basin and surrounding infrastructure have included the introduction of a range of mixed uses with cafés, bars, restaurants and retail outlets.

Opposite: The Point viewed across the rooftops of Paddington Station.

Top: Farrells' masterplan of Paddington Basin.

Middle: The Point sits right next to the canal.

Bottom: Entrance area cladding design for The Point.

Right: The curved façades echo the curve of the canal and present a 'prow' to the water.

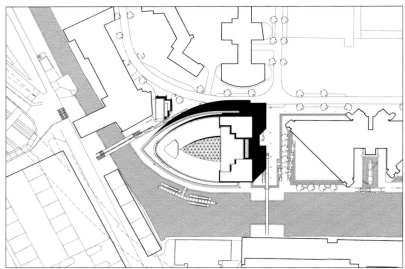

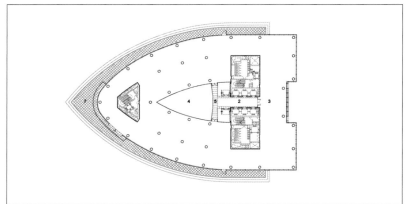

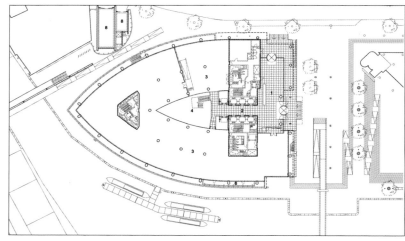

Top left: Looking up in the atrium to the tensioned cable glass roof.

Bottom left: Timber louvres provide solar shading and bounce light further into the floorplate.

Top: Site plan.

Centre: Typical floor plan.

Bottom: Ground floor plan.

LONDON CLINIC

The London Clinic in Harley Street is one of the UK's longest established and largest independent hospitals. The masterplan looked at new buildings and the refurbishment of the existing estate, part of a multi-site development programme.

The scheme was phased to enable an economic restructuring and expansion of the existing facilities whilst responding to the needs of a fully operational hospital. Sensitive issues concerning the conservation area and residential properties that adjoin the sites were key considerations.

This state-of-the-art facility houses 25 modern consulting suites and a number of out-patient clinical services such as cardiology and endocrinology. There are also x-ray, ultrasound, pharmacy and pathology departments. A broad range of outpatient facilities provides patients with a seamless one-stop service on site to provide diagnostic and other clinical support to the consulting practices.

Extensive consultation with the hospital's clinical staff resulted in emphasis on the delivery of patient-focused care. The quality and feel of the existing London Clinic Consulting House has been combined with the latest technology to create a classic interior with reference to contemporary design.

The refined detailing of the interiors compliments the Georgian-style façade to Devonshire Place. Colours, finishes and artwork have been carefully chosen throughout the building to respond to patients' well-being and to create a calm, familiar and reassuring environment. New glazed roofs bring natural daylight to the heart of the building and existing external lightwells have been transformed into landscaped gardens. Within the design, care has been taken to provide wayfinding for those unfamiliar with the building. Inclusive access is provided and each diagnostic department has been designed as a self-contained unit to provide privacy for patients.

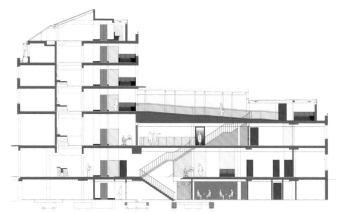

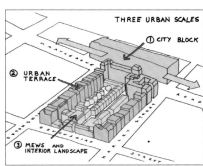

Top left: Cross-section of the building.

Top right: Sketch showing the building in its urban context.

Right: The central staircase at the clinic with artwork features at landings. (Inset: courtyard garden and café area in the centre of the building).

THE HOME OFFICE

Farrells have had a long involvement with the former Department of the Environment site, previously occupied by the Marsham Street Towers. The consensus was that they were inappropriate as a backdrop to a World Heritage site adacent to the Palace of Westminster. Throughout the 1990s Farrells produced masterplans advocating reinstating the area's historic pattern and replacing the overscaled, impregnable podium and towers by erecting separate buildings and re-making lost street frontages/public spaces. Farrells took the opportunity to address issues of sustainability on one of the few inner-city sites large enough to permit it and to develop big-picture urban masterplan thinking.

In 2000, Farrells' contribution to the winning PFI bid launched by the Home Office demonstrated the feasibility of a low-rise mixed-use scheme, with the capacity for office, residential and retail accommodation with non-intrusion of the superb skyline views. The delivered scheme provides a similar overall gross floor area to the previous structure of 1 million sq. ft., with approximately 800,000 sq. ft. of office space sufficient for 3,500 Home Office staff in three inter-connected low-rise buildings, and the remainder in three residential blocks, providing 140 private and affordable apartments, 9 shops and 3 kiosks.

Farrells fulfilled the aspirations of the original masterplan by their alternative use of the site, and further enhancements to the masterplan and built project were incorporated throughout the programme. The scheme recognised that the existing development restricted public circulation. The desirability of creating an inclusive, civic community and enhancing the public realm, coupled with high-quality architectural design, was emphasised and this vision has been realised.

Left: The 'gentle giant' concept used in the Home Office building design also informed Farrells' study for the Hong Kong and Shanghai Bank's former city headquarters in Gresham Street.

Top: Before – on the original site stood the 'three ugly sisters', housing the Department of the Environment.

Bottom: After – the new Home Office building delivered the equivalent space through thoughtful design.

Opposite: The Home Office entrance elevation with Liam Gillick artwork in the foreground and the curved 'pavilion' building wing in the background.

This Page

1. The development within its urban district. The new Home Office is located within the urban district of Westminster, a neighbour to schools, hospitals, housing and listed buildings. Its setting is quite distinct from Whitehall's monocultural environment, a highly specialised arena of state buildings that includes the Royal Horseguards, Banqueting Hall and Palace of Westminster. The Department of Environment was built in the 1960s at the scale of the Whitehall buildings. Its successor is an urban planning exercise that inserts a non-pompous 'gentle giant' headquarters building into the neighbourhood.

2. Urban design site plan. Permeable streets, new squares and mixed-use accommodation harmoniously sit within the adjacent listed buildings and street patterns.

3. Axonometric view from the north-west.

4. Axonometric view from the south-west.

5. The urban design of the exterior is followed into the building's interior planning. An internal street with subsidiary side streets and main squares form community spaces, accommodating up to 5,000.

Below: Long section through the site.

Opposite: A confident and welcoming new entrance to the Home Office.

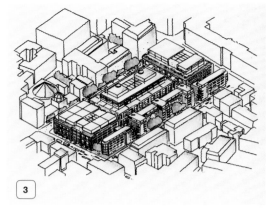

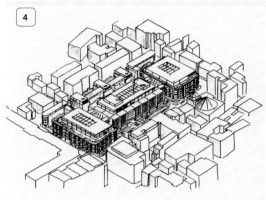

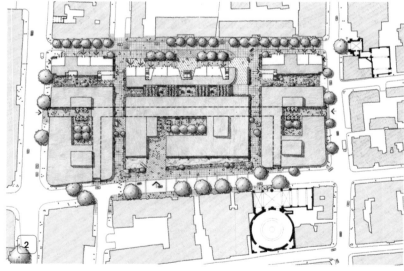

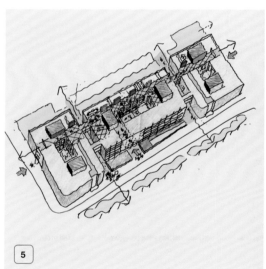

The construction programme spanned a total of 34 months, of which the first 17 months was the demolition phase – the new build phase overlapped with the demolition (a high proportion of materials from the old buildings were recycled in the current complex and off-site). The construction programme was accelerated by use of a hybrid construction technique – in situ concrete columns and pre-cast concrete beams and floor planks. That meant that 4,200 sq metres of floorplates could be erected every 11 days (cutting down on the disruptive period for local residents).

A collaboration between Farrells and artist Liam Gillick introduced a generous use of colour on the lightweight glass canopy, giving the complex exterior visual interest along the elevations. Coloured glass vitrines enliven the office space, creating a positive impact for the area and privacy for personnel.

As a government building, part of the design brief was to achieve an 'Excellent' BREEAM rating. This scoring is based on energy performance, sustainability, building construction methods and management and the desirability of the resulting environment for the occupants. To achieve the 'Excellent' rating the project was monitored throughout design and construction and modifications introduced as appropriate.

The development was completed on time and on budget and original and subsequent objectives were met. A flexible, cost-effective headquarters building was delivered, which fosters a new community – the antithesis of its predecessor. The new building blends into the district, weaving urban design issues and architectural solutions into this strategically important area and injecting a strong sense of place.

Left: The atrium space interacts with the 'street' – a colourful arrangement of 'communal' functions across all flow to improve inter-departmental communications.

Insets: 'Internal urban design': interior photos of the 'street', a linear feature on each floor physically joining departments and improving dialogue between the many sub-groups and employees at the Home Office.

FOUNDER'S PLACE

The Founder's Place development, opposite St Thomas' Hospital, focused on regeneration founded on a health-led development brief. This was a richly diverse mixed-use scheme, which aimed to create a new community in north Lambeth linked to the hospital, yet integrating seamlessly with the neighbourhood – the area between Waterloo Station, Lambeth Palace Road and Archbishop's Park.

The design team encouraged a masterplan approach in order to overcome the problem of the severance of the site from its neighbours and to enhance the quality of the public realm and significantly contribute to the regeneration of Lambeth, with the creation of a new urban quarter. The development was to include: affordable housing for key workers and local people, 300 private flats, a nursery, accommodation for parents of sick children and a patient hotel.

Public realm improvements included landscaping, restoration of the railway arches and improved connectivity with the Lower Marsh shopping centre.

Farrells architectural approach to Founder's Place emerged from the masterplan analysis. Creation of a 'campus' was advocated as a way of remedying past problems and unifying the various elements of the scheme.

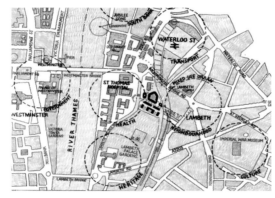

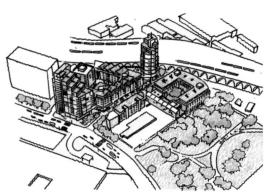

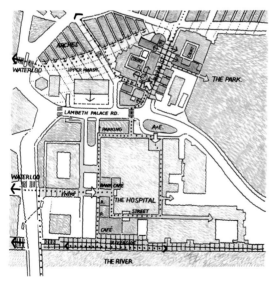

Above: Location plan showing railway and hospital.

Centre left: The development within its urban context.

Centre right: Concept sketch.

Right: The scheme in context with Westminster Palace and London Eye in the background.

LOTS ROAD

The redevelopment of the landmark Lots Road Power Station and site will unify an important but fractured district of London with physical, social and visual permeability. The power station, built in 1904, occupies a wide concave bend of the River Thames. The site is split between two boroughs: Kensington & Chelsea and Hammersmith & Fulham, with the boundary running through the centre line of Chelsea Creek. The power station occupies a highly visible location which, after a century of industrial use, has remained largely undeveloped.

The scheme illustrates how good-quality design and urban planning can make the best of limited land resources, delivering world-class design on an important brownfield site. The mixed-use scheme includes approximately 800 apartments, with some commercial space and retail outlets for neighbourhood-type shops. It incorporates both private and affordable housing, as well as improvements to public amenities. It is both sustainable and integrated with substantial transport improvements. Support for the original scheme has come from the public and heritage bodies along with the GLA and TfL.

The intention is to create a 'new village' to connect the Lots Road neighbourhood on one side with Chelsea Harbour and Imperial Wharf on the other. It will create one of the largest covered public open streets in London and open around 600 metres of river and creek to public use for the first time in over a hundred years. The creek will become a new linear park and water garden.

The proposals focus on the retention and conversion of the historic power station building. The shell will be transformed into a unique mixed-use community development.

Two new residential towers located on either side of the creek entrance have been carefully conceived to form a powerful visual grouping. The power station sits comfortably between the uniquely slim 37-storey south tower and the 25-storey north tower, which contain a mix of apartments with spectacular penthouses under the sloping glass roofs. The long east-west orientation of the two towers ensures maximum optimisation of views. This arrangement is a sensitive response to the inflection of the Thames and of Chelsea Creek itself. It reinforces their sentinel role at the mouth of the creek, framing both the creek's opening and the power station. Like a dancing couple, the pair of towers will create a dynamic form when seen from different viewpoints.

The riverside scheme will create an expanded village centre to a true mixed-use urban quarter with ideal pedestrian and transport connectivity.

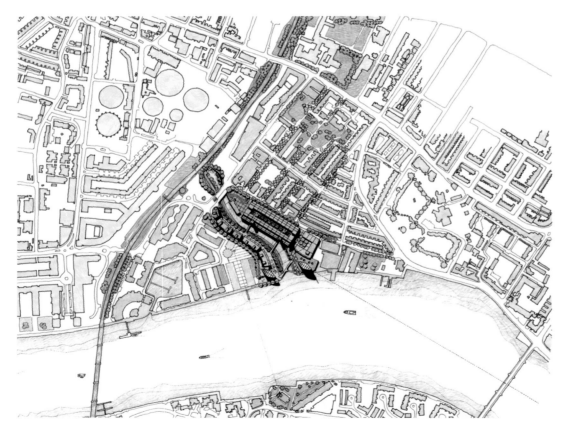

Above: Currently an industrial brownfield site, the masterplan intends to create permeability and the transformed power station will become a landmark.

Main image: Artist's impression of the two towers in their river context with Montevetro to the left and Worlds End development to the right.

Top left: Historic photograph of the Lots Road power station.

Top centre: Lots Road is one of three great power stations

(the others being Battersea and Bankside).

Top right: Proposed cross-section of the power station.

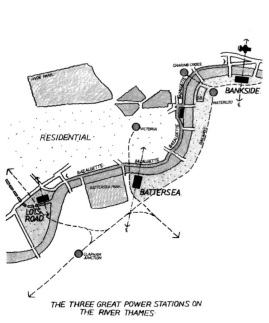

THE THREE GREAT POWER STATIONS ON
THE RIVER THAMES

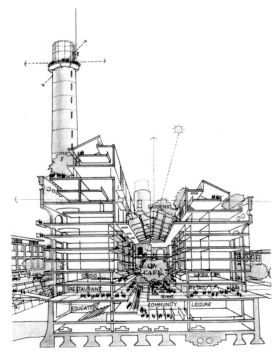

SWISS COTTAGE

Swiss Cottage is an existing urban village, which together with Highgate, Hampstead, Chalk Farm, Camden and Kilburn form inner north-west London. Farrells' aim was to create a new cultural heart that realised the original concept for a civic-cultural centre at Swiss Cottage, whilst unifying this fascinating and varied site.

The scheme retained the grade II listed library but removed the existing leisure centre, replacing it with a mixed-use complex comprising a new leisure centre, community centre, doctor's surgery, children's play areas, cafés, new public entrance and amenities to the library, and affordable housing. This accommodation sits beneath a unifying roof, which is located in a new landscaped open public park, linked to the new Hampstead Theatre. This public space is linked to all adjacent roads and amenities by pedestrian-only routes, allowing greater access and identity for the development.

Unlike the existing leisure centre, the development is completely transparent. This allows the swimming pools, state-of-the-art gyms and sports halls to be visible from the exterior, providing animated and vibrant views of the building during the day and night. This scheme is an innovative community-based leisure complex providing genuine mixed use and shared amenities that has become a landmark in the immediate and local area.

The leisure centre plan is arranged to allow a significant proportion of its mass to be housed below ground. The lower ground floor contains the sports hall, changing rooms and the swimming pools. Using a natural form of spectator seating, the large glass façade is completely glazed to let passers-by enjoy and connect with the activities of the pool and the gym beyond. The compact planning of the leisure centre's overall height remains comparable to the adjoining library. The entrance façade and link are light, transparent expressions of steel and glass, signalling a welcome entrance to both the leisure centre and library.

The new centre has four lively façades. The main Adelaide Road façade is dominated by a climbing wall – with all the colour and paraphernalia that goes with the sport. The theatrics of the climbing wall create a striking night view, with a show of colour, changing floodlights, fluorescent lights, UV cannon lights on fluorescent painted climbing walls and LED lights embedded in the climbing surface.

Farrells' designs have provided much improved facilities to the community centre, including a café terrace towards the park, a multi-purpose hall, meeting rooms and a crèche. There is affordable housing above the leisure centre, pool and sports hall, and from this position the tenants have panoramic views over London and the landscaped open spaces.

Throughout the scheme open spaces have created new routes. Reinforcing the site's permeability, they create improved physical and visual links around the centre and surrounding area. The redevelopment is a good example of architecture growing from urban design; with its outdoor market, local offices and the close proximity of public transport, the scheme has established a vibrant cultural heart in a new urban quarter.

Top: Aerial view of the Swiss Cottage buildings organised around a central landscaped space.

Opposite page
Top: The climbing wall reveals the activity of the leisure centre with library behind.

Centre left: A sketch showing the urban neighbourhood.

Bottom left: Farrells masterplan.

Bottom right: The landscaped area that forms the heart of the development.

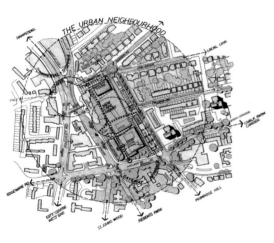

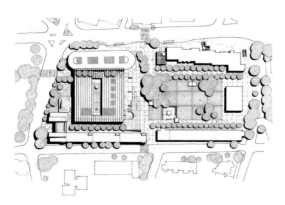

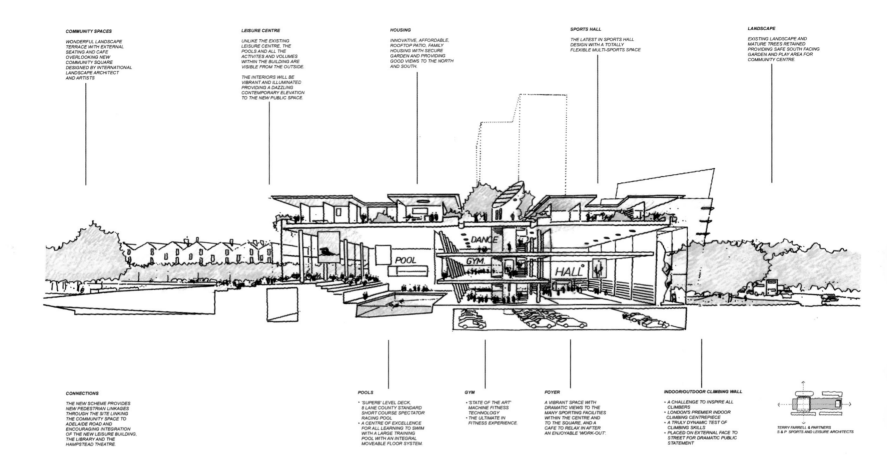

COMMUNITY SPACES

WONDERFUL LANDSCAPE TERRACE WITH EXTERNAL SEATING AND CAFE OVERLOOKING NEW COMMUNITY SQUARE DESIGNED BY INTERNATIONAL LANDSCAPE ARCHITECT AND ARTISTS

LEISURE CENTRE

UNLIKE THE EXISTING LEISURE CENTRE, THE POOLS AND ALL THE ACTIVITES AND VOLUMES WITHIN THE BUILDING ARE VISIBLE FROM THE OUTSIDE.

THE INTERIORS WILL BE VIBRANT AND ILLUMINATED PROVIDING A DAZZLING CONTEMPORARY ELEVATION TO THE NEW PUBLIC SPACE.

HOUSING

INNOVATIVE, AFFORDABLE, ROOFTOP PATIO, FAMILY HOUSING WITH SECURE GARDEN AND PROVIDING GOOD VIEWS TO THE NORTH AND SOUTH.

SPORTS HALL

THE LATEST IN SPORTS HALL DESIGN WITH A TOTALLY FLEXIBLE MULTI-SPORTS SPACE

LANDSCAPE

EXISTING LANDSCAPE AND MATURE TREES RETAINED PROVIDING SAFE SOUTH FACING GARDEN AND PLAY AREA FOR COMMUNITY CENTRE

CONNECTIONS

THE NEW SCHEME PROVIDES NEW PEDESTRIAN LINKAGES THROUGH THE SITE LINKING THE COMMUNITY SPACE TO ADELAIDE ROAD AND ENCOURAGING INTEGRATION OF THE NEW LEISURE BUILDING, THE LIBRARY AND THE HAMPSTEAD THEATRE.

POOLS

• 'SUPERB' LEVEL DECK, 8 LANE COUNTY STANDARD SHORT COURSE SPECTATOR RACING POOL
• A CENTRE OF EXCELLENCE FOR ALL LEARNING TO SWIM WITH A LARGE TRAINING POOL WITH AN INTEGRAL MOVEABLE FLOOR SYSTEM.

GYM

• 'STATE OF THE ART' MACHINE FITNESS TECHNOLOGY
• THE ULTIMATE IN FITNESS EXPERIENCE.

FOYER

A VIBRANT SPACE WITH DRAMATIC VIEWS TO THE MANY SPORTING FACILITIES WITHIN THE CENTRE AND TO THE SQUARE, AND A CAFE TO RELAX IN AFTER AN ENJOYABLE 'WORK-OUT'.

INDOOR/OUTDOOR CLIMBING WALL

• A CHALLENGE TO INSPIRE ALL CLIMBERS
• LONDON'S PREMIER INDOOR CLIMBING CENTREPIECE
• A TRULY DYNAMIC TEST OF CLIMBING SKILLS
• PLACED ON EXTERNAL FACE TO STREET FOR DRAMATIC PUBLIC STATEMENT

TERRY FARRELL & PARTNERS
S & P SPORTS AND LEISURE ARCHITECTS

Top: Internal section of the leisure centre with roof top housing above.

Bottom left: The shared glazed link between the new leisure centre and the refurbished listed library building.

Bottom right: The affordable housing with its unique bay windows and coloured render artwork.

ROYAL INSTITUTION

The Royal Institution (Ri) is the oldest and one of the most prestigious scientific establishments in the world. It has been continuously housed in the same buildings in Albemarle Street since around 1800 and contains the oldest research laboratories in the world. Within these buildings, 10 of the 100 or so chemical elements that constitute the known visible universe have been discovered, and 14 Nobel prizes are associated with Royal Institution scientists.

The building is made up of a row of Grade 1 listed Georgian townhouses and is within the Mayfair conservation area. The Ri took over these houses and amalgamated them into one building. Over time, the many layers, additions and reconfigurations of the internal spaces had created a largely incoherent building with inefficient use of space and very poor circulation. Farrells were appointed as masterplanners and lead designers for its restoration and refurbishment and subsequent emergence as a 'salon for science', widening the audience for science to as many children, students, and scientific and lay members of the general public as possible. Planning took a total of six years and involved extensive dialogues with various heritage groups and statutory authorities.

One of the key design principles was to make the building much more accessible to the public. As well as rationalising the circulation and providing deep views into the building from street level, Farrells' aim was to reinstate all the heritage rooms and make them accessible to the public – the improvement work has increased the public space within by 40%. Where possible all heritage rooms were reinstated using like-for-like materials and colour palettes. A clear distinction can be drawn between the heritage rooms and new spaces, not just in terms of design but in use of colour and materials. The heritage colours and materials used have been reinterpreted in a contemporary way. Glass and stainless steel have been used in the new atrium area to juxtapose against the existing design, and this glazing has enabled the daylight to pour into the rear of the building, which was previously dark and oppressive. In terms of improving the general circulation each floor has a central corridor spine with level or low level ramped access.

Apart from the existing exhibition space in the basement which primarily centred on Faraday, the building itself did not tell a story, the richness of its history. Explaining the mission of the Ri was done by extending the exhibition areas and using the whole fabric of the building to show its collection of paintings and drawings. Displaying objects and telling the stories behind the artefacts led to a complete rethink of the basement exhibition area. The Ri is now reconfigured, not as a museum but as a living, working, lively and engaging institution.

All of the interventions and improvements to the building were done in a way that kept the best of what was already there. This was possible because so much of it was hidden away from the public as storage and back rooms. It was possible to create this new feeling without destroying the principal parts. Through both architectural work and masterplanning Farrells contributed much to the reinvention process of the Ri, rethinking the building and rethinking its mission statement. The holistic masterplan was instrumental in establishing a new vision for the Royal Institution.

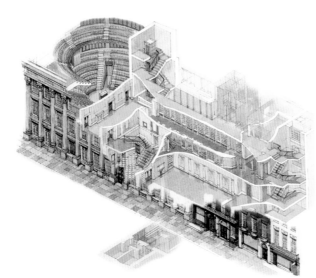

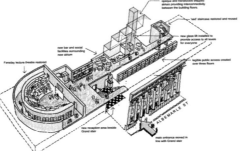

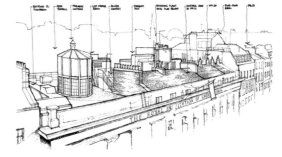

Above: Exploded view of the original building.

Top right: The 'grand' frontage of the Royal Institution belies its original composition as a row of Georgian townhouses.

Right: Axonometric view of the proposed interventions.

Far right: View of existing building from Albemarle Street Rooftops.

Top to bottom, left: Display of the 14 Nobel Prize winners with views through to the café area.

The 'Time & Space' bar provides activity onto Albemarle Street.

The restored entrance hall with sweeping staircase and open connections to public areas.

Top to bottom, right: The basement exhibition with its 'experimentation' theme.

The 'Conservation Room' utilises the refurbished library as a contemporary restaurant.

Restored Faraday Lecture Theatre, the venue for the annual Christmas Lectures.

Opposite: The new atrium space connects all levels of the building and has allowed for the exhibition of scientific artefacts never before seen by the public.

NINE ELMS

The masterplan for a new mixed-use area at Nine Elms, the area between Vauxhall and Battersea, is a 15-acre site around the proposed new US Embassy. The area has great potential for connectivity with its close proximity to central London, the River Thames, Westminster, the West End and the South Bank. The site currently reflects its past of industrial and small-scale usage, lacks connectivity to its surrounding area and is not pedestrian-friendly.

Farrells masterplan process identifies opportunities and challenges, and also urban design principles that will inform key interventions. These include a new network of streets and spaces, green linkages, a variety of uses, active frontages and a well thought-out public realm, creating a vibrant new urban quarter for London. The new development brings with it the potential for 16,000 new homes and 25,000 new jobs, and Farrells are working closely with the local council and the Greater London Authority, who recognise that the developments have far-reaching potential to create a fantastic new district for central London.

The relocation of the US Embassy to the area will bring with it further growth and it will be one of the key addresses in the future of developments south of the river.

Main image: The masterplan within the context of the emerging schemes of the wider area of Nine Elms and Vauxhall.

Bottom left: The part completed Battersea power station.

Bottom centre: Completed power station, fully operational.

Bottom right: The site as it exists today.

Opposite page
Top left: Urban design principles that show the strategies for connections and movement both in and around the masterplan.

Bottom left: Artist's impressions of how the site could look.

Top right: The masterplan forms the setting for the new US Embassy.

Bottom right: Framed by active ground floor uses on either side, the park provides a rich environment for recreation.

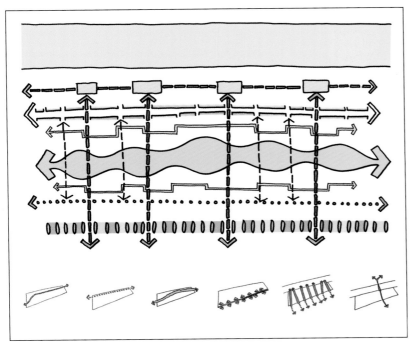

EARL'S COURT

The entire area around the Exhibition Centre in Earl's Court is to be redeveloped, and will see three major landowners working in collaboration. The site is an isolated area to the rear of the exhibition building, a vast 28 hectares of under-utilised land in a high-value location. The exhibition centre forms part of the 'Valley of the Giants' – a string of vast industrial, institutional and transport complexes along the previously industrialised 'lost river', in an area that is well connected to central London and the A4/M4.

Through routes are currently non-existent and there is very little connection to the surrounding urban area. The exhibition venue has been in decline over the past few years as bigger and better venues have opened in East London.

The masterplan concept is a vision based on the idea of four urban villages and a high street. These four new London villages are at the key corners of the site and would be named after their locations: West Kensington village, Earl's Court village, North End Village and West Brompton village. This scheme will grow inward from the edges and the emphasis is on place not buildings. A new north-south broadway will serve as an urban and cultural magnet whilst a new high street will run on the east-west axis.

The masterplan form will evolve over time – but with a robust strategic framework of agreed and consistent principles the vision will remain strong.

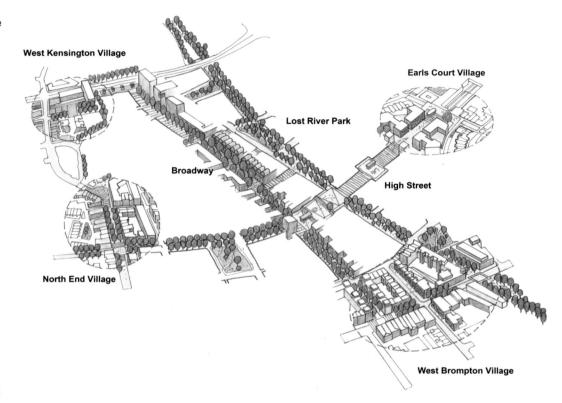

Above left: Aerial photograph of the site in its London context.

Above right: Original concept sketch by Terry Farrell: a network of disaggregated spaces that create value across the masterplan and enable the delivery of places in each phase.

Top: Masterplan components: four villages, a high street, broadway and Lost River Park.

Right (clockwise from top left): Artist's views of the masterplan proposals: West Brompton village; Earl's Court village; a bird's-eye view of the development; high street and broadway junction.

Opposite: Illustrative masterplan.

**Four Villages and
a High Street**
1. The proposed high street
looks to combine retail,
community and A3 uses to
create a vibrant new focus
for the development
2. Earl's Court Village
3. West Brompton Village
4. North End Village
5. West Kensington Village

Opposite: Masterplan model
with first-phase Seagrave Road
development in the foreground.

PETERSHAM HOUSING

Three contemporary homes were built in Petersham, on the east bend of the river Thames, to the south-west of London. The site is set away from the outside world down a 50m winding lane and is obscured by established trees, shrubs and high fences. The planning authority stipulated that the development should be low profile and should not be seen from outside the site – a height of seven metres was agreed.

The design concept creates three individual family homes that form part of a high-quality architectural grouping while remaining totally private. Each house is conceived as a linear arrangement of rooms consisting of dining room, kitchen, study and bedrooms accessed from a double-height gallery that runs the length of the house.

The northern wall of the gallery is two storeys high and windowless and therefore presents the adjoining property with a boundary wall ensuring complete privacy. A glazed living room pavilion plugs into the spine and sits within the enclosed garden. As a result, the living accommodation is pulled as far as possible away from the site boundaries, existing properties and the immediate neighbours on the site, ensuring completely private external space and living accommodation that does not overlook, and is not overlooked by, any of the surrounding properties. The architectural language for the building consists of a range of materials, which with the building form create a contemporary classic modern profile and a scheme of the highest architectural quality.

White rendered walls cut through the landscape and the accommodation is enclosed in lightweight elements of timber and grey metal. A full-height sliding glass door system is used in all rooms. The three houses use three different stones for the ground level floor and three complementary timbers for the stairs and upper floor.

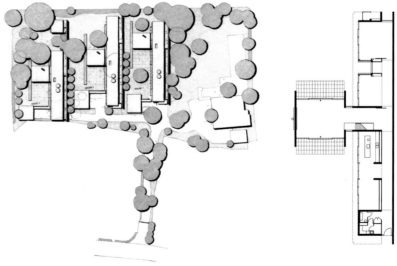

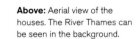

Above: Aerial view of the houses. The River Thames can be seen in the background.

Centre left: The site plan showing all three houses and their courtyard gardens.

Centre right: Floor plan of the courtyard house.

Bottom left: The development is in close proximity to Richmond Park and the leafy suburbs of Richmond and Twickenham

Bottom right: 3D view of the three courtyard houses.

Opposite: A private idyll – a courtyard in one of the Petersham houses.

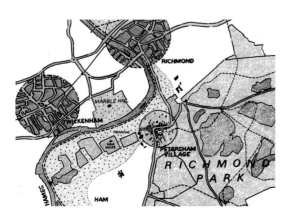

Top to bottom, left: Generous private garden spaces provide the setting for the house.

Hardwood louvres shade the highly glazed façade and invest the elevation with dynamism.

High ceilings in the living rooms exaggerate the sense of space and light.

Top to bottom, right: The house has great street presence.

The living accommodation is immersed in the garden.

Full-height glazed doors allow indoor space to flow into outdoor space.

BISHOPSGATE

Bishopsgate Goods Yard covers an area of approximately 4.7 hectares and lies between the diverse neighbourhoods of Shoreditch, Spitalfields and Banglatown, close to the northern edge of the City of London. The site spans the boundary between the London Boroughs of Hackney and Tower Hamlets. The site has an interesting history, and the structures remaining on the site help define its unique character. These include the listed Braithwaite viaduct, the listed forecourt wall and gates to Shoreditch High Street, the railway arches

west of Braithwaite Street, the former weaver's cottages on Sclater Street and the boundary wall to Sclater Street. The area is currently extremely well served by public transport with bus routes, five mainline rail and underground stations within a short walk from the site.

Farrells are developing the masterplan and urban design framework for a new 2m sq. ft. mixed-use scheme, with the intention of submitting a first phase planning application by early 2012. The proposal includes restoration of listed arches, a

new high-level park on top of the retained historic viaduct, new public squares and routes through the site. The varied context of the immediate areas presents opportunities for a variety of building scales and architectural character. There will be transition in scale and building height across the site from west to east.

Bishopsgate Goods Yard offers an exciting opportunity for a sustainable form of high-density development closely linked to excellent public transport access.

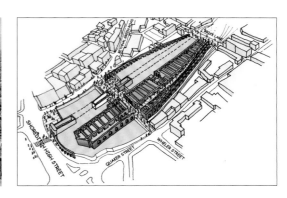

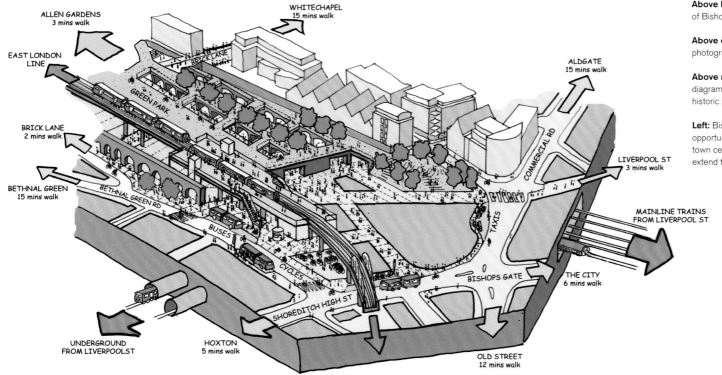

Above left: Historic photograph of Bishopsgate Goods Yard.

Above centre: Aerial photograph of the site today.

Above right: Axonometric diagram illustrating the existing historic structure.

Left: Bishopsgate: an opportunity to create a new town centre and massively extend the public realm.

THAMES ESTUARY

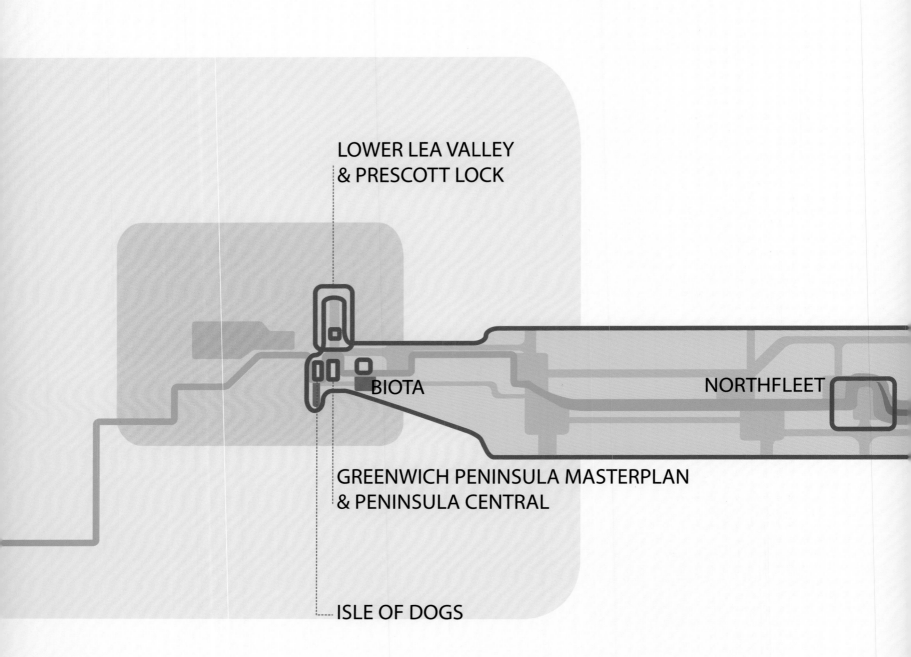

LOWER LEA VALLEY
& PRESCOTT LOCK

BIOTA

NORTHFLEET

GREENWICH PENINSULA MASTERPLAN
& PENINSULA CENTRAL

ISLE OF DOGS

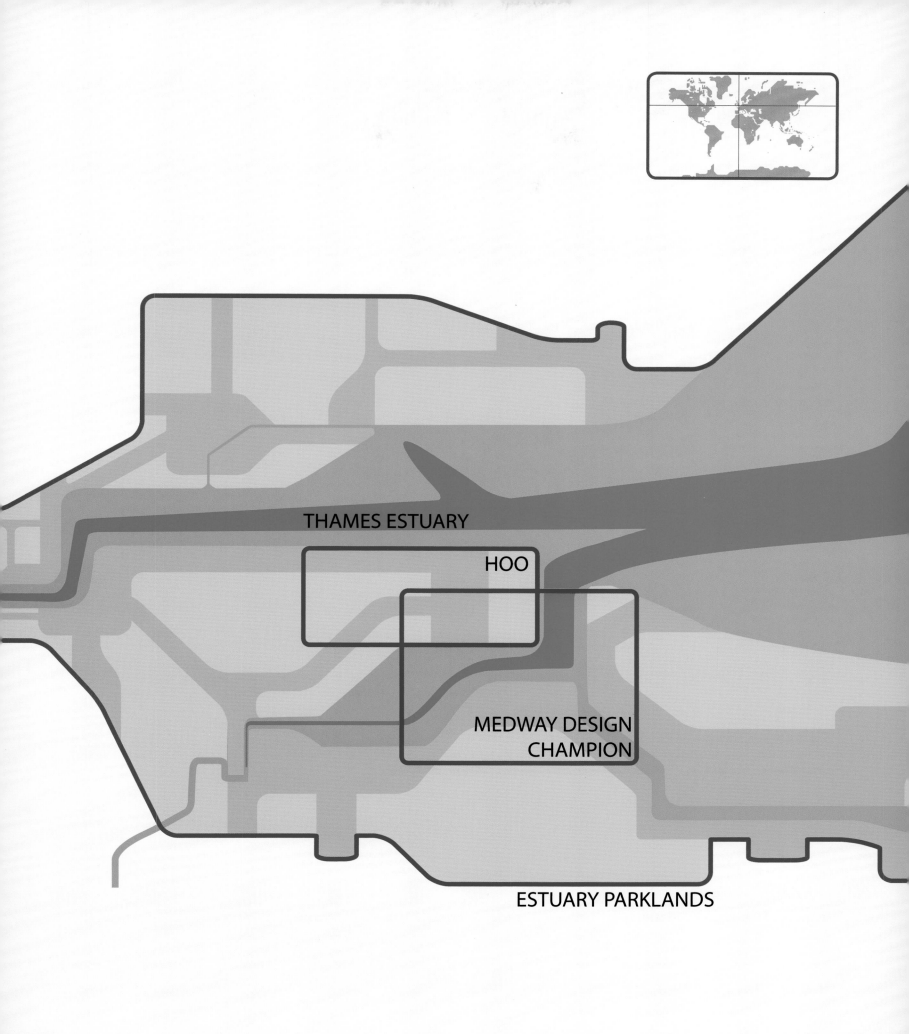

THAMES ESTUARY

HOO

MEDWAY DESIGN
CHAMPION

ESTUARY PARKLANDS

THAMES ESTUARY

For centuries the Thames Estuary has acted as London's engine room. It is the place which supported the exploration and scientific endeavour of the 16th, 17th and 18th centuries. It supported the globalisation and empire-building that occurred in the 19th century. Its docks welcomed migrants to the UK in the 20th century.

The Thames Estuary has for centuries been the focus for trade and exchange. It helped to reinforce London's role as the world's first metropolis. It supports London's status as a world city to this day generating 10% of the UK's power, and it imports a similar percentage of the raw materials needed to generate its energy. The new container port at London Gateway will maintain its status as an international port. It is the lifeblood of the whole region.

Despite its continuing significance, the estuary has been in decline for the last 50 years. It has lost its role as a large-scale centre for manufacturing and the labour-intensive employment that went with 19th- and 20th-century methods of distribution are long obsolete. This means that it has the greatest potential to absorb the growth, but the rationale for new growth does not currently exist here.

What the Thames Estuary does have is enormous potential to become the engine room of the region for the 21st century. It is undoubtedly the place with the most natural advantages to develop the new environmental industries and the low carbon technology that will be necessary to maintain the region's competitiveness on the world stage.

As well as its coherence as an economic asset, the Thames Estuary has a natural coherence as the tidal part of the River Thames. It has sites internationally designated as important areas of nature conservation, and its salt marshes, mudflats, wetlands and wildernesses are the starting point for its reinvention as the region's focus for growth in the 21st century. Using these natural assets must form the basis for this reinvention. The Estuary will not attract the people, the new environmental industries, or the infrastructure that is needed to secure the region's future unless this is based on making the most of its natural assets to transform its quality of life.

"Bottom up regeneration but with a picture on the box"

Above: 'One Vision – A Thousand Projects'. The Parklands vision supports bottom-up regeneration but with a picture on the box.

Bottom left: Oare slipway, Faversham.

Bottom right: Cliffe Pools, north Kent.

Opposite: Sunrise on the Thames Estuary, looking towards the sea.

ESTUARY PARKLANDS

The Parklands vision: regenerate and develop urban and rural open spaces which are connected together to create an accessible and coherent landscape. This will improve the quality of life for people who live in the Thames Gateway, and the experience for those who visit and work in it. Parklands spaces should be sustainable and contribute towards the development of the Gateway as an eco-region. The vision can be implemented over time by a variety of organisations at national, regional and local level.

Parklands' aim is to help make the Thames Gateway a special place drawing on the Thames Estuary's unique landscape, its rich history and its vibrant mix of cultures and communities. A vision has been created that connects these communities – both existing and new – to the river, its tributaries and the Estuary landscape.

Parklands will help to breathe new life into the area by contributing to a high-quality environment. This in turn will help the Gateway's communities meet the challenges of the future. The environmental improvements described in the vision will encourage increased growth, economic development and investment in the region, by creating an attractive business and residential environment for both existing and new communities.

This is not a masterplan. It is a spatial framework that suggests ways in which public, private, third sector and local organisations can help shape the future of the Gateway through the development of its green infrastructure. It is intended to help in strategic decision-making and provide a context for the implementation of projects at local level. Parklands is designed to adapt to new challenges and change.

Parklands will make a contribution to the development of the Thames Gateway as the UK's first eco-region. The evolving landscape – including the urban landscape – can be a showcase for sustainability in response to climate change and the demand for finite resources. By drawing inspiration from nature, landscape and history, and by taking a respectful approach to the adaptation of existing resources including our built heritage and the culture of place, we are creating an environment within which low-carbon growth can thrive.

Parklands is about improving a landscape that continues to inspire great writing, art and architecture. It is our aim – along with those that have participated in this process – to put forward an ambitious vision that is worthy of this special and diverse place.

CENTRAL LONDON
PARTNERSHIP ZONE
16,000 HECTARES
1.5 MILLION POPULATION

90%

10%
of New Housing
in Rural Areas

SCALE
COMPARISON

10% in the park

= 4000 HECTA

= 200 000 HO

TO SAME SCALE
AS MAIN DRAWING

@ 50 HOME
PER HECTA

THAMES GATEWAY
95,000 HECTARES
1.5 MILLION POPULATION

PROPORTION
OF BUILT
& UNBUILT
AREAS

EXISTING
BUILT AREA
OF THAMES
GATEWAY

PROPOSED
ADDITIONAL BUIL
AREA TO ACHIEVE
200 000 HOMES,
OF WHICH 90%
COULD BE WITHIN
THE EXISTING
BUILT AREA

REMAINING
UNBUILT AREA
OF THAMES
GATEWAY

Below left: The Parklands concept linking communities to Parklands and to the River Thames and its tributaries.

Below middle: Concept sketch of Parklands formed by the combination of blue, green and brown landscapes.

Below right: The urban Parklands concept – greening the urban landscape and improving access for existing and new communities to significant landscapes.

Bottom: The Parklands spatial framework masterplan drawing, presented in 2008.

Opposite page: A demonstation that the Gateway project is about landscape first, not new housing.

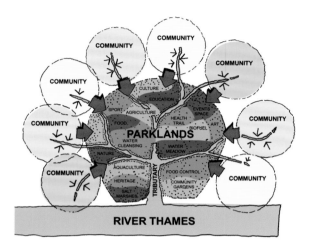

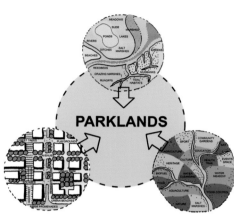

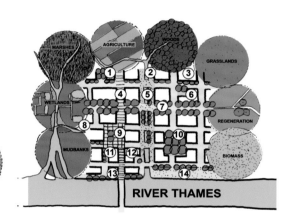

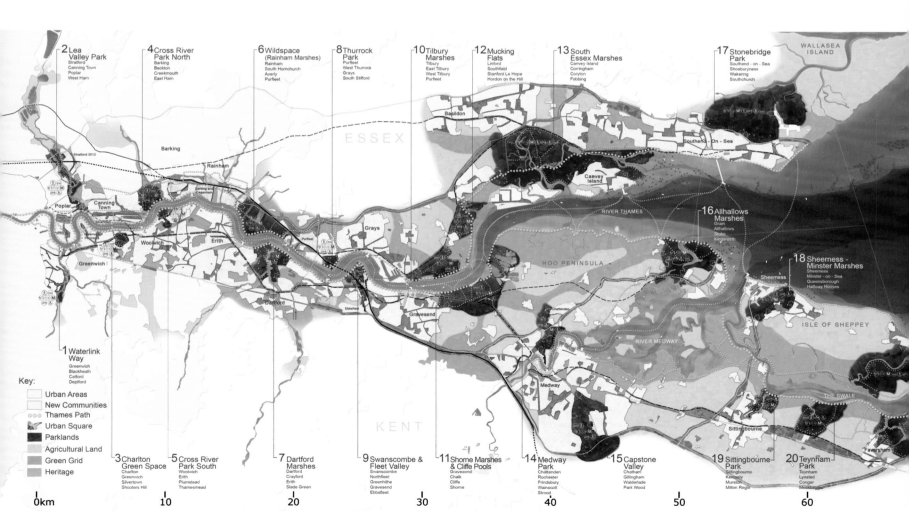

Key:
- Urban Areas
- New Communities
- Thames Path
- Urban Square
- Parklands
- Agricultural Land
- Green Grid
- Heritage

1 Waterlink Way
Greenwich
Blackheath
Catford
Deptford

2 Lea Valley Park
Stratford
Canning Town
Poplar
West Ham

3 Charlton Green Space
Charlton
Greenwich
Silvertown
Shooters Hill

4 Cross River Park North
Barking
Beckton
Creekmouth
East Ham

5 Cross River Park South
Woolwich
Erith
Plumstead
Thamesmead

6 Wildspace (Rainham Marshes)
Rainham
South Hornchurch
Aveley
Purfleet

7 Dartford Marshes
Dartford
Crayford
Erith
Slade Green

8 Thurrock Park
Purfleet
West Thurrock
Grays
South Stifford

9 Swanscombe & Fleet Valley
Swanscombe
Northfleet
Greenhithe
Gravesend
Ebbsfleet

10 Tilbury Marshes
Tilbury
East Tilbury
West Tilbury
Purfleet

11 Shome Marshes & Cliffe Pools
Chalk
Cliffe
Shorne

12 Mucking Flats
Linford
Southfield
Stanford Le Hope
Hordon on the Hill

13 South Essex Marshes
Canvey Island
Corringham
Coryton
Fobbing

14 Medway Park
Chalkenden
Gravesend
Chalk
Wainscott
Strood

15 Capstone Valley
Chatham
Gillingham
Walderslade
Park Wood

16 Allhallows Marshes
Grain
Allhallows
Stoke
Kingsnorth

17 Stonebridge Park
Southend - on - Sea
Shoeburyness
Wakering
Southchurch

18 Sheerness - Minster Marshes
Sheerness
Minster - on - Sea
Queensborough
Halfway Houses

19 Sittingbourne Park
Sittingbourne
Gillingham
Kemsley
Murston
Milton Regis

20 Teynham Park
Teynham
Lynsted
Conger
Moddington

0km   10   20   30   40   50   60

NORTHFLEET

In 2009 Farrells were appointed to devise a concept masterplan for Northfleet, which is located on the River Thames next to the historic town of Gravesend. The site is adjacent to the international high-speed rail station in Ebbsfleet, and was formerly occupied by cement works and warehouses.

A previous masterplan proposed low-rise suburban development on the site. Farrells' propose a high-density mixed-use riverside community which makes better use of the investment in infrastructure that has already taken place in the area. The rail service provides access to central London at St Pancras in less than 20 minutes, which justifies a high-density, urban approach to the development of the site.

As well as proposals for new development, the plan integrates Northfleet with existing communities at Swanscombe, Gravesend and Ebbsfleet, as well as providing direct pedestrian and cycle routes to the international railway station.

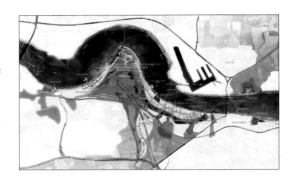

Top: Proposal for a new eco-city within the Thames Estuary Park.

Above: Aerial perspective of the riverside development and its connection to the high-speed rail service.

Left: Creating a cityscape on the Thames.

LOWER LEA VALLEY

The conceptual masterplan for the Lower Lea Valley – the main site for the UK's 2012 Olympic Games – mirrored the goals set out in the Olympic Charter and formed the basis for the creation of a potentially great city quarter. The aspirations focused on inclusiveness, diversity, compassion and cohesiveness to remake a large part of London via the challenge of the regeneration of the Lower Lea Valley and the opportunities presented from holding the Olympics in London.

The masterplan formed the inner layer of a three-level plan linking the Lea Valley to London, and London to the whole world for the period of the Olympics. It formed the northern arm of four axes of regeneration, which converge at the point where the Lea meets the River Thames. The western arm embraces the financial district of Canary Wharf, City Airport and the Royal Docks, opening up a new techno pole to the east. Greenwich Peninsula, to the south, has already undergone a major transformation. The legacy of the London Olympics will be the global villages of the Lower Lea Valley. Within the plan the idea was challenged that all of the Lower Lea Valley-based Olympic events need to be clustered at the northern end. To secure the regeneration of the whole area and complete the park connection to the Thames, a broader disposition of the facilities should be investigated. Each existing local node grows to drive regeneration whilst the continuation of the Park mirrors the flood plain. The Lower Lea Valley is tied through a myriad of local connection projects celebrated by a new Aerial Cable Tram Car linking Stratford to North Greenwich.

Farrells' approach was that the masterplan should be, first and foremost, about the regeneration of the Lower Lea Valley, allowing the Olympics element to 'plug in' seamlessly.

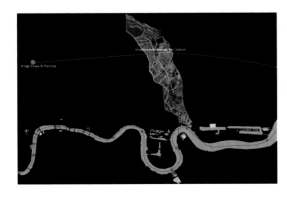

Left: Lea Valley and Olympic Park within Parklands.

Above: Concept model showing the growth of existing villages and the cable car connection between the O2 centre and the Olympic Stadium.

ISLE OF DOGS

Previously part of East London's dock complex, today the Isle of Dogs is a place of contrasts. Along with Canary Wharf, which is the largest financial centre in Europe after the City of London and one of London's greatest concentrations of wealth, it is home to some of the most deprived and isolated communities in London.

The last 10 years have seen rapid large-scale development in the area, and further growth is planned, notably at Wood Wharf and on Pan Peninsula. Recently it has become clear that much of this activity has been piecemeal and uncoordinated, to the detriment of this area in general.

In 2007 Farrells were commissioned by Ballymore, the Canary Wharf Group and the London Borough of Tower Hamlets to develop a strategy that would provide context and coherence to all the plans that were being made for the Isle of Dogs. The practice's concept was to regard the disused docks as an integral part of the public realm, and to connect the water space seamlessly with the streets, squares, parks and gardens that define successful places.

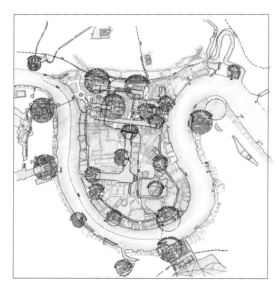

Above: The Isle of Dogs is made up of a number of urban villages; with Canary Wharf to the north and Mudchute to the south.

Right: Integrating the exemplar wildlife and ecological habitat as an amenity to the peninsula.

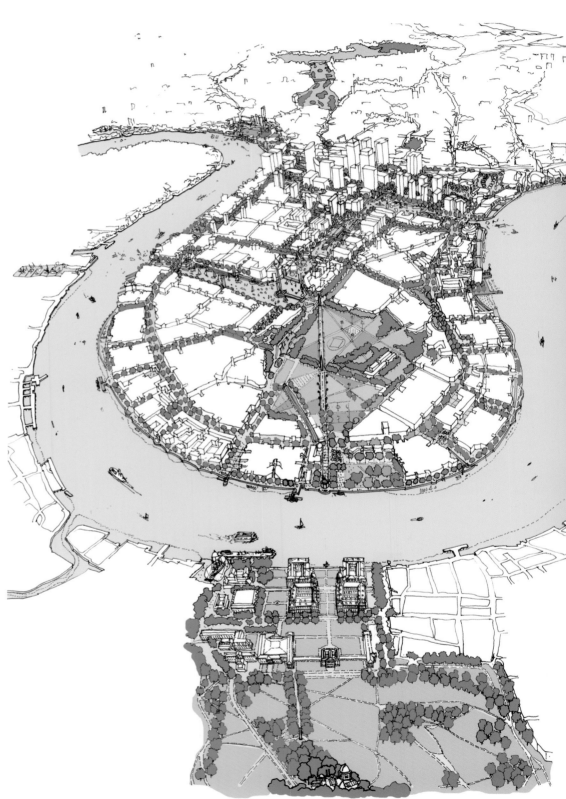

PRESCOTT LOCK

In 2007 Farrells were commissioned by British Waterways to design a new lock and associated landscape for the new Three Mills Lock at Prescott Channel, Bromley-by-Bow. This is the first new lock to be built in London for 20 years. For more than 50 years, the Bow Back Rivers in East London lay derelict, under-used and almost forgotten. The completion of the new Three Mills Lock has revived this fascinating network of waterways and made it part of the 2012 Olympic Park.

The lock was designed to enable boats to carry construction material to and from the Olympic Park and also form part of the Olympic legacy by opening up the Bow Back Rivers network, which runs in and around the Olympic site, for water taxis, waste removal and recreation. This project forms part of British Waterways' restoration programme to bring canals back into active use and help to improve water quality and flood management in the area. The £20m Three Mills Lock structure at Prescott Channel includes a tidal lock, a weir and a fish pass.

By creatively reinterpreting the engineering constraints on the structures and their function, Farrells' concept design incorporated a pedestrian and cycling bridge across Prescott Channel separate from the lock structures, landscape and public realm improvements to the surrounding area, and an artistic intervention in the form of a screen on the tidal lock gates, which celebrates the kinetic nature of the lock and signifies the gateway to the Olympic park.

Three Mills Lock was constructed by civil engineering contractor VolkerStevin, and was officially opened in June 2009.

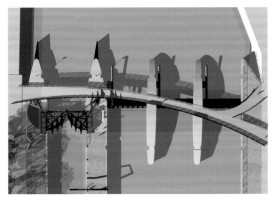

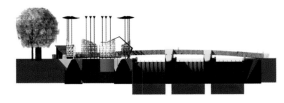

Top right: The new lock facilitating the construction of the Olympic site – concept image.

Centre left: The bridge connection in place today.

Right and above: Sketch proposals for new lock and linking parklands footpath and bridge.

GREENWICH PENINSULA MASTERPLAN

The Greenwich Peninsula has a diverse history. It was originally marshland and after subsequent draining in the 16th century became agricultural land. In the late 18th and early 19th centuries industrial use including ship building took precedence.

Its comprehensive regeneration marks one of the largest planning consents ever achieved in London. The site covers an area of around 75 hectares and has 2.5 kilometres of waterfront. However, a seemingly simple brownfield area was in fact a highly complex and constrained site with soil contamination, seawall defences, road and tube tunnels, listed buildings, arterial roads and flight paths for London City Airport all needing careful consideration.

The masterplan retained the O2 (then known as the Millennium Dome), station and park as they were

valuable resources for the area's future success. Core strategies for the masterplan were to create value, utilise existing infrastructure and make logical connections with the existing development. Office and retail districts were placed around the transport nodes at the heart of the peninsula and residential developments were sited near picturesque areas.

There were four new residential neighbourhoods, each positioned to make the most of the proximity of the river and park. Each neighbourhood has its own distinct character and identity. The masterplan also incorporated 5 new public parks and 12 public squares – forming a network of urban greenery.

A series of linkages connects the parks and squares to create a comprehensive network of pedestrian routes, extending beyond the boundary

of the masterplan to connect residents with local transport, schools and retail and employment areas.

The plan creates a new urban quarter for London. The pattern of streets, squares and parks ensure clear lines of connection north and south. The cross streets connect both sides of the peninsula to its heart, ensuring that all parts connect to the river. By creating a series of distinctive urban districts, i.e. the four neighbourhoods, public parks and the squares the scheme has facilitated a sustainable urban quarter for London, embodying the concept of growth, renewal and rebirth while embracing existing infrastructure. The proposals demonstrated a comprehensive and sustainable approach to the planned development of a complete and holistic new urban district.

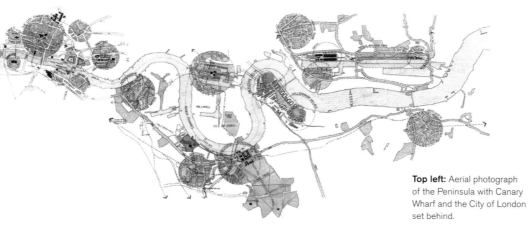

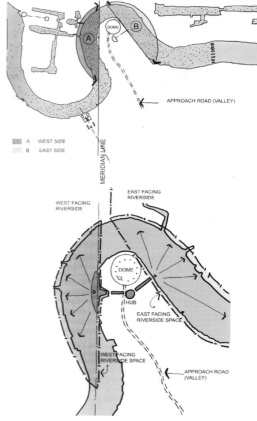

Top left: Aerial photograph of the Peninsula with Canary Wharf and the City of London set behind.

Left: Docklands urban villages.

Above: Peninsula with parklands and meridian line.

Opposite: Masterplan model with principal connections highlighted.

Inset: Masterplan concept diagrams.

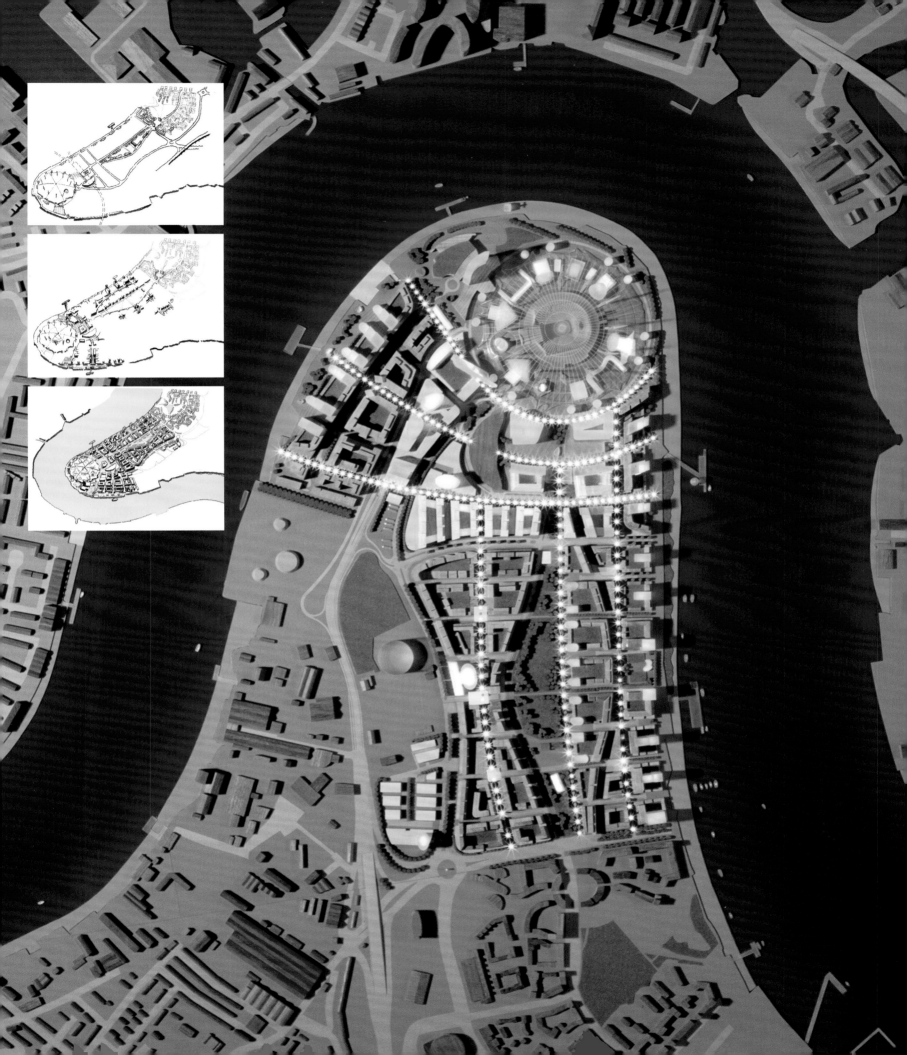

PENINSULA PLACE

The project site set within the Greenwich Peninsula masterplan consists of two office buildings: to the north, 14 Pier Walk is split in height and provides 7 – 8 levels of approximately 26,700 m² (GEA) of office, retail and parking space. To the south, 6 Mitre Passage provides 13 levels of approximately 15,600 m² (GEA), again comprising office, retail and parking space.

By taking its formal inspiration from the masterplan geometry and translating it into three dimensions, the new buildings create a strong visual presence which addresses both Peninsula Square and the new Green Place to the south.

The buildings' concept is of three sliding 'blades' of office accommodation and a fourth landscape 'lane' on the ground plane, which establishes a new public space separating the two buildings and creating a strong linear route across the site. The building 'blades' have different heights, colours, levels of transparency and reflections but form a family of dynamic shapes, which trace the strong underlying geometry of the masterplan. In addition, they follow the stepping down of the buildings' form established in the masterplan principles. The form of the buildings is dynamic and broken down in response to the masterplan concept. A new presence on Peninsula Square has emerged, creating a counterpoint to the O2, and at the same time opening itself to the new Green Place to the south.

The concept for the design of the buildings' elevations is inspired by the Paul Klee painting *Fire at Evening* (*Feuer Abends*, 1929). Following the buildings and massing concept, a modular tapestry-like architectural idea was developed where the pattern of the façades responds to the orientation and aspect of the buildings.

Entirely new London districts come along maybe once a generation. But an area of sheer quality, scale and beauty that is Greenwich Peninsula is a once-in-a-lifetime event. Peninsula Central will offer flexibility of design, exceptional environmental performance and excellent value for money.

These two office buildings are exemplars of the most sustainable commercial buildings in the country, having achieved a BREEAM rating of

Right: Office building 'the three sliding blades' (Terry Farrell's concept diagrams on right) with the new Ravensbourne College and Dome in the distance.

'excellent' and set a benchmark for the rest of the masterplan. The buildings not only incorporate some of the best green technologies, but are very well connected to the transport infrastructure, just metres from the Jubilee Line, a bus station, water taxis, as well as being on the doorstep of the world's most popular music venue – the 02. Within a generation, Peninsula Central will provide 3.5 million sq. ft. of commercial space across 14 buildings, developed in tandem with 10,000 new homes, 48 acres of open green space, shops, restaurants, schools and community facilities – a truly sustainable community.

Top: View of the development from the Jubilee Line station.

Above: Close-up view from Millennium Square.

Opposite page: Façade detail of the 6 Mitre Passage building.

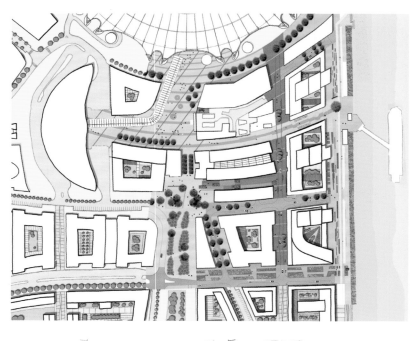

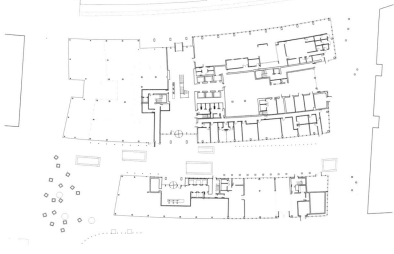

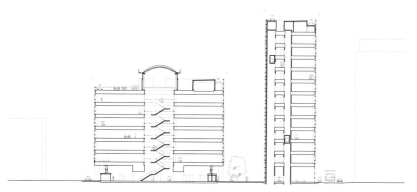

Top: The masterplan and site context.

Above, centre and bottom: Plan and section of the buildings.

Top: Staff rest area.

Bottom right: Canteen area with its views to the O2 centre.

Opposite: The long staircase within the 14 Pier Walk atrium.

BIOTA!

On the north bank of the River Thames at Silvertown Quays, on a peninsula bordered by water on its north, south and west sides, was the site for a National Aquarium. The Zoological Society of London (ZSL) sought to build a world-class, conservation-led public aquarium that would become a major attraction, an iconic building and a recognisable addition to London's landmarks. The objective was to inspire visitors by presenting to them the beauty and wonder of underwater life, so that more people would be committed to learning and caring about the aquatic environment.

The principles of conservation and sustainability were key to the design of the aquarium that would represent the global diversity of aquatic life through four strongly contrasting biomes recreating complete ecosystems with plants, fish, free-flying birds, mammals and other animals. The design for the building was arranged around a central atrium. The first floor houses the open ocean and coral reef exhibits with day-lit biomes on the upper floors. The exhibit areas represent diverse world habitats – the Amazon, the British Isles, the Indo-Pacific and the Atlantic Ocean. The fifth exhibit area, 'Living Conservation', focuses on protecting aquatic species and their habitats, the underlying message of Biota!

The building was part of a larger masterplan for the regeneration of the area around the Royal Docks as a whole and included a pedestrian-friendly plaza and esplanade along with new homes, offices, workspace, retail, leisure, entertainment and community facilities.

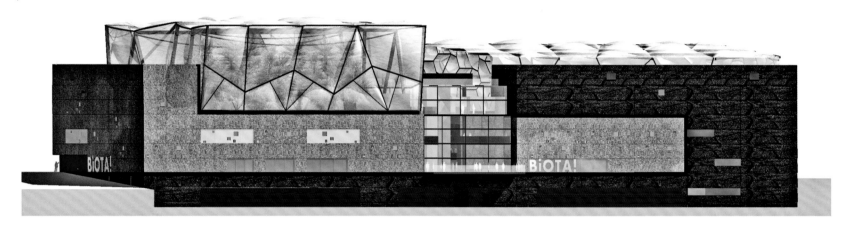

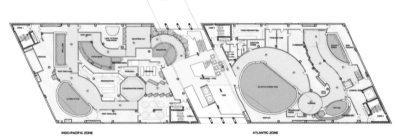

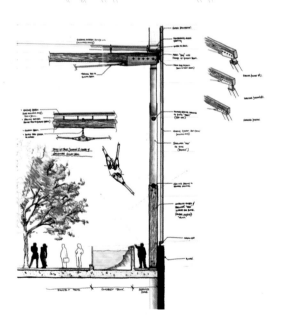

Opposite page
Main image: View of the esplanade with consented façade design.

Inset: Artist's impression of the aquarium in its urban context.

Top: Southern elevation facing the Docklands Light Railway.

Centre left: Ground Floor Plan.

Centre right: Upper Floor Plan.

Bottom left: Section detail of façade.

Bottom centre: The link building.

Bottom right: Overall context masterplan and River Thames with tidal barrier.

LONDON-ON-SEA

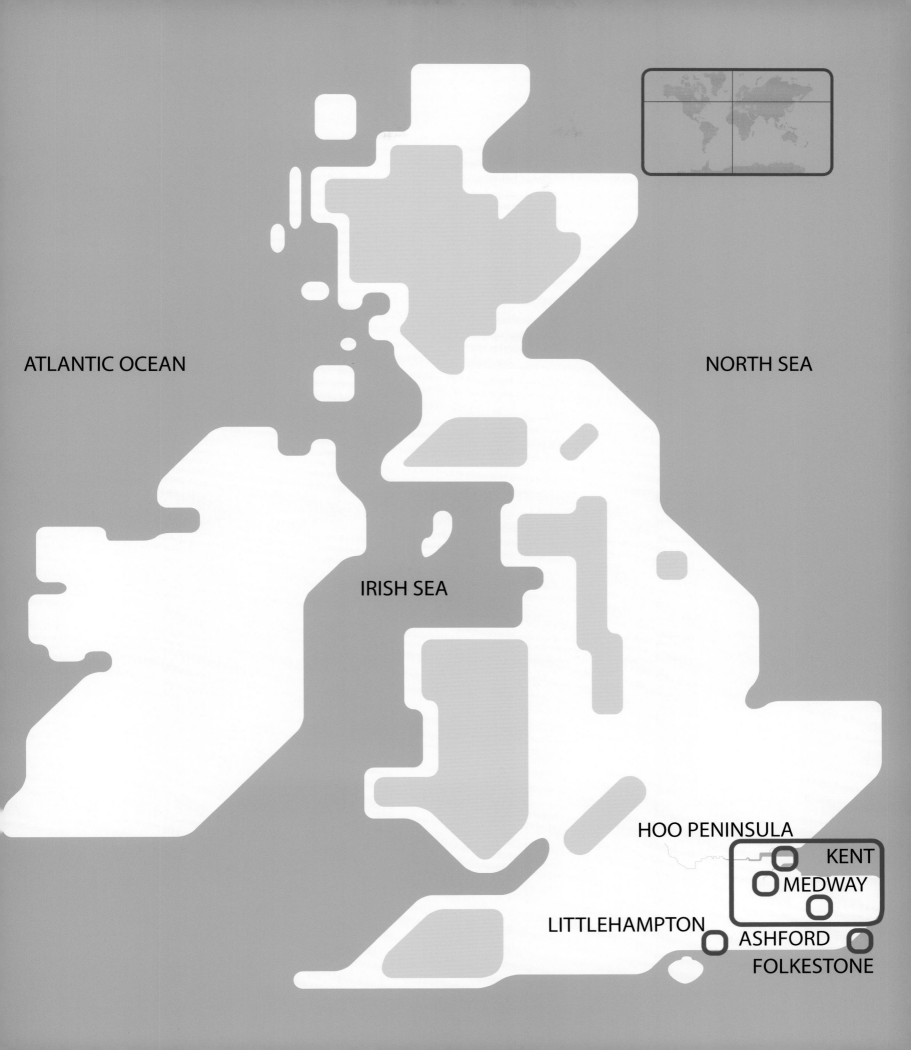

ATLANTIC OCEAN

NORTH SEA

IRISH SEA

HOO PENINSULA

KENT

MEDWAY

LITTLEHAMPTON

ASHFORD

FOLKESTONE

LONDON-ON-SEA

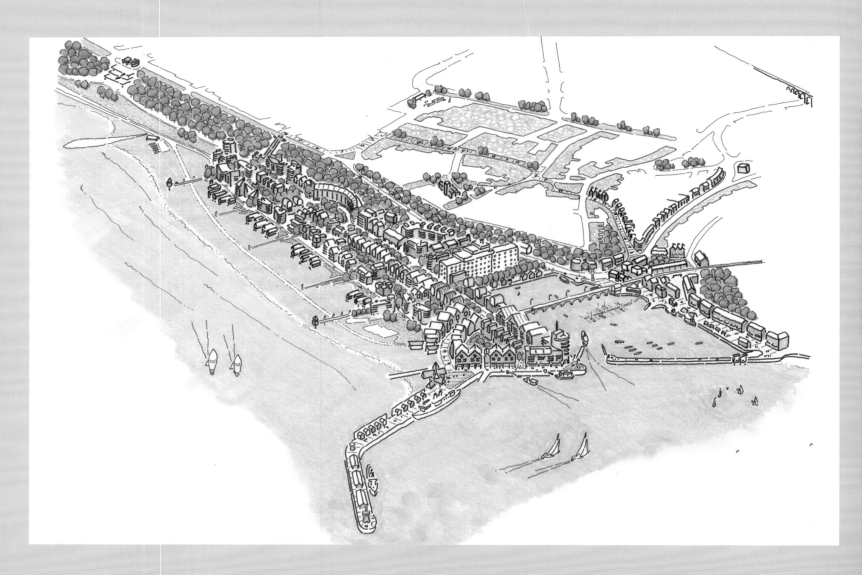

Building on the core message of Farrells' Thames Gateway – that landscape is the starting point, the first infrastructure, and that interventions, whether economic or indeed physical, should work with the essence, the grain of the 'place' – Terry Farrell was appointed successively 'Design Champion' for Kent, for the Medway, and for the Isle of Wight.

Themes running through the studies that followed from these commissions include the effect and desirability of improved connectivity and transport links, the need for a unified approach to the public realm, and the importance of understanding the underlying structure of these places – the shape of the place. These themes are also integral to a series of studies around the coast, in coastal towns and sub regions increasingly subject to the economic and cultural influence of London – 'London-on-sea' as it were.

Central to the Hoo Peninsula study is the planning – in the bigger context of the Thames Gateway – for growth in an area previously dominated by strategic infrastructure. Farrells' work at Littlehampton has also created a bigger picture for individual public realm interventions and drivers such as flood defence, which has resulted in an overall public realm strategy. Ongoing work at Folkestone continues these themes, building on the philanthropic work of the Folkestone Harbour Regeneration Board to formulate a masterplan for the regeneration of the seafront, an area that had lost its identity following the economic forces acting on the former Channel ferry port.

Above: Sketch view of Folkestone showing the seafront development linked to the harbour and the Old Town Creative Quarter.

Opposite top left: Regeneration of Folkestone and its Creative Quarter; the Quarterhouse (to the right), Folkestone's performing arts and business centre, opened in March 2009.

Opposite top right: Droit House on Margate Pier, with its modern rotunda designed by Farrells providing a visitors centre and exhibition space.

Opposite bottom: The longest bench in Britain by Studio Weave forms part of Farrells' seafront strategy for Littlehampton.

KENT & ASHFORD DESIGN CHAMPION

In 2009 the practice was asked to devise a strategic vision for Kent following the success of the Thames Estuary Parklands project. Kent County Council was keen to apply the concept of environmental infrastructure and quality of life as the basis for the whole county's future growth and regeneration. The other main impetus behind the project was the fact that it has the UK's only high-speed domestic rail service. This reinforces its historic role as the UK's 'front door' to Europe and the rest of the world. The essence of the strategy is to capitalise on all the investments that have been made over several decades in rail, road, maritime and landscape infrastructure.

Kent is arguably the UK's most diverse county. Its countryside has the magnificent chalk cliffs facing the English Channel, the drama of the Kent Downs, and the orchards and vineyards that define it as the garden of England. It has a constellation of hamlets, towns and villages which are extraordinarily different from one another. The county epitomises a multi-centric settlement pattern. It has many famous places – Canterbury, Tunbridge Wells, Margate, Folkestone – but none of these dominate, unlike other parts of the UK which have recognised 'capitals'.

Our strategy for Kent emphasises the natural and urban diversity of the county as the basis for its future plans. Urban regeneration must aim at increasing its pattern of local distinctiveness. Along with an emphasis on place, the strategy argues for focusing growth on Kent's most accessible locations, in particular taking advantage of rail infrastructure which sets it apart from other parts of the UK. Places that were previously more than an hour from London can now be reached in half the time.

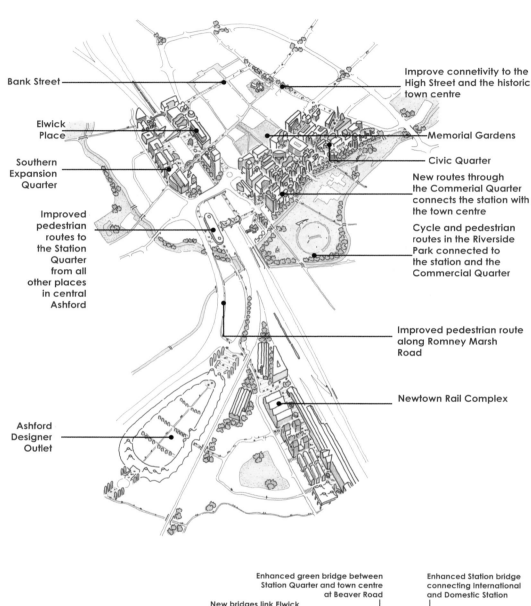

Bank Street

Elwick Place

Southern Expansion Quarter

Improved pedestrian routes to the Station Quarter from all other places in central Ashford

Ashford Designer Outlet

Improve connetivity to the High Street and the historic town centre

Memorial Gardens

Civic Quarter

New routes through the Commerial Quarter connects the station with the town centre

Cycle and pedestrian routes in the Riverside Park connected to the station and the Commercial Quarter

Improved pedestrian route along Romney Marsh Road

Newtown Rail Complex

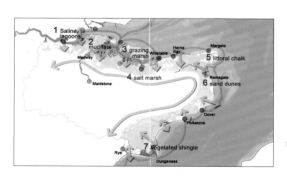

Above: The coastline has a diverse mix of environments and inhabitants.

Right top: A vision for Ashford.

Right bottom: A vision for new bridges across the railway line.

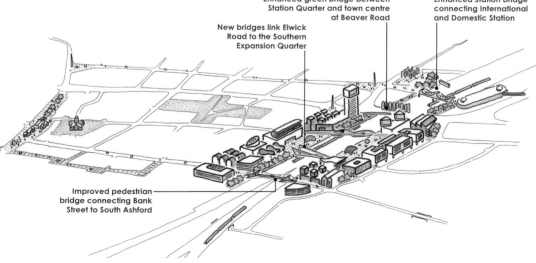

Enhanced green bridge between Station Quarter and town centre at Beaver Road

Enhanced Station bridge connecting International and Domestic Station

New bridges link Elwick Road to the Southern Expansion Quarter

Improved pedestrian bridge connecting Bank Street to South Ashford

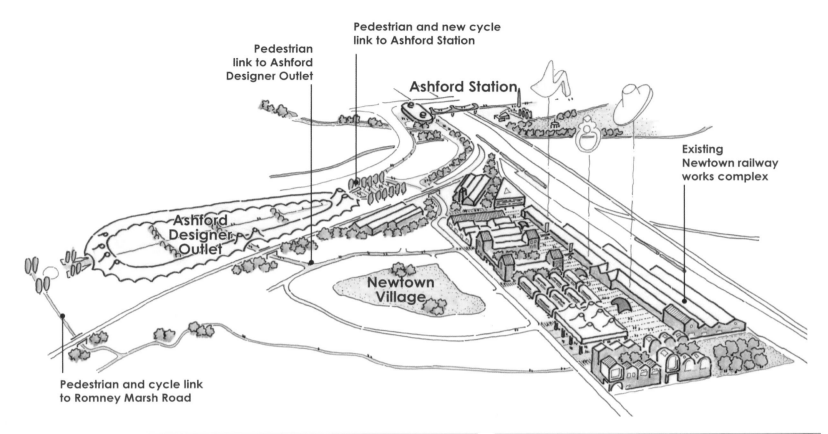

Pedestrian and new cycle link to Ashford Station

Pedestrian link to Ashford Designer Outlet

Ashford Station

Existing Newtown railway works complex

Ashford Designer Outlet

Newtown Village

Pedestrian and cycle link to Romney Marsh Road

Above: A new mixed urban quarter at Newtown.

Right: Railside Studios.

Far right: A vibrant and permeable Commercial Quarter.

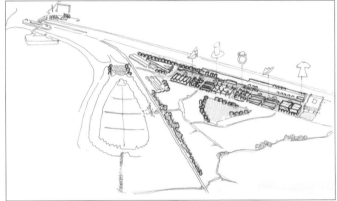

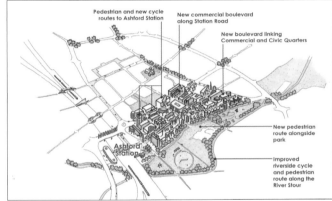

Pedestrian and new cycle routes to Ashford Station

New commercial boulevard along Station Road

New boulevard linking Commercial and Civic Quarters

Ashford Station

New pedestrian route alongside park

Improved riverside cycle and pedestrian route along the River Stour

Terry Farrell was appointed as Design Champion for Ashford in March 2010 by Ashford's Future, the agency overseeing the £2.5bn investment programme which aims to double the size of the town by 2031. The main reason for this growth is due to the arrival of high-speed rail. This transport connection has changed prospects for Ashford's forever, helping to redefine its role as a centre for innovation and design excellence within Kent, the South-east and the rest of the UK.

Ashford is set to become 'the powerhouse of Kent', built on an ambitious programme of major new public transport projects, a regenerated Station Quarter and a Commercial Quarter, pioneering shared streetscapes, iconic new bridges across the motorway and railway line, three new parks and a host of other eye-catching improvements.

Some of the main strategic principles identified as central to Ashford's future development are centred around the station. One of the key aims is to link Ashford International Station to the town centre, integrating the 'currently remote' station with its surrounding areas. In recent years high-speed rail stations have been shown to be place-makers, and properly designed station quarters can become magnificent expressions of civic endeavour. Alongside this, benefits would come from creating new 'iconic' pedestrian bridges across the railway line, linking south Ashford with the town. Complementing the increased accessibility of the station would be the transformation of the ring road as a shared surface, an opportunity for Ashford to lead the UK in the development of pioneering shared space urban streetscapes.

Ashford has strong links with an historic past and this should be celebrated in the town's transformation by reinvigorating the historic high street, to reinforce its distinctive identities. Creating a mixed urban quarter at the old Newtown railway works, a great heritage complex has the potential to attract creative and design-led businesses.

The Design Champion's role is to help the town articulate and elevate its ambitions for the future, to promote high-quality design, and to explore further opportunities to enhance its potential. Farrells have created a blueprint for a vibrant, sustainable and prosperous future for this ancient Kent market town and a vision that can be shared and spread to a national and international audience.

MEDWAY AND HOO PENINSULA

Sir Terry Farrell was commissioned as Medway's Design Champion in 2006 as a consequence of independent strategic work undertaken by the practice and its multi-disciplinary collaborators within the Thames Estuary. This initiative gained widespread recognition in the professional community and within government. Our appointment by the Medway Renaissance partnership was the first formal commission, which resulted from many years of pro bono work in this area.

We felt at the outset that the role of a Design Champion should involve more than the review of work by others. As a result a series of commissions were undertaken, each of which put forward strategic propositions for specific places within Medway, which is defined by the river of the same name, a major tributary of the Thames.

This work focuses on urban Medway, which includes the medieval city of Rochester with its famous cathedral, Chatham with its historic naval yard, Strood, Gillingham and Rainham. This area has a population greater than many major UK cities such as Bristol and Newcastle, but the relocation of the Navy to Portsmouth and Southampton has left an 'empty stage' on the river itself.

The main strategic idea is captured in the phrase 'Five Towns make a City'. This involves re-occupying and reintegrating riverfront land vacated by the Navy, connecting urban Medway's high streets to create a city centre of extraordinary vitality, and taming the urban motorways which blight the various towns and disconnect them from one another. A key part of the plan is to urbanise a low-density industrial peninsula and to connect this by means of bridges, ferries and a cable car to the rest of the centre. This work has generated millions of pounds of investment in public realm and transport projects and has reinforced the growth of the university, which in less than 10 years has gained 6,000 students where no university existed before.

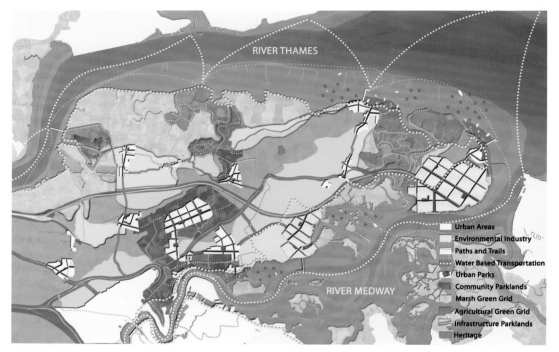

Urban Areas
Environmental Industry
Paths and Trails
Water Based Transportation
Urban Parks
Community Parklands
Marsh Green Grid
Agricultural Green Grid
Infrastructure Parklands
Heritage

RIVER THAMES

RIVER MEDWAY

Top: Masterplan drawing identifying the rich range of ecological habitats of Hoo Peninsula.

Centre: Re-occupy the land by Medway vacated by the Navy.

Bottom (left to right):
1. Create a sustainable and truly integrated transport system.
2. Create a continous high street and ecological framework.
3. Connect and heal the high streets.
4. Re-inhabit the empty stage.

1

3

2

4

LITTLEHAMPTON

In 2008, we were asked to help create a waterfront strategy for Littlehampton, to help the town to articulate its ambition not only to restore the former grandeur of the place but to change and adapt it to the needs and requirements of a seaside town in the 21st century. The seeds of regeneration have already begun to take root in surprising and unexpected ways, through the development of a small but iconic seafront restaurant designed by the artist Thomas Heatherwick and the construction of the world's longest bench by Studio Weave – ideas developed and promoted by imaginative local entrepreneurs Jane Wood and Peter Murray.

Littlehampton has the most magnificent seafront and a very walkable scale but, as is too often the case in our towns and cities, the legibility of the place has become muddled and disconnected by the over-dominance of the motor vehicle. Our proposals focus upon re-establishing the town's identity through restoring its public realm in simple and pragmatic ways. A clear 'mental map' is created through simple improvements to the landscape: pedestrian connections between the rail station, the towncentre and the sea-front are simplified and signposted by greening streets and by removing the one-way traffic system; car and coach parking which dominates and diminishes the seafront is

hidden in side streets; the promenade along the seafront is enhanced and made continuous; cycling is welcomed and accommodated; passive flood measures are recommended to ensure the town is not disconnected from the river; and the east and west banks are connected to give access to both tamed and wild landscapes.

Our study looks to build on the existing identity and the good work that has already begun in Littlehampton to create a clear strategy for a way forward. Regeneration and change here should begin by evolving a commonly held and inclusive vision – a step change in the quality of the public realm in Littlehampton will need energy and commitment from everyone.

Main image: Aerial perspective of the town with 'reinforced' public realms and improved waterfront connectivity.

Bottom left: Aerial photograph of Littlehampton.

Bottom centre: Studio Weave's 'The Longest Bench'.

Bottom right: Thomas Heatherwick's East Beach Café.

FOLKESTONE

Farrells' proposed plans commissioned by the Folkestone Harbour Regeneration Company for the redevelopment of Folkestone Harbour and Seafront will be residential-led, and aim to create a vibrant public realm enlivening the seafront with a mix of new uses. The ambition is to build upon the substantial regeneration work that has already taken place in the Creative Quarter in Folkestone's Old Town.

Back in the late 1800s and early 1900s the town was a vibrant holiday destination, but in the intervening years the seafront lost its identity as the heart of Folkestone, and this problem is exacerbated by the fact that the seafront is physically disconnected from the town. The seafront is an empty space that needs a new approach that is not dependent on large upfront investment in infrastructure.

The core of the plan is to create a series of character areas that can be introduced phasically, making it realistic and achievable given the prevailing economic situation. The main character areas would be: the Creative Quarter, Harbour Square, Harbour Front, Outer Harbour, the sand beach, Marine Parade and shingle beach, Pier Head Quarter, Harbour Arm, Lower Lease Costal Park and the green walk.

Regeneration depends on a many-pronged approach: by revealing the rich history of the seafront and looking at new uses for the redundant historic setting; reinforcing the varied landscape character along the seafront and looking at creating active frontages on the buildings along there; making the quayside vibrant and lively perhaps by using different designers to create diversity of styles; and creating a strong linking boulevard along Marine Parade.

The future success of Folkestone is dependent on better connectivity and this could be achieved in several ways: creating strong connections between the harbour and town centre and shaping a new public square to connect the harbour and town centre. Also, utilszing what is already there but no

Top: Seafront elevation looking north – the grain of the buildings sit comfortably with their surroundings.

Bottom left: The spectacular waterfront and defensive harbour arm.

Bottom right: The masterplan displays a layered approach to developing the waterfront and linking back into the town centre.

longer used: the former railway line could become a green pedestrian and cycle route. Pedestrians and cyclists would also benefit from making the waterfront a continuous public domain, with safer pedestrian crossings, reducing the width of vehicle carriageways and looking at humanising the one-way system to make it pedestrian-friendly.

This project sits comfortably with the Design Champion roles such as the Thames Gateway, Kent, Medway and Ashford. Folkestone's seafront will be part of Kent's continuing regeneration and recognition of design and planning as crucial to future success.

Left: A selection of historic and present-day photographs of Folkestone.

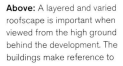

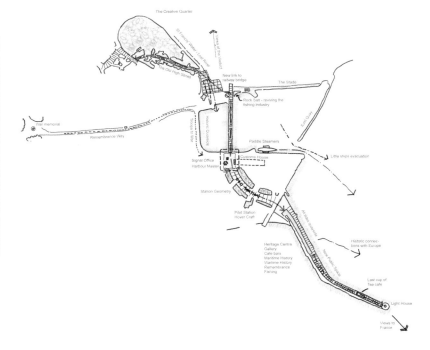

Above: A layered and varied roofscape is important when viewed from the high ground behind the development. The buildings make reference to the architecture of harbour warehouses and beach huts.

Right: Concept sketch illustrating the integration of Folkestone's historical and cultural heritage into the masterplan.

MANCHESTER

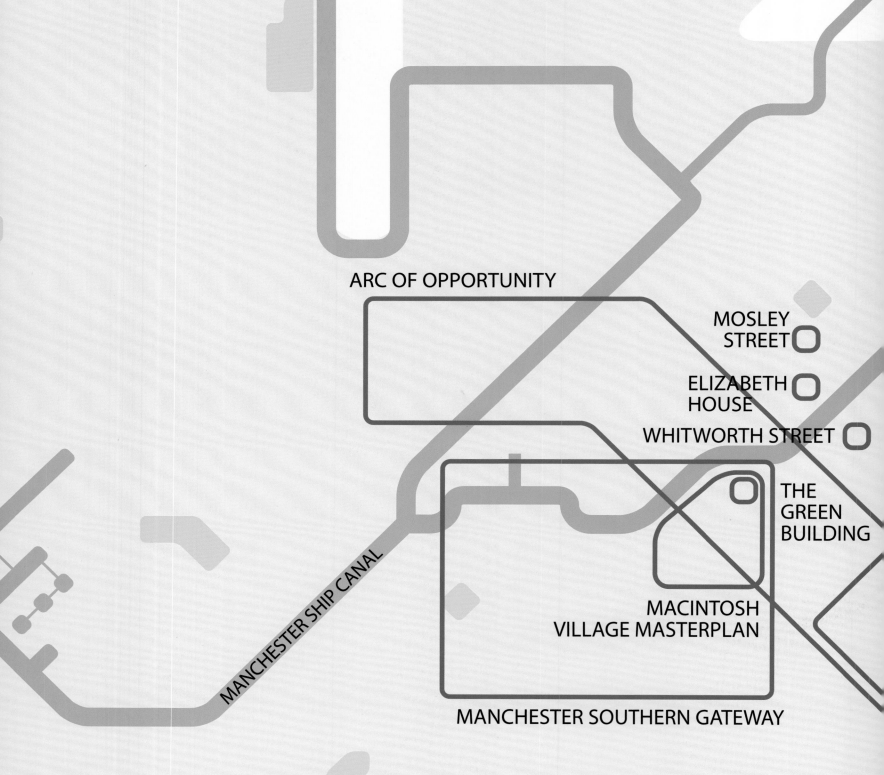

ARC OF OPPORTUNITY

MOSLEY STREET

ELIZABETH HOUSE

WHITWORTH STREET

THE GREEN BUILDING

MANCHESTER SHIP CANAL

MACINTOSH VILLAGE MASTERPLAN

MANCHESTER SOUTHERN GATEWAY

SPORTCITY

MANCHESTER UNIVERSITY
MASTERPLAN

MANCHESTER

The 19th-century industry that arose from a new form of global economy has its origins in northern England, most notably in Manchester. Here, around an ancient, but small and inconsequential settlement, a new type of city was created structured around a new type of work based on industrial methods of manufacturing in giant factories. The forces that shaped Manchester also created many factory towns in the north but it is Manchester that stands as the complete archetypal model. The city core provided finance, insurance, and a market place for exchange. A ring of factories surround the core, in turn ringed by the terraced houses of the newly invented working class. Beyond this belt are the leafy suburbs all clearly indicating the class of its residents.

In the mid-20th century the economic system that had created the city collapsed when the focus of global manufacture moved away to lower cost centres in Asia and elsewhere. By the 1970s large parts of the city were derelict or in steep decline. Complete oblivion or complete reinvention were the stark options faced by the city authorities.

Selecting the more optimistic and courageous path, the Work Foundation led by the economist Will Hutton prepared a seminal document to set the course for reinvention. The resulting short book entitled *Ideopolis* identified Manchester as having, latent within its people, culture and institutions, the ingredients necessary for a second revolution that would reinvent the city as a new type based around the work of making ideas rather than products – the so-called knowledge economy.

All of Farrells' work in the city, across many projects, focused on various aspects of the work required to realise the reinvention outlined in the *Ideopolis* report.

Fundamental to an ideas-based economy is the quality of the city's university. Manchester decided to create the UK's largest by unifying the University of Manchester Institute of Science and Technology with the University of Manchester to create a single world-leading institution of learning. Farrells

Top: Bridgewater Canal in the 1950s; alongside runs the Altrincham railway line.

Above: Image of the Macintosh Mills (in 1857); the area still survives, a remnant of 19th-century industrial Manchester.

Right: The Arc of Opportunity: encompassing Oxford Road through Manchester City Centre to Salford.

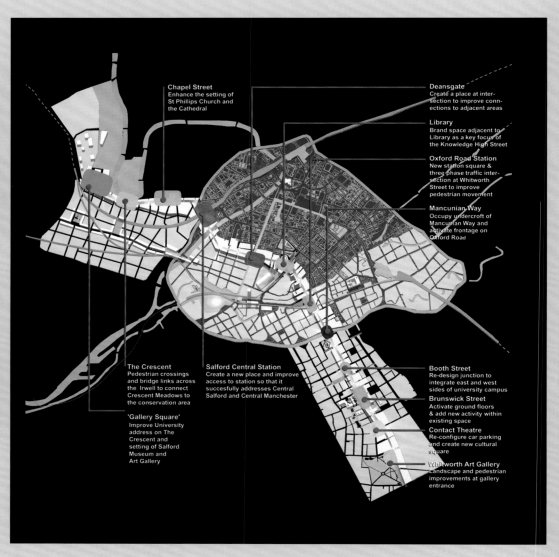

Chapel Street
Enhance the setting of St Phillips Church and the Cathedral

Deansgate
Create a place at inter-section to improve connections to adjacent areas

Library
Brand space adjacent to Library as a key focus of the Knowledge High Street

Oxford Road Station
New station square & three phase traffic inter-section at Whitworth Street to improve pedestrian movement

Mancunian Way
Occupy undercroft of Mancunian Way and activate frontage on Oxford Road

The Crescent
Pedestrian crossings and bridge links across the Irwell to connect Crescent Meadows to the conservation area

Salford Central Station
Create a new place and improve access to station so that it succesfully addresses Central Salford and Central Manchester

Booth Street
Re-design junction to integrate east and west sides of university campus

'Gallery Square'
Improve University address on The Crescent and setting of Salford Museum and Art Gallery

Brunswick Street
Activate ground floors & add new activity within existing space

Contact Theatre
Re-configure car parking and create new cultural square

Whitworth Art Gallery
Landscape and pedestrian improvements at gallery entrance

prepared the masterplan to facilitate this change reconnecting the university into the city.

Farrells' Southern Gateway masterplan reinvented part of the old factory belt as a place for new knowledge-based businesses. At Macintosh Mill, a former rubber factory was transformed into a place to live for the new creative city centre inhabitants. The Green Building forming part of the same project explored urban living in high-density sustainable architecture.

In Mosley Street, Farrells proposed reinventing an historic street that had fallen into decline. Public realm improvements were combined with selective replacement of poor quality buildings. The process of change was managed by the strong city planning authority, resulting in the complete transformation of the street and its surroundings.

Across the north-west of England a similar spirit of reinvention that characterised the Manchester approach is in progress.

In Preston, the ancient county town of Lancashire, the city embarked upon an ambitious plan to reinvent the commercial core of the city with a retail-led regeneration strategy that sought to regain Preston's position as a county town and attractive shopping destination. Farrells created a plan that repaired the core of the city broken by neglect and inappropriate traffic-centred planning of the 1960s. Pedestrian priority was set as a guiding principle across the plan. Lost streets were rediscovered, new functions were found for disused listed buildings, empty sites were in-filled with a mix of shopping and residential uses and a new streetscape of paving and planting was proposed.

In the great north-west port of Liverpool reinvention of the city core through a retail-led scheme was also proposed. Farrells' competition proposal explored the urbanisation of the shopping centre form based on ideas first explored in their work in China. The proposal fixed malls within a pattern that connected into the surrounding city streets; mixed-use development was proposed for the resulting urban blocks, and a dramatic covered urban space formed the core of the proposal.

Top and far right: The Green Building in its urban setting.

Above left and centre: Macintosh Mills – so called as this was where they manufactured the waterproof rubberised cloth invented by Charles Macintosh.

ARC OF OPPORTUNITY AND MANCHESTER UNIVERSITY MASTERPLAN

The historic core of Manchester was based on an industrial city that was simple and mechanical but disconnected. The strategic overview plan looked at four main areas: a spatial framework that would create 100 linked places, a development framework that would open and expand the city, a movement framework that would improve connections, and lastly an environmental framework that would help the city continue into the 21st century with a greater awareness of green issues and sustainability.

The key principles for the spatial framework were: a flexible urban grid, a clear sense of identity and place for inhabitants and visitors – connected and clear orientation signage, improvement to street lighting, contained waterfront areas – and most importantly the linking up of 100 public spaces, which would include parks, gardens, squares, pocket spaces, waterways and walks.

The spatial plan looked at public access to the higher levels to facilitate views across the city. The goal for a fully accessible core would also depend on interventions such as: establishing new pedestrian routes and connections across the ring road, the removal of one-way road systems and the widening of pavements and improvements to pedestrian crossings. The movement framework looked at the strategic integration of transport and its important role in place-making, along with increased priority for pedestrians and cyclists with improved crossings, improved way-finding, less obstructive street furniture and wider pavements – it promoted a connected city that would knit together the core and the suburbs.

The development framework focused on place-making by celebrating the city's fascinating history, creating harmony in diversity, ensuring architectural quality, active street frontages and development clusters around transport nodes.

The Arc of Opportunity is a framework that seeks to improve not only the core area but to improve its connections to the suburbs, by rediscovering the lost grids and developing the existing character.

Left: Unification and reinvigoration through place-making: the University of Manchester masterplan, organised around 15 new places/academic centres.

Below left and right: The masterplan components.

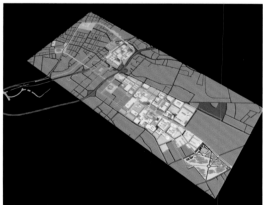

MANCHESTER SPORTCITY

Manchester has a unique place in the history of urbanism, having transformed itself during the 18th century from a village to the world's first industrial city in only 100 years.

Our work in Manchester, which has been extensive over the last decade, has principally focused upon thinking at a strategic level, understanding and anticipating future change and transformation both for the forward-looking City Council as well as for a variety of local and national developers. This work culminated in our developing a 'Manifesto' for Manchester – the Coherent City' – which we presented to Sir Howard Bernstein, the Council's Chief Executive, in 2004. Whilst recognising Manchester's considerable achievements in recent years, our 10-point manifesto for a more coherent city

included proposals for more focus upon a healthy and high-quality public realm with less reliance on the car and more focus on diversity and place-making, much of which has been embraced and implemented over time. It was from this standpoint that we were invited by developers Quintain to articulate a masterplan proposal for Manchester's Sportcity, a project aimed at building a tangible legacy to follow the 2002 Commonwealth Games.

Our vision for Sportcity was for a new sustainable city quarter for Manchester and the North-west region created around the world-class sports campus, through the introduction of a diverse range of new residential and commercial uses. At the core of the masterplan was a new neighbourhood woven into the sports complex of 2,500 new homes based around a new local high street, as

well as a hotel and casino complex, new shops and restaurants, the conversion of the main stadium into a new home for Manchester City FC and a brand new stadium for Lancashire Cricket Club.

The new facilities at Sportcity complex already provide world-class venues for use by the existing local community and grass roots sports development as well as by elite athletes. The ambition of our masterplan was to use this success to grow a new diverse community in and around the successful sports complex to more fully integrate it within the urban fabric of regenerated East Manchester.

Below: 3D image of Manchester Sportcity masterplan.

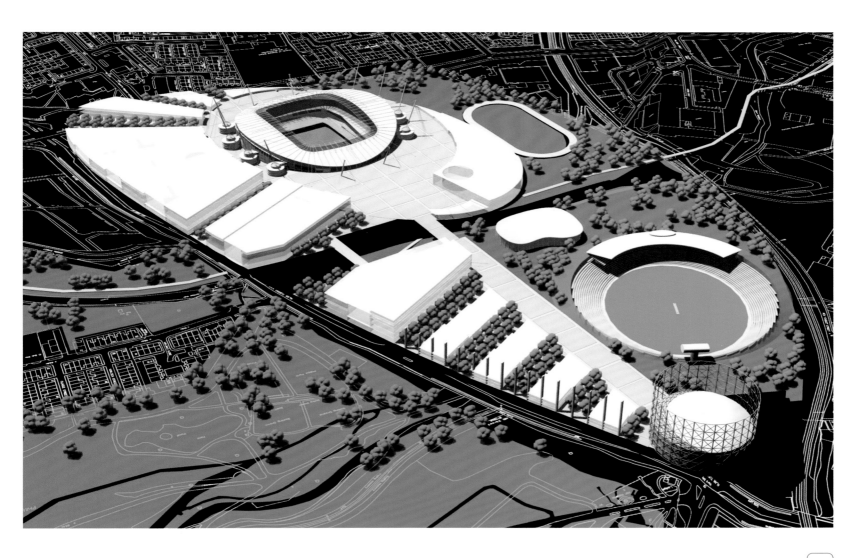

MANCHESTER SOUTHERN GATEWAY

Manchester's Southern Gateway is on the southern fringe of the city centre between Castlefield Basin and Oxford Road. The masterplan project was won in an open competition. The team worked with Manchester City Council and numerous landowners and stakeholders to create a scheme that was part of the greater vision for Manchester – to be a city that was continuously being renewed, reinvented and reinterpreted.

The conceptual framework for Manchester's Southern Gateway region sets out an innovative vision for the future of the principal entrance to the city core from the south. The aim was to create a new public realm to serve the area, which would become a location for world-class knowledge-economy businesses.

The project offered an exciting opportunity to develop a vibrant, mixed-use zone within the southern arc of the city centre, an area that houses a critical mass of higher education facilities and provides two key gateways into the city centre (southern and eastern). The axis from the airport to the city centre forms a spine through the southern gateway of the knowledge arc.

There are obvious advantages associated with this location – the site is on the international axis of the city and is well-served by the transport infrastructure. There is a graduate talent pool and thriving commercial core immediately adjacent. Road improvements and tree-planting would transform Medlock Street into an urban boulevard, whilst Albion Square forms a new civic heart at the focus of the main through routes.

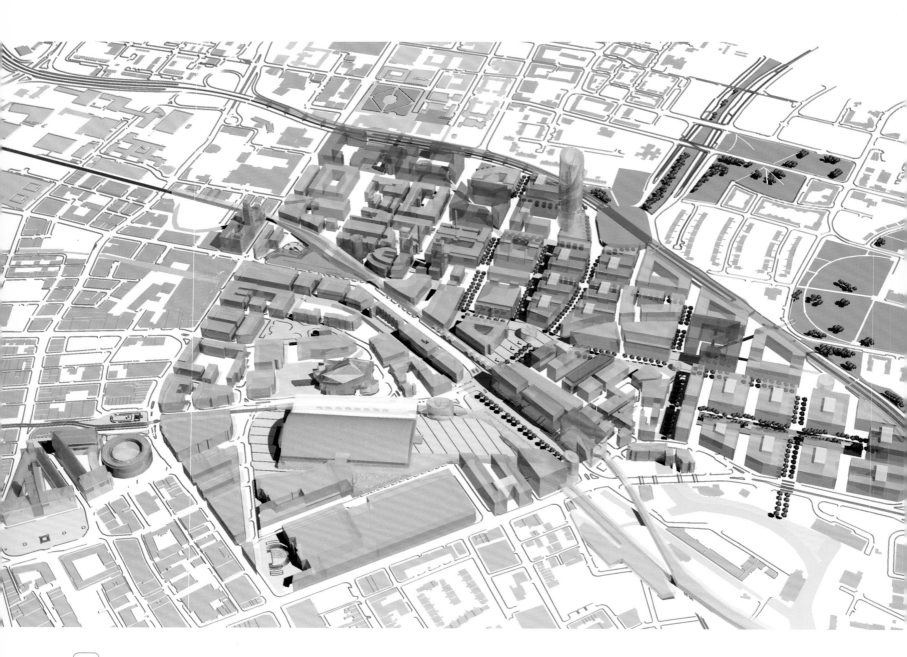

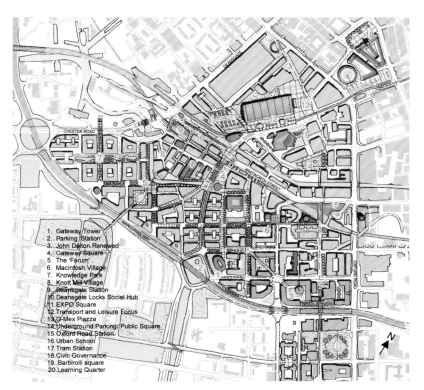

1. Gateway Tower
2. Parking 'Station'
3. John Dalton Renewed
4. Gateway Square
5. The 'Forum'
6. Macintosh Village
7. Knowledge Park
8. Knott Mill Village
9. Deansgate Station
10. Deansgate Locks Social Hub
11. EXPO Square
12. Transport and Leisure Focus
13. G-Mex Piazza
14. Underground Parking/ Public Square
15. Oxford Road Station
16. Urban School
17. Tram Station
18. Civic Governance
19. Barbirolli square
20. Learning Quarter

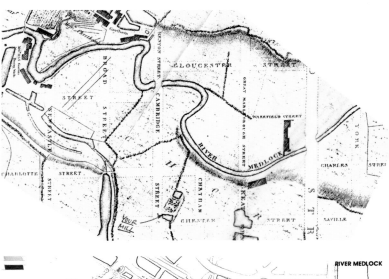

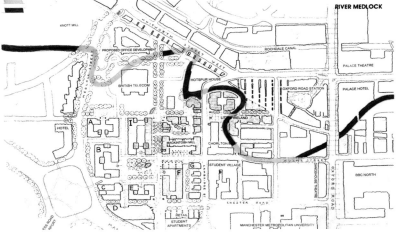

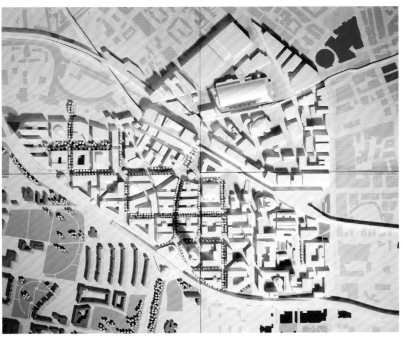

Bottom left: Illustrative masterplan.

Top left: Model photo of the Southern Gateway illustrating the proximity to the university and its good transport links.

Top right: Historic map of area.

Centre right: Early masterplan study.

Bottom right: Model photo of the Southern Gateway.

Opposite page: 3D study of the Manchester Southern Gateway masterplan viewed from the north.

MACINTOSH VILLAGE MASTERPLAN

The proposals for Manchester's Macintosh Village masterplan combine a significant 2-hectare site with detailed plans for 1.7 hectares of refurbished historic warehouses and new buildings. This unique urban district is just a short walk from the city centre.

The scheme comprised the refurbishment of the remaining historic mill buildings, the construction of a new block and two new 21-storey towers. The buildings, containing 700 residential units plus a number of live/work units, sit within the masterplan designed to reconnect the former Southern Gateway industrial quarter to the commercial core of the city. The scheme reverses the fortress-like nature of the existing factory buildings, where public access has traditionally been denied. Two abandoned streets have been reinstated to enhance permeability; two new public spaces form the nucleus for a network of pedestrian and cycle routes.

The two new towers provide a symbolic gateway and iconic signpost for the area, which would harmonise with the existing layout whilst visibly landmarking the site to and from the city centre. The tower form is used to release land at ground level for a new civic space that creates a gateway square at the threshold to the scheme.

The masterplan scheme was welcomed by English Heritage and the Commission for Architecture and the Built Environment (CABE) and cited as an exemplar for both the quality of design and the contribution it will make to the area in urban design terms.

The restoration of original mill buildings and the creation of stunning new constructions, superb landscapes and newly designed public spaces would combine to create a stylish and environmentally friendly community. The masterplan objective was to create a long-term permanent and sustainable centre. The emphasis was on regeneration, restoration and reconnection.

Central to the idea is a commitment to opening up the existing Macintosh Mill site, building on the experience of the past and having respect for what has gone before – modifying and re-using the best of what has been handed down rather than demolishing it. Restoration of original buildings would be approached sympathetically, preserving the pattern of age and richness of character of the buildings. Macintosh Village would open up and link the whole Southern Gateway area to central Manchester. The planned development would have established pedestrian links in all four directions. A new civic space at the gateway to the scheme would be a new heart for the local community, integrating it into the urban fabric.

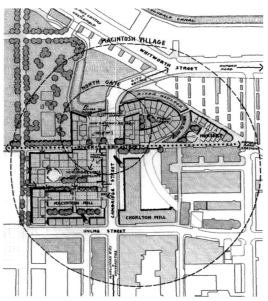

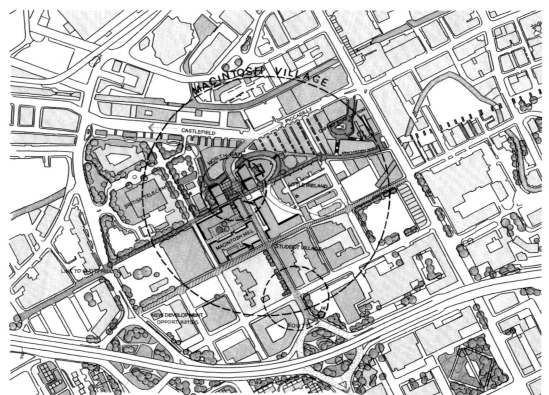

Top left: Masterplan model illustrating the layers of historical and present-day infrastructure that serves it from the city centre.

Bottom left: The Macintosh Village masterplan was conceived to incorporate a diversity of uses as part of a bigger vision for a new urban neighbourhood.

Above: Macintosh Village masterplan – the wider context.

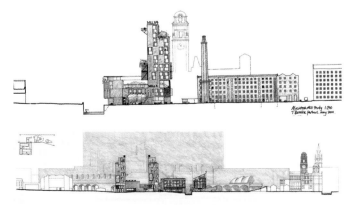

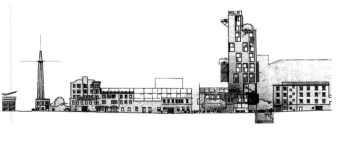

Top: Elevation of the masterplan. The Green Building can be seen on the far left.

Centre: Old and new: Macintosh Mill restored with new complementary buildings. Together they create a place and a beacon for regeneration.

Left: Elevations of the masterplan, showing new buildings integrated in the gaps between the historic mill buildings.

THE GREEN BUILDING

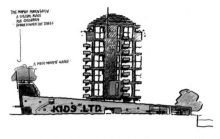

The Green Building is set in Macintosh Village, occupying a site adjacent to the River Medlock, and is an important component of the Macintosh Village masterplan. The iconic, circular structure of the Green Building makes the most efficient use of its quirky triangular site, creating a dramatic impact within its landmark setting.

Conveniently located for the city centre, the Green Building provides a mixed-use complex, created for comfortable, modern and sustainable use. In addition to 32 apartments, there is a 120-place pre-school nursery, a doctor's surgery and almost 2000 sq. ft. of commercial accommodation set over three floors.

The Green Building has a number of striking design elements, including a high-specification 10-storey cylindrical 'drum' housing the apartments, a dark blue-brick 'plinth' designed for the nursery school, complemented by a timber-faced rectangular 'prow'. The nursery accommodation is enclosed by a sloping wall with playfully composed openings allowing differing height views for children and adults. This wall terminates with a corner feature that marks the doctor's surgery at an entry point to the site's historic core.

Designed with environment-friendly issues high on the agenda, the Green Building is one of the most advanced ecological residential and educational developments in Britain of its time. The circularity of the Green Building is more than a striking architectural statement – it offers the smallest surface area related to the volume of the structure, providing optimum insulation and making measurable energy consumption savings possible all year round. Every aspect of the construction and maintenance of the Green Building has been examined to minimise energy wastage through radical design. Energy consumption is minimised 'passively' through the design of a highly energy-efficient envelope wrapping the structure of the building and 'actively' through installing highly efficient plant and equipment for heating, ventilation and light. Yet the Green Building is designed in such a way as to ensure that nothing is lost aesthetically in aiming for ecological soundness. The exterior and bright, flexible interiors have been devised to respond to demand for the best in comfortable and stylish living.

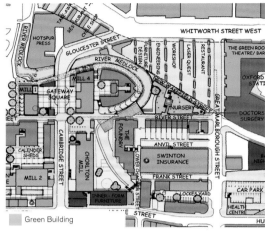

Green Building

Top: Macintosh Mill masterplan.

Above: Elevation with ground floor Kids' Nursery and upper floor residential uses.

Below: Rooftop view over Manchester. The solar panels and wind turbine on the roof of the building can clearly be seen and juxtapose the masonry features of the area.

Opposite: The cylindrical shape of the building was chosen for its energy efficiency.

Inset: Green Building interior.

HULL

RIVER HUMBER

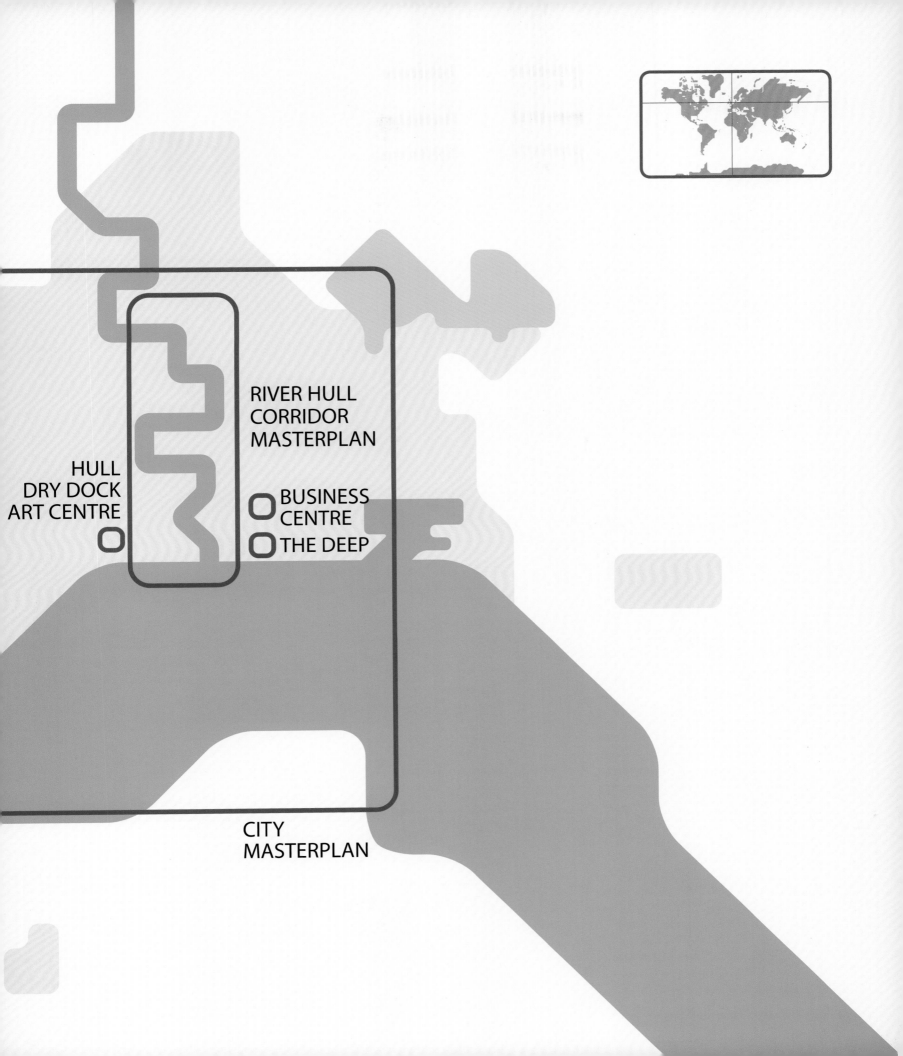

RIVER HULL
CORRIDOR
MASTERPLAN

HULL
DRY DOCK
ART CENTRE

BUSINESS
CENTRE

THE DEEP

CITY
MASTERPLAN

HULL

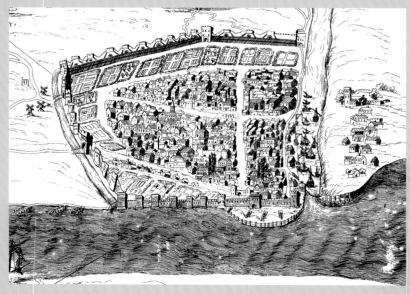

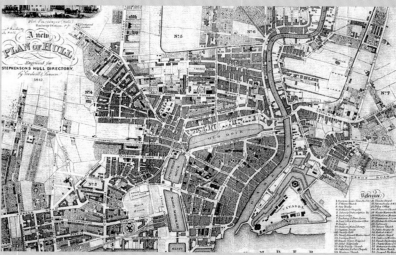

Hull, once a prosperous port city trading with European ports across the English Channel, now seems isolated and cut off from the UK's inland north-south flow of commerce. In common with all the northern cities its industrial base has declined, leaving Hull with a fragile economic base from which to develop. The potential for the city lies in marshalling the power of small-scale incremental change over time.

Farrells masterplan for the city was a response to this economic context and proposed a fine-grained series of interventions to repair and remake the preserved medieval centre of the city within the line of the original protective walls. By removing car parking from the historic centre to a site outside the walls, a large number of modest-sized development sites became available for mixed-use infill and development. Public realm improvements restored the attractiveness of the centre for pedestrians and reinforced the civic qualities of the principal civic monuments. Outside the historic centre the plan focused on the potential to regenerate the city's waterfront areas with new, larger scale development of former industrial sites.

Farrells' project for The Deep formed part of this waterfront regeneration strategy. The Deep, described as a submarium, is one of the world's great aquariums, combining a tourist attraction with a research centre on marine life. It created a dramatic architectural landmark on the water's edge to draw visitors to this formerly abandoned corner of the city. The building has become a new emblem for the city as it strives to reinvent its economy and purpose.

Top left: A historic map showing the walled city.

Above left: A historic map of the city from 1842. The Citadel in the lower right corner marks the site of The Deep project.

Top right: Aerial photograph showing the convergence of the River Hull and the Humber River and the wider area prior to construction of The Deep.

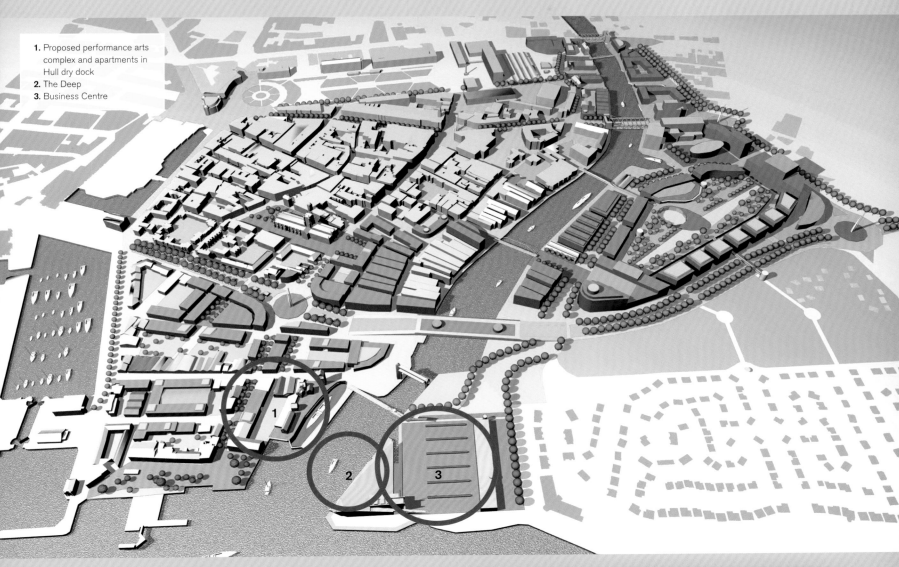

1. Proposed performance arts complex and apartments in Hull dry dock
2. The Deep
3. Business Centre

Top: The Deep was part of Farrells' River Hull corridor masterplan.

Left: Hull dry dock was the proposed location for a performance-based arts complex with the dock decked over to be used as an outdoor arena.

Above: An apartment block is canted over the performance facility, providing dramatic waterfront accommodation and helping to generate interest in the Fruit Market district.

THE DEEP

Situated on a 2.45-hectare brownfield site at Sammy's Point, at the confluence of the River Hull and the Humber estuary, The Deep began its life as an urban renaissance scheme. In this respect, it reaches beyond architecture to become enmeshed with the infrastructure of the River Hull corridor, as well as the economic, social and cultural renewal of the city in general. Hull's economic decline over the last 50 years has been extreme – the development of The Deep was viewed as being part of a large-scale urban strategy.

The Deep submarium is public architecture at its most populist. The aim at Farrells is to create buildings that win popular support by bridging the gap between elite and populist causes. As a comprehensible, iconic building, The Deep looks for inspiration to a range of precedents and the design conjures up metaphorical associations with wave or glacier-like forms.

The £45.5 million scheme was the second of Farrells' landmark millennium projects (the other being the International Centre for Life in Newcastle), based in two buildings. The main building, located at the south-west point of the site, houses the visitor attraction, the Learning Centre, the Total Environment Simulator and the University of Hull's research facility. The other building, a simple linear structure close to the site's western edge, is a business centre that will help fund and contribute research to the educational part of the scheme.

The design of The Deep captures the image of an eroded monolith. Over time, fractures, fissures and fault lines will create a complex pattern on the monolith's surface. Man's intervention halts the process of decay and transforms the vision of abandonment into one of optimism and regeneration. The design exploits the natural metaphor of land form versus sea form.

Below: The Deep in context with the city of Hull viewed from the south bank of the River Humber.

Opposite: Early design studies.

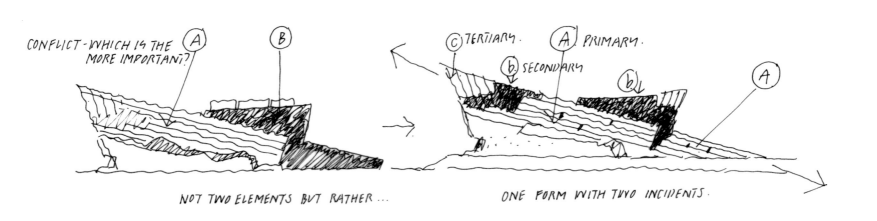

CONFLICT — WHICH IS THE MORE IMPORTANT? Ⓐ Ⓑ

NOT TWO ELEMENTS BUT RATHER ...

Ⓒ TERTIARY. Ⓐ PRIMARY. ⓑ SECONDARY ⓑ Ⓐ

ONE FORM WITH TWO INCIDENTS.

Like the Peak Tower in Hong Kong and Newcastle's International Centre for Life, The Deep is a building that revels in its metaphorical associations. At an extreme point in the landscape, the visitor attraction rises in a wave-like form, amplifying the geography of the site and the oceanographic function of the building. The exterior is treated as an eroded rock face using organic forms and lines, while irregular recessed strata on the façades provide points of access and openings for windows. The roof plane is treated similarly to the wall surfaces so that the building is read as a three-dimensional object rather than as a series of two-dimensional planes. Similar qualities of natural erosion inform the interior spaces, where a rich and varied spatial sequence makes the most of the views. The interior spaces were strongly influenced by the physical nature of the ocean: rather than imitating the usual aquarium form of a linear procession of tanks, Farrells made full use of the three-dimensional space. The building's section offsets the solid (water) and void (circulation space), giving visitors a sense of immersion within an ocean environment.

While the main mass of the building is treated as natural metaphor, two architectural elements are placed within the composition. These are an observation point at the form's pinnacle, with unrivalled views across the River Humber to the great Humber Bridge, and an entrance lift, stair core and walkway that bridge out of the main structure.

A central objective was to create a building with a bold, pioneering image for the city of Hull. The four-storey visitor attraction housing a world-class aquarium exhibition was designed to be a dramatic icon. The barrenness of the site and its powerful seascapes is the perfect environment for this iconic glacier-like building.

Above: The Deep: a bold pioneering image for Hull.

Opposite: The design of The Deep captures the image of an eroded monolith.

Opposite: View from the
River Hull of the observation
point at the form's pinnacle.

Above left: Layered strata of
the elevation.

Above right: View showing
the 'punched' windows on
the entrance tower.

Overleaf: Immersion within
an ocean environment, interior
design in conjunction with
Csaky Associates.

BUSINESS CENTRE

Comprising a linear two-storey building, the Business Centre's simple profiles and serene stance contrasts with the soaring pinnacle of the main submarium building, and provides a calm backdrop, underlying the controlled but essential function of the building as a component of the establishment as a whole.

The building forms the east edge to the development, containing and defining the car park and pedestrian circulation areas, framing and screening the site.

Red brick and charcoal render provide background tones to allow highlight colours from the window mullion panels and tiled stair tower to sparkle with maritime colours, reflecting the waterside setting and similar colour palettes from The Deep's prow.

Main image: Business centre offering modern space for marine science companies.

Inset: Plan and elevations of the business centre.

Top: Tiled stair tower.

LEEDS

EASTGATE

QUARRY
HILL

AIRE VALLEY

LEEDS

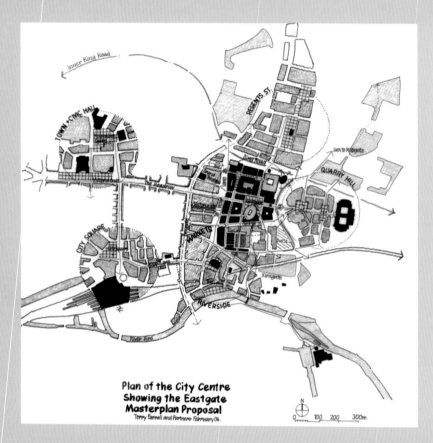

Plan of the City Centre
Showing the Eastgate
Masterplan Proposal
Terry Farrell and Partners February 04.

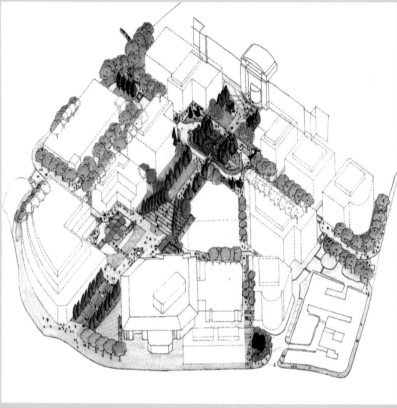

Leeds is one of Britain's big proud core cities and one, to use Simon Jenkins' phrase, 'that understands its urbanity'. Following its rapid growth, boosted at first by the river navigations which connected Leeds to Manchester and the North Sea, and then by the railways, which smashed their way across the southern part of the city, Leeds became a place with a rich, complex but sometimes fragmented urban fabric, a place where commerce had begun to push mills and factories away from the city centre.

Studded throughout the compact city centre are many fine individual buildings, including Cuthbert Broderick's town hall. Echoing Nash's Regent Street intervention in the organic fabric of London, Reginald Blomfield's boulevard-like Headrow of 1924 runs like a spine through central Leeds from the Town Hall to the Eastgate, opposite the site of the former Quarry Hill flats.

The Eastgate is the location of two successive Farrells masterplans and works of urban repair in central Leeds, both occasioned by the damage wrought by the inner road road, which very efficiently disconnected these formerly thriving city quarters from their hinterlands.

The first of these masterplans was for the site of the Quarry Hill flats, cleared some years previously as a failed continental experiment in housing, both mono-cultural and totalitarian. Farrells' main task was to provide a plan to develop an area of mixed use, overcoming this mono-cultural history and the isolated nature of the site, which had been reinforced by opportunistic road building around the temporarily empty and available site.

In terms of historical continuity there was little upon which to build, apart from the area's strong axial relationship to Blomfield's Headrow running as a spine through Leeds up to the Town Hall. The masterplan naturally continues this axis onto the site, and transforms it into a sequence of wide formal public spaces, leading up the slope of the site with steps and terraces.

From the Eastgate end of the site, a court forms the pedestrian gateway, linked to the pre-existing Playhouse Theatre. The central sequence of spaces is terminated by the main square at the most elevated point of the site, which is surrounded by new buildings, and the new DHS headquarters. Secondary routes cross this main pedestrian route,

linking into the existing pattern of surface and bridge crossings and forming plots for the phased completion of the masterplan. Farrells' work at the eastern end of the city centre has continued with the major Eastgate masterplan, a retail and residential-led scheme to regenerate an entire quarter of the city centre.

The Eastgate masterplan was undertaken for commercial clients, but very much in concord with John Thorp, who held the crucial role of Leeds City Council Civic Architect for Leeds from 1996 until his recent retirement. Here, we have been pushing at an open door in terms of understanding the underlying forces shaping the city, of repairing and reinforcing the street pattern, and the incremental art of shaping places in the city.

John Thorp has also mapped the wider metropolitan city of Leeds, characterising it as a city of petals radiating from the city centre, as part of his Renaissance Leeds programme. Our work (shown on the following pages) on visioning a sustainable future for the lower Aire Valley has built on this analysis, seeking to connect city and country, and to provide a sustainable new city district.

AIRE VALLEY

The commission for the Aire Valley masterplan required the production of an illustrative masterplan for various sites to the south-east of Leeds city centre, taking particular account of constraints and advocating a masterplan approach that realistically addressed these with a sustainable and robust urban design proposition. The 98-hectare site is to accommodate 2,200 new homes, as well as 100,000 square metres of commercial development, with new road infrastructure and enhanced landscape amenity, and a new light rail system triggered by the new settlement.

This process involved a series of workshop meetings, design review sessions, presentations, site visits and liaison with relevant bodies from Leeds City Council Planning Department and other appropriate consultees, including Leeds' last Civic Architect, John Thorp. The evolution of the design has therefore been an iterative one, responding to constraints as material has become available and to feedback from other consultants and key stakeholders.

The masterplan was brought forward through its Accelerated Development Zone status and this has allowed proposals that address the constraints, and in particular the ground conditions, to be considered in a way that might be more difficult to address through a more conventional design and planning process.

The substantially undermined site (through a variety of mining interventions) has influenced the history and pattern of development over centuries, and has now been able to suggest forms for a new sustainable settlement that, through energy initiatives, can start to repay its carbon debt by establishing an exemplar of place-making centred on connected communities and responsible energy management through transit design and settlement efficiency.

Opposite page left: The urbanity of Leeds: urban villages set around the formality of Blomfield's Headrow.

Opposite page right: The Quarry Hill masterplan organised around the extended axis of the Headrow.

Top: Aerial view of the masterplan with residential and recreational uses in the foreground, new retail by the junction with the M1 and commercial development further towards Leeds city centre forming a link with the grain of the city.

Right: A continuous network of place-making opportunity links Leeds' City Centre to the Aire Valley and its settlements connected across the valley.

Far right: New neighbourhood centres connect with existing landscape and settlement fragments to form communities.

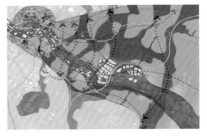

EASTGATE

Alongside the growth of high-density urban living, and with the demise of out-of-town shopping centres, residential and retail activity has again become a driver for city centre regeneration.

Farrells' Eastgate masterplan seeks to harness these forces, and to reconnect and regenerate an entire quarter of the city centre. Spanning the 1930s boulevard-like Headrow as it descends towards Quarry Hill, the masterplan seeks to repair the damage caused by the insertion of the inner ring road around this quarter of the city, which left the area isolated from both its hinterland and from the city centre.

The masterplan includes the restoration of listed buildings, new public squares and spaces, community facilities, homes and a re-engineered transport and roadways network. The project also offers the potential to develop a new 'ramblas', reinvigorating the stalled 1930s masterplan of

Sir Reginald Blomfield and tying into the Farrells' masterplan for the adjacent Quarry Hill site.

Leeds' unique position amongst competing retail centres is partly due to the substantial amount of surviving Victorian arcades and pedestrianised streets – the Eastgate masterplan naturally extends this pattern of activity, anchoring the end of the city centre retail activity with a large John Lewis department store, in a location that can accommodate these types of large space users. A dramatic 21st-century arcade, extending the axis of the existing arcades, leads from one of the main cross streets to the department store, with transverse routes repairing the medieval based street pattern and reconnecting the quarter into adjacent areas, and back to Blomfield's Headrow.

At the eastern end of the Headrow, the scheme removes a traffic roundabout, rescuing a unique Blomfield listed filling station from isolation, and

continuing the gradual urban design moves to reconnect the Quarry Hill area to the city.

Above the city centre retail, a rich mix of uses can be provided, including 600 residential units, making a natural part of the city centre a true 24 hour multicultural place.

Achieving real design diversity in tandem with variety of use is a fundamental tenet of Farrells' urban design – the urban design framework at Eastgate was partly produced by collaborating with designers, working almost as orchestra players under the light direction of Farrells as conductor, in harmony rather than in an architectural zoo. A similar tenet is the need to implement places gradually and in increments, and this is how the overall Eastgate masterplan will be realised, with one of the masterplan districts being achieved first, reflecting ever-changing market and urban forces.

Right: Isometric drawing of the extensive and connected public realm that underpins the proposal.

Inset: Concept sketch - acheiving diversity through collaboration.

Opposite page: Model photo illustrating the Bloomfield's axis running through the development and its seamless integration into the surrounding area.

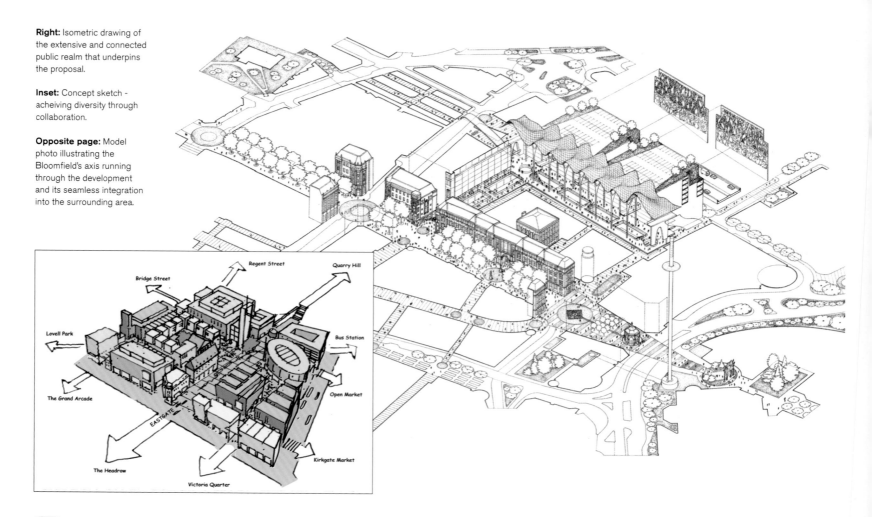

NEWCASTLE

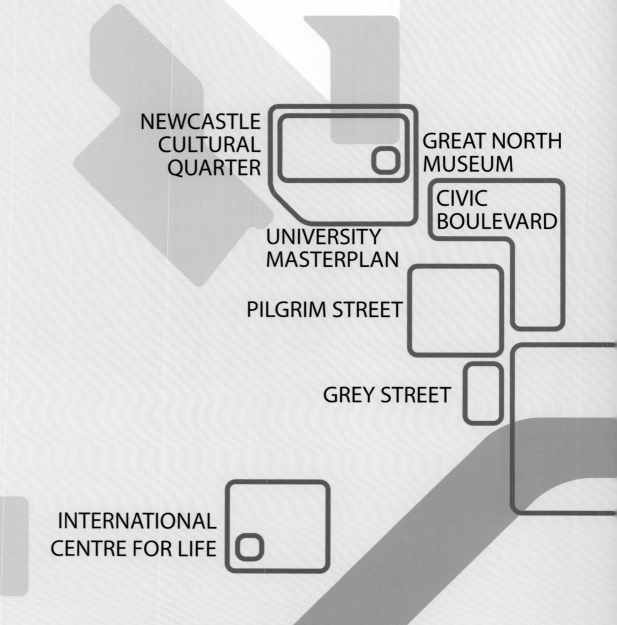

NEWCASTLE
CULTURAL
QUARTER

GREAT NORTH
MUSEUM

CIVIC
BOULEVARD

UNIVERSITY
MASTERPLAN

PILGRIM STREET

GREY STREET

INTERNATIONAL
CENTRE FOR LIFE

RIVER TYNE

OUSEBURN
MASTERPLAN

QUAYSIDE
AND OUSEBURN
GATEWAY HOUSING

QUAYSIDE

NEWCASTLE

Newcastle and Gateshead have parallel histories of separation and connection, from the river that simultaneously unifies and divides the cities, to the railway and former Great North Road that joins their city centres to Scotland and the South.

The past, which needs to be understood in order to speculate about the future, provides insights into the physical and cultural nature of these cities and how they may continue to evolve in a meaningful and contextual way. The building of the railways, and the deep valley cut by the Tyne, have both created cities that primarily exist at a 'high level', and that, ironically, have sometimes failed to engage with one another along the unifying river frontage.

The Gateshead Millennium Bridge goes some way towards addressing this divide by providing part of a route connecting the city centres, particularly with the new cultural facilities on the Tyne's South Bank, but real legible routes are still to be clearly established. Farrells have propounded a 'Geordie Ramblas' – a great route through Newcastle to Gateshead, linking Exhibition Park to the north, through Newcastle University and the Great North Museum, for which Farrells were architects, rediscovering clear walking routes along great streets, leading down to the Tyne and back up to Gateshead city centre. This can operate in parallel to other more familiar routes such as that along Grey Street, but has the advantage of recentering the city to bring in cultural and civic elements like the two universities. Recently the practice has been involved in a piece of public realm planning at the Civic Centre, which allows Newcastle City Council and the

Top: The Tyne River gorge, with high- and low-level bridges linking Newcastle and Gateshead.

Universities of Northumbria and Newcastle to co-exist and form a 'Civic Boulevard'. The ambitions of the three parties include bringing definition to the city centre without it being perceived as retail activity-led, whilst allowing more focused and complementary retail and cultural activities (like at the revitalised Laing Gallery, which Farrells are helping regenerate) to be enabled with a mutually supporting renewal strategy.

Although the East Quayside masterplan (which Farrells led on in the '90s and which has now been fully realised) has allowed the 'low level' cities to be rediscovered, and has helped to form a connection to the burgeoning cultural activities at the river's edge, there are still areas to be resolved, such as the route from Central Station, still obscure and confusing, and a proper understanding of an appropriate mix of waterside activities and uses that do not rely on 'horizontal drinking' as the main attraction.

The river and its vistas hold the key to the future of both cities. There are large swathes of land, close to both city centres, that, in most other cites, would themselves be thought of as 'city centre' sites. These, with their considerable heritage of historic buildings and structures, now need to be harnessed, to form new creative and vibrant quarters that can provide both access and renewal to the nearby fading city edges. Innovation has long been a distinctive characteristic of the North-east, and now can be used in the imaginative re-use of land by the Tyne, allowing the cities to exist in a genuine cultural and economic partnership that will provide shared benefits and identity.

Top left: Celebrating the regenerated Quayside: fireworks during the Tall Ships race.

Top middle: International Centre for Life: delivering urban repair, new routes and connections, and through the entrance a new public square.

Top right: Grey Street – a mixed-use, re-use and renovation of Grade II listed buildings.

Bottom left: Gateshead Millennium Bridge: a new vibrant walk between the river banks.

Bottom middle: True mixed-use in a city centre environment: research, teaching, education and outreach in one building.

Bottom right: New buildings are incorporated within the historic fabric of the city.

NEWCASTLE CULTURAL QUARTER MASTERPLAN

Newcastle University is located at the northern gateway to the city adjacent to the Civic Centre and University of Northumbria. A major part of the estate's strategy masterplan focuses on the relationship between the university's central campus and Newcastle city centre – 'Town Meets Gown'. The Cultural Quarter proposal seeks to draw together the dispersed and hidden treasures of the university and several learned societies into a Cultural Quarter within the renewed university campus.

As part of a wider vision for connecting the cultural assets of Newcastle and Gateshead,

the proposal is for a 'Geordie Ramblas' (taking its inspiration from Barcelona's La Rambla – a wide connecting boulevard with varied active frontages, markets and cafés) running down the axis of Northumberland Street, Pilgrim Street and down the City Road to the practice's celebrated East Quayside. The dramatic Millennium Bridge forms a direct connection to Gateshead Quayside and the emerging cultural south bank of the Tyne.

The Cultural Quarter is focused on the Grade II* listed Hancock Museum, the adjoining buildings and Claremont Road and Eldon Place.

Dramatic improvements have been made: creating the new Great North Museum (see page 226) has improved the physical and intellectual accessibility of the collections, and the museum has been integrated into a whole new programme of exhibition design and interpretation. The lawns at the front of the museum have been re-landscaped to provide a new accessible setting for the building, removing unsightly car parking to a more carefully considered location.

Above: University and Cultural Quarter masterplan:
1. Robinson Library
2. Northumbria University
3. Civic Centre
4. St. Thomas Church
5. Haymarket Metro Station
6. Refectory / Students' Union
7. King's Hall
8. Hatton Gallery
9. Playhouse
10. Allied cultural uses

Above: The 'Geordie Ramblas' defines a civic route through Newcastle, connecting Exhibition Park, Newcastle University and the city centre with the East Quayside, where it accesses the Gateshead arts quarter via the Gateshead Millennium Bridge.

NEWCASTLE UNIVERSITY MASTERPLAN

The masterplan for the University of Newcastle-upon-Tyne provides the opportunity to take an overview of the university's accommodation requirements and sets out proposals for the ongoing physical development of the university. This particular study focused on the university's central campus and its relationship with Newcastle city centre.

The relationship with the city is key to establishing a clear identity for the university. As the university seeks to attract and retain the highest calibre of staff and students, putting a 'face to the place' is critical. The masterplan makes proposals to reinforce the physical identity of the campus by creating 'four new Quadrangles' to enhance the setting of the university buildings and faculties. The identification and strengthening of pedestrian routes through the campus reinforces the relationship between the university and all of its neighbours.

Within the university campus, the concept of the Foyer building on the Barras Bridge site and the link to the Great North Museum (originally the Hancock Museum) form a key component in the overall cultural strategy.

The proposed academic restructuring of the university brings into sharp focus the relationships between the different schools and departments and the central student and administrative support functions. The opportunities this restructuring present have been investigated with particular reference to their physical requirements.

Newcastle University is located at the symbolic northern gateway to the city adjacent to the Civic Centre and the University of Northumbria. The strong axis of Northumberland Street and Pilgrim Street links these centres of learning and local government to all of the major cultural elements in the city centre.

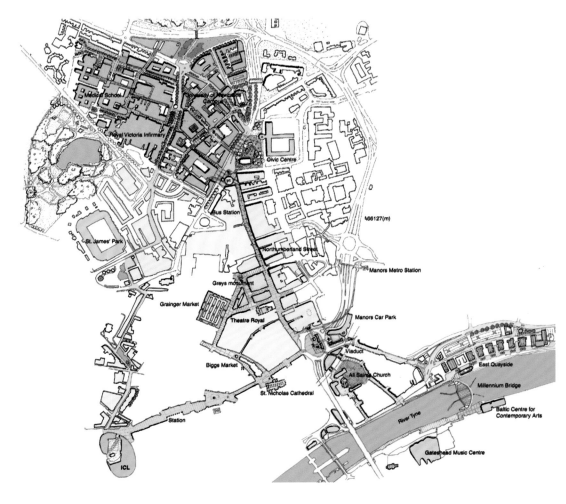

Above: The university masterplan proposes a series of routes and spaces that are linked with recognisable thoroughfares through the city.

New quadrangles and courts are proposed to provide identity to existing buildings and new development opportunities within the campus.

Top right: The university masterplan proposes a series of routes and spaces that are linked with recognisable thoroughfares through the city.

Above: The new quads (left) highlight how the campus is evolving in a coherent way, rather than responding to short-term requirements.

NEWCASTLE CIVIC BOULEVARD

One of the defining characteristics of Farrells' urban design is the attention paid to place-making. The creation of places needs to be incremental and considered sequentially to knit with complex layered cities. The almost fully implemented masterplan for the University of Newcastle, and the subsequent initiatives of the Cultural Quarter and the Great North Museum, have firmly placed the new physical and intellectual front door of the university to face the traffic-dominated, fragmented and nameless area around the Civic Centre.

With the University of Northumbria also realising that their own front door should face the city, the City Council commissioned Farrells to develop the merging idea of a civic precinct focusing on the links between these front doors and the Civic Centre.

The resulting 'Civic Boulevard' concept drew together all the prior pieces of work into a proposal organised into projects capable of implementation sequentially and incrementally.

Central to the Civic Boulevard is the overarching concept to re-integrate the Civic Centre, and the uses and activity that flow in and out of it into the public domain, enabling and facilitating the emerging Cultural Quarter. In turn, this reinforces the big picture desire to rebalance the centre of Newcastle with an attractive 'top of the town' place, brimming with activity and life.

Components of the Civic Boulevard include urbanising the big roads to make streets, making the place legible, coherent and pedestrian-friendly by linking the civic gardens into the surrounding context, defining and revitalising the settings of the gardens, Church and Civic Centre, and exploiting the entire precinct for arts and cultural activity.

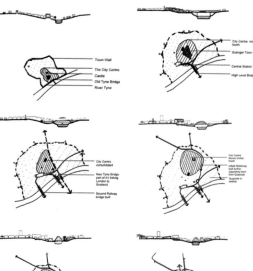

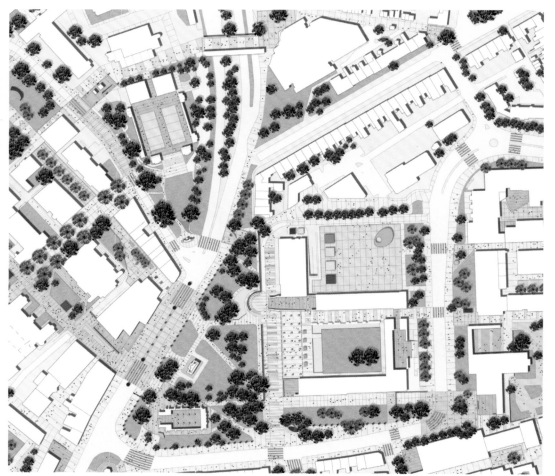

Top left: Aerial view of Newcastle Civic Boulevard study area.

Sketches: An understanding of the development of Newcastle's roads and railways lies at the heart of being able to propose solutions to improve circulation and accessibility. These diagrams show how the railways, bridges and eventually urban motorways have resulted in the current state of affairs.

Above: The Civic Boulevard links the Universities of Newcastle-upon-Tyne and Northumbria with the Civic Centre to engage the city centre in a vibrant flow of spaces and uses.

PILGRIM STREET

In the 1960s the natural order of Newcastle, collectively planned over time, was overlaid and significantly disrupted by an urban ring motorway, which cut off the city centre from its hinterland, and severed some of its organically grown main streets.

Typical of these is Pilgrim Street, which at its northern end becomes Northumberland Street – the shopping street with the highest footfall in the UK – but which now terminates in a complex and impassable traffic gyratory, leaving the street bereft of life and activity. The gyratory also very effectively blocks the most direct route from the city centre to the Quayside, the Millennium Bridge and Gateshead beyond, further damaging the vitality of this part of the city.

Farrells' 'Geordie Ramblas' study sought to repair this significant route, by devising a legible and coherent pedestrian route through the gyratory, fed by a new diagonal street through a derelict and now underused part of the Pilgrim Street area.

The potential for this street to reconnect and re-activate the lower part of Pilgrim Street and to remake the retail heart of Newcastle was recognised by several major retailers and developers, who worked with Farrells to produce an holistic vision, revitalising Pilgrim Street and naturally extending city centre retail activity down from Northumberland Street toward the Quayside.

Farrells' vision retained the best of the found places and buildings in this hitherto derelict quarter of the city, extended the surrounding city patterns and uses, and found space for a large department store whilst repairing the medieval grain of the city fabric.

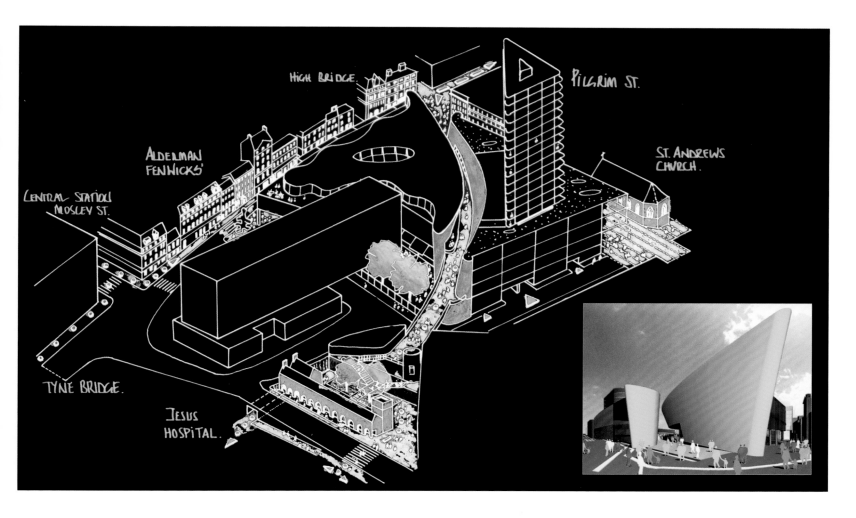

Above: The existing street levels meet at the heart of the site.

Inset: New retail buildings marking the new diagonal street as it joins Pilgrim Street.

THE GREAT NORTH MUSEUM

The Great North Museum in Newcastle brings together for the first time the North-east's premier collections of archaeology, natural history and geology. The project sits within the practice's Cultural Quarter masterplan, occupying a prominent site on the Great North Road. The brief was to address its setting in relation to the city, limited exhibition and storage space, unsuitable environmental conditions for the collections and, working with exhibition designers Casson Mann, to reinterpret a varied collection.

The redesigned galleries of the Grade II* listed building open up vistas and communication routes around the building, making the museum more coherent to the visitor, the collections themselves inhabiting these reinvented spaces. A new central axial route through the galleries and new extension forms a vista between the university and city. Cross views via side galleries to the outside provide orientation and contrast.

The extension complements and contrasts the existing Hancock Museum in form and use; they are separated visually and physically by a double-height glazed 'galleria' allowing their identities and forms to read strongly whilst providing appropriate scale against adjacent buildings and providing new positive west/east entrance points.

The new building contextually derives its form, size and elemental composition from the Hancock building: form and size from the volume

Top: Illustrative concept section. A new route through the museum, connecting existing with new.

Bottom (from left to right): Site and ground floor plan; first floor plan.

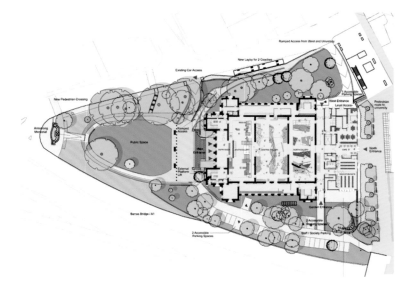

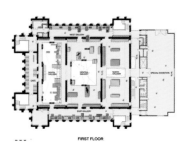

FIRST FLOOR

of the existing central gallery; strong horizontal datums and vertical rhythms transfer from the existing building across to the new building. The refurbished natural stone, new traditional zinc roofing, lead, timber flooring and lime plaster detailing to the existing building is contrasted by the reconstructed stone cladding, aluminium roofing, modern render and planar glazing.

The Great North Museum is zoned with retail and hospitality to the front spaces and galleria.

Circulation is ordered about the four existing stone stairs and new galleria stair; education, special exhibition and society spaces are stacked vertically through the new extension. The special exhibition area has been designed to accommodate large touring animated exhibitions and provides access into the space via a 4.5m² glazed steel door, with the public library and archive facilities above accommodating the most prominent societies' collections.

The landscaping around the museum is Northumbrian-themed, with colours extracted and interpreted for this local landscape to enliven and animate the new extension. They are used through the interiors of both buildings.

The Great North Museum project began in 2003, was granted planning permission in 2005 and opened in May 2009 to unprecedented acclaim, taking 50,000 visitors within the first week alone and more than 800,000 in its first year.

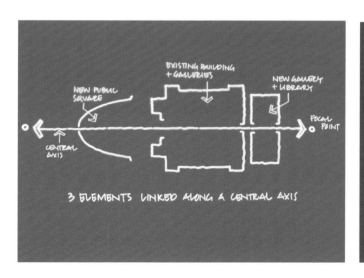

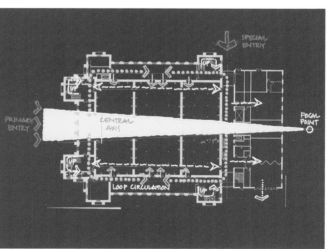

Left: Concept diagrams illustrating connectivity.

Overleaf top: Revival and refurbishment of the Grade II* listed building façade, with new accessible routes to the front entrance.

Overleaf bottom: The appropriate scale of the new extension sits between the existing building and the closely neighbouring large-scale university buildings.

Overleaf top and bottom: The new temporary exhibition gallery provides a unique space for display and performance.

Previous page: The new extension complementing and contrasting against the existing Hancock Museum.

Top left: Simple patterns and materials together with bold windows bring richness to the new exterior.

Bottom left: Stone staircases repaired, cleaned and enhanced to 21st-century accessible standards.

Top right: A simple glazed link articulates the junction between old and new.

Bottom right: The new café that looks out onto the newly landscaped entrance and path.

Opposite: Revitalised existing galleries improve the conservation, display and interpretation of the combined collections.

Overleaf: New interiors of the restored museum.

QUAYSIDE & OUSEBURN GATEWAY HOUSING

The Ouseburn Gateway site marks the meeting point of the River Tyne and its tributary, the River Ouseburn. This area sits within the city centre and in a conservation area at the eastern end of the Newcastle quayside, at the southern end of the Ouseburn Valley.

It was important that the proposals took account of the Gateway's setting and the links to its neighbours so that it settled into the surrounding context in a seamless way but nevertheless asserted its 'village' identity on the city stage.

The brief was set out by Newcastle City Council, which delineated the proposals for the regeneration of the Ouseburn Gateway site to be a mixed-use scheme, combining residential and commercial components. The council's desires have been honoured with the provision of near-equal amounts of residential and office space. The former responds carefully to the brief so that the eighty homes are a combination of one-beds, two-beds and duplex apartments.

The duplex apartments are organised at the lower levels, providing individual front doors, which

are essential for creating the required ground-level activity. In the main plaza, the main entrance to the residential building looks north to the Ouseburn River and is set back allowing the landscaping to wash into its open light-well. Opposite sits the restaurant, building overlooking the connection through to the valley. On the small building's northern side, a newsagent is located under the office building, where a pint of milk can be purchased – serving the local community in an area devoid of primary retail.

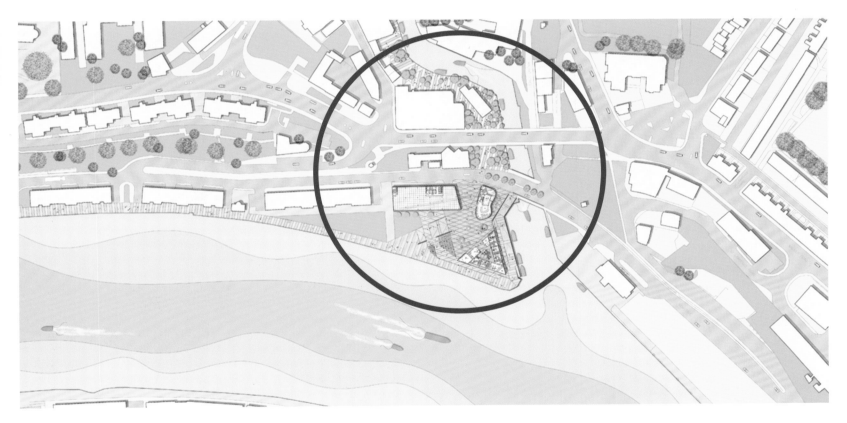

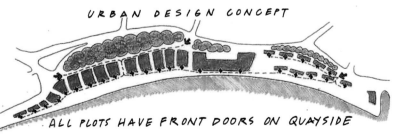

URBAN DESIGN CONCEPT

ALL PLOTS HAVE FRONT DOORS ON QUAYSIDE

Top: The proposals mark the meeting point of the Tyne Gorge and the Ouseburn Gateway.

Bottom left: Early concept drawing.

Bottom right: Quayside masterplan drawing.

The office space provides flexibility, with a variety of floorplates and levels that can be subdivided for multi-tenancy. To create variety in the office uses, additional entrances have been planned to allow for different types of occupiers and a perceived increase in movement of people into the building.

The sloping form of the office's roofline forms part of a carefully designed massing sequence with its important residential associate. The building's heights build from Mariner's Wharf adjacent, framing the St Lawrence Road view, before the prism continues upwards to a zenith pointing to the historic centre of settlement. The sequence leads to an interesting 'dance' of one building around the other as the observer's

viewpoint changes, whilst acknowledging the duality of the site with each incline in turn focusing on Byker and the Quayside.

At ground level, and on a more local scale, the rich brief of uses has been blended to create a vibrant and active series of spaces. The residential building exhibits a gallery in its most westerly angle, pointing towards the Baltic Flour Mill and Sage Music centre, embracing those culturally enriched pedestrians moving east, continuing along the promenade.

Together the three buildings and their public realm dramatically improve the area, promoting physical, social and economic benefits to the local community, the Ouseburn Valley and future development in the wider Tyne River corridor.

Above: The main plaza surrounded by the office building to the left and residential building to the right. The low-level restaurant building and the angled façades of its neighbours preserve views from St Lawrence Road and Byker beyond.

Opposite: The prism residential building marks and responds to the unique site and the curve of the River Tyne.

EDINBURGH

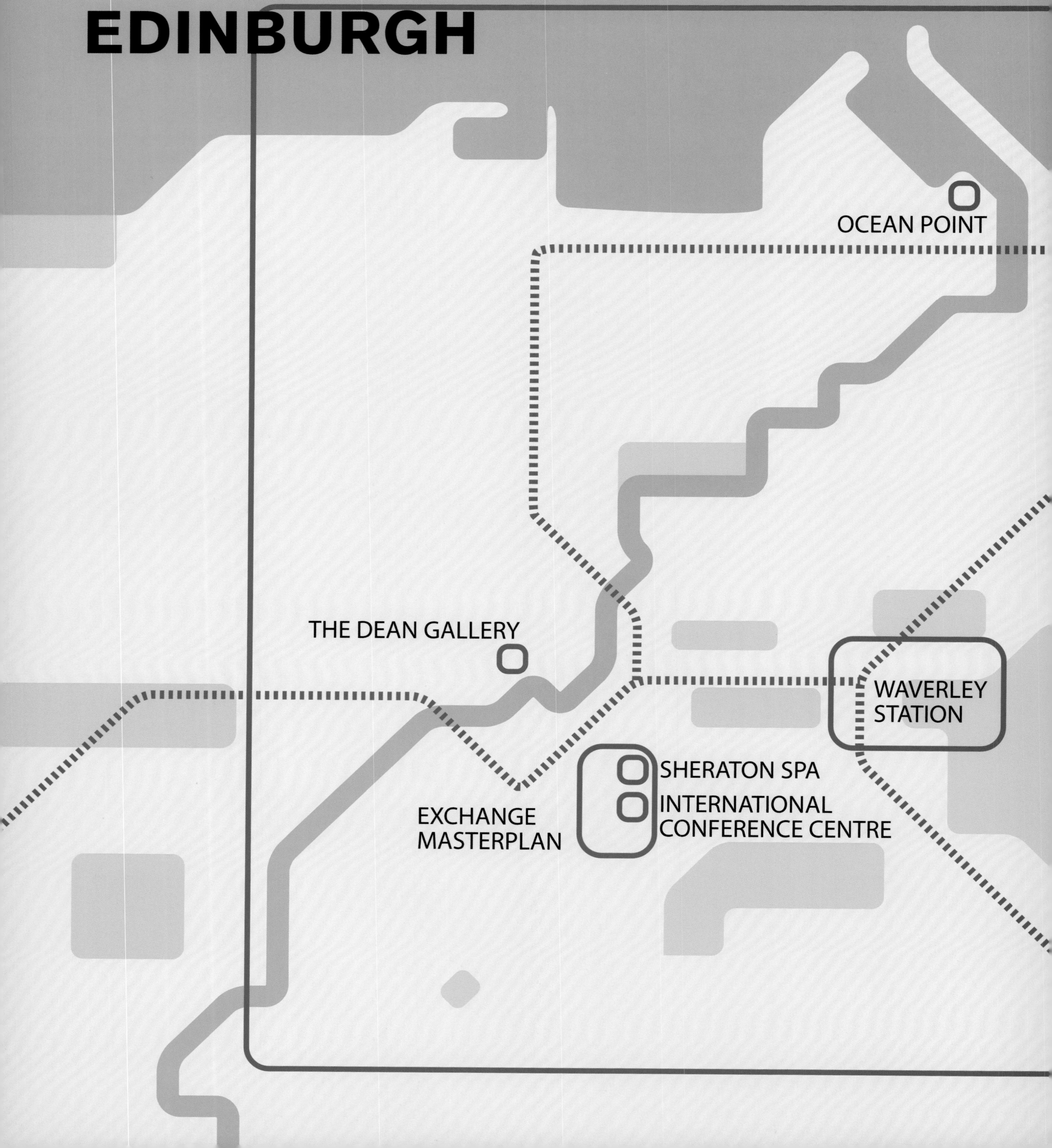

OCEAN POINT

THE DEAN GALLERY

WAVERLEY STATION

SHERATON SPA

EXCHANGE MASTERPLAN

INTERNATIONAL CONFERENCE CENTRE

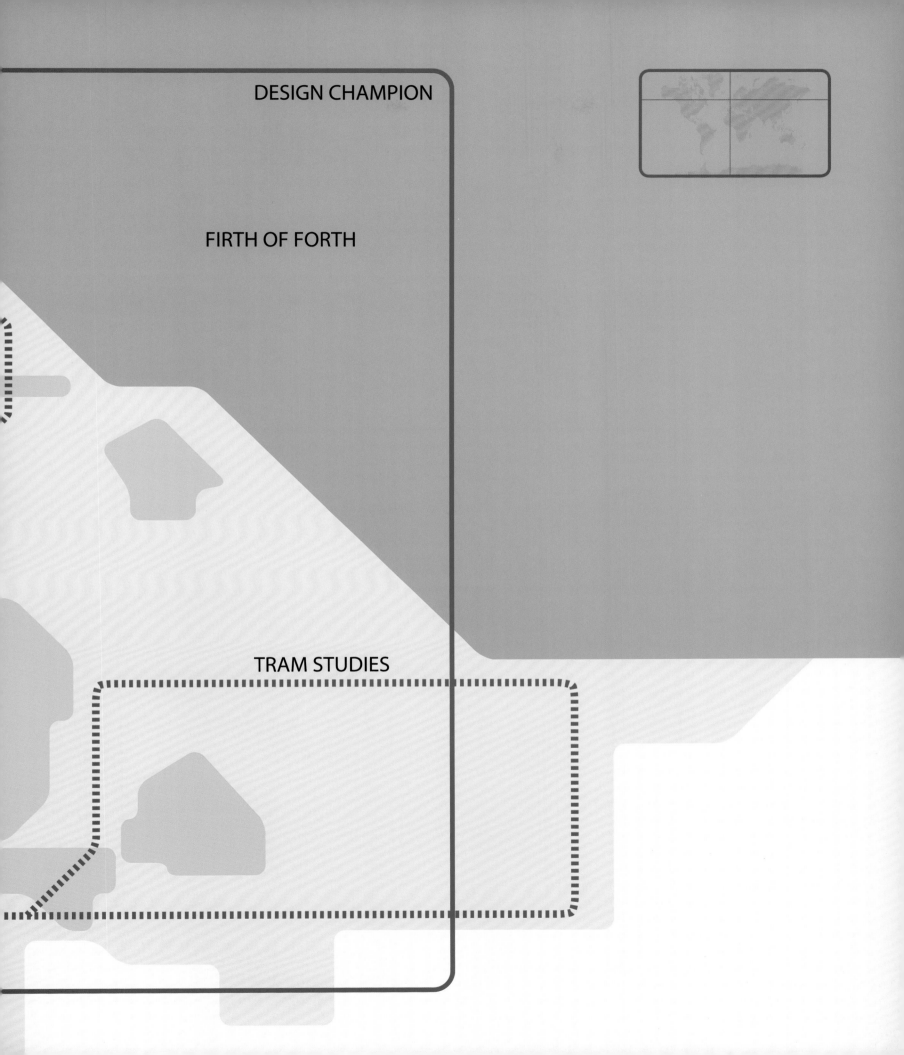

DESIGN CHAMPION

FIRTH OF FORTH

TRAM STUDIES

EDINBURGH

Farrells' work in Scotland's central belt has involved tackling projects that seek to reunify components of neighbourhoods, districts, cities and regions at a variety of different scales.

The Dean Gallery was designed as an orphanage, with the boys' and girls' accommodation separated by a wall constructed through the centre of the building. Farrells not only removed this wall to reunite the two halves of this symmetrical building as part of their radical conversion, but formed a cascade of new openings, rooflights, internal vistas and connections. This made the building open to sunlight and visitors' gaze alike, allowing the exhibits, building and landscape to form a seamless experience that permits an interpretation of the displayed works (and shop and café – and even the building's security area) as a microcosm of the city's creative energies.

The National Galleries of Scotland's two buildings off Belford Road were united as part of a new Arts Campus masterplan. This formed part of a broader cultural project to rediscover the Water of Leith and to connect the city through specifically commissioned sculpture (most recently by Anthony Gormley) back to the sea via the Port of Leith. Roads and paths were re-routed, and building entrances and movement hierarchy reconfigured. This allowed the buildings and their parkland settings to address each other in a legible way most conducive to the enjoyment of art in its context – either outside in various landscape locations, or internally in two contrasting gallery settings.

The Exchange Financial District was conceived, in the late 1980s, as a key component in uniting two city fragments, sitting as it does at the fulcrum between Edinburgh's Old and New Towns. The neighbourhood that it represented had been dissolved by railways, local (short) express roads and clusters of development, fracturing the site from the West End, city centre and medieval city grain alike. Farrells skilfully knitted back the connecting urban fabric, rediscovering old routes and inventing new ones, allowing a cascade of other developments to follow. This provided this forgotten city quarter with new arterial access and economic life-blood in the form of international financial headquarters, cultural buildings, including the conference centre designed by Farrells. In addition new public spaces were delivered, designed around pedestrians, improving circulation between the adjacent neighbourhoods.

The Design Champion initiative – with Terry Farrell appointed as Edinburgh's first Design Champion – allowed the whole city to be properly reviewed from an urban design perspective, arguably for the first time since the creation of the New Town. The constituent projects were many and diverse, but jointly had the aim of uniting the component parts of the city. Some had been overlooked and undervalued for decades if not generations, but the role sought to provide a contemporary interpretation and a dynamic manifesto for the city creatively to reassert itself with relevance and verve. The impetus for these challenges has been triggered with imagination and skill that will allow Edinburgh to flourish – if it holds its nerve – in decades to come.

Terry Farrell was instrumental in promoting a city cooperation initiative between Edinburgh and Glasgow, traditionally a notion that would not always chime naturally with these two rivals. Heritage and precedent for collaboration was explored – from the building of Roman fortifications, canals, railways, roads and new towns linking Glasgow and Edinburgh over two millennia, as well as learning from other city regions working in association by sharing commerce, international travel hubs and apportioning local skills and traditions. A credible picture emerged for a future for Scotland's Central Belt that proposed a lively, jostling relationship bringing hitherto inaccessible benefits to both parties. There is now a distinct possibility of these two cities setting up a product and destination that would challenge the most successful British regional partnerships for global esteem and value.

From a building interior, to a pair of buildings, to a city quarter, to a conurbation, to a regional cluster containing two international cities to rival any world capital – the work in and around Edinburgh has demonstrated the practice's ability to work simultaneously on a number of levels, and to understand 'big picture' thinking and the value of operating simultaneously on crafting small components, whilst stoking the engines of culture and commerce that in turn create further opportunity for growth and renewal at each scale.

Right: Diagrammatic artworks by Terry Farrell, for design champion conference delegates. The city plan form as a work of art.

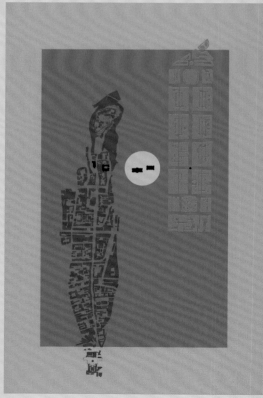

Above left: Bird's-eye view of Edinburgh with Farrells Exchange masterplan in foreground.

Above right: The Dean Gallery's ground floor corridor spine has been recreated and extended, with a dialogue between all three storeys allowed through use of new openings, new flights, integrated display cases and glazed walkways.

Left: The Edinburgh conference centre, a flexible facility that includes an auditorium with up to 1,200 seats.

DESIGN CHAMPION

Terry Farrell was appointed Edinburgh Design Champion by Edinburgh City Council in February 2004. This was originally a three-year role which was subsequently extended by two years, until May 2009. During this period Scotland gained substantial political independence and experienced significant economic changes. As an independent design champion, Terry Farrell sought to address place-making issues across the city and the surrounding region through a proactive planning approach. In leading the Edinburgh Design Initiative, he brought together a range of people with an interest in the city and place-making to think about future directions for the Scottish capital.

After four years in the role Terry Farrell reviewed what had been achieved and what continued to be the ambitions and challenges for the city; these were published in *Prospect* magazine (a design quarterly) under the title: 'Edinburgh is changing…12 challenges from the design champion'. These challenges set out his intentions and plans for the Design Initiative that would radically change not only how Edinburgh saw itself but also its position as a world-class city. It is a truly extraordinary place, however; its exceptional civic and urban qualities come hand in hand with some of the worst problems of the modern age: traffic congestion in the city centre, depredation of pedestrian routes and grim social housing juxtaposed alongside a city that regularly wins awards and is a World Heritage site. Added to this was the introduction of the city's tram line, possibly the most challenging urban design and planning project undertaken in the city for 100 years.

Terry Farrell's proposals endorsed the actions already being progressed by the City of Edinburgh Council and challenged the Council to be even more ambitious in taking these forward.

In particular, he highlighted the need for a continued focus on reinventing Princes Street. The street had long suffered from commercial decline and was characterised by too many second-rate buildings, too much clutter and bottlenecks. It should be one of Europe's finest promenades yet shops above street-level are hardly used and many only for storage. He

recommended a range of new uses such as flats or boutique hotels that will see people, rather than shoeboxes enjoying the view of Edinburgh Castle.

Another area for focus was redeveloping the waterfront. Edinburgh's waterfront offers outstanding opportunities for regeneration and the creation of a new kind of waterfront city. The redevelopment of the waterfront as new urban territory with housing, offices, entertainment and leisure facilities would be a spectacular addition to Edinburgh, and would have as great an impact as the New Town and Old Town had when they were first developed.

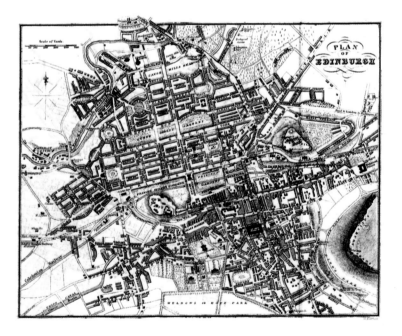

Bottom Left: Edinburgh won The Academy of Urbanism's European City of the Year Award 2006 (from left to right: Sir Terry Farell, Edinburgh Design Champion; Michaela Sullivan, Forth Ports; Riccardo Marini, City Design Leader; Stewart Mackintire, National Grid; Trevor Davies, Convenor of Planning CEC; Zoe Clark, Edinburgh World Heritage; Martin Perry, Henderson Global; Isabella Miller, John Lewis).

Left: Plan of Edinburgh, 1820 (Aickman).

Bottom: Aerial view of Princes Street and the New Town.

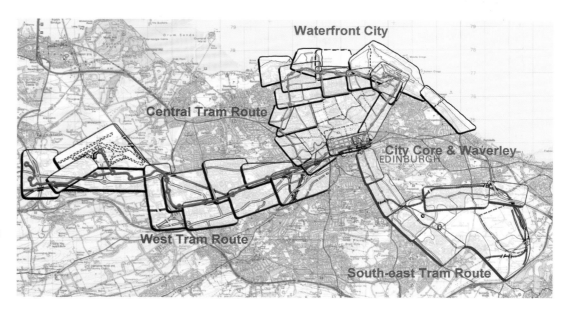

Waterfront City

Central Tram Route

City Core & Waverley
EDINBURGH

West Tram Route

South-east Tram Route

Amongst the 12 challenges Terry Farrell highlighted were that Edinburgh and Glasgow were setting aside their historic rivalries and were beginning to work more closely together. He recommended that this should continue with a focus on delivering real benefits if they are to compete on a global scale with other large cities. Already they form Scotland's economic and cultural backbone, and are placed in an amazing setting of water, rural and urban terrain that faces both across the Atlantic and across to Europe. By retaining their individuality but working and planning together, he believed that a strong union would help them address their future needs.

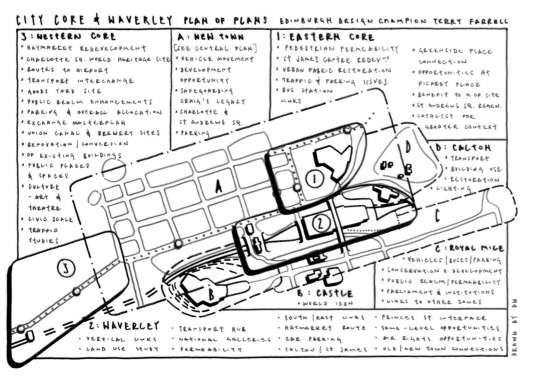

CITY CORE & WAVERLEY PLAN OF PLANS EDINBURGH DESIGN CHAMPION TERRY FARRELL

Top: The *Plan of Plans*, the key to all the masterplan tiles, primarily following the projected future tram routes.

Above: A later plan showing the city core and Waverley areas.

Right: Making headlines: Sir Terry Farrell, Edinburgh Design Champion, addresses Edinburgh's place-making issues.

Edinburgh champion

Ten reasons to avoid Princes Street

Edinburgh at risk from lethargy and lack of vision, says architecture guru

Design tsar wades in to attack city Waterfront

DESIGN GURU'S ROAD RAGE OVER TRAFFIC SCHEME

THE TRAM – DESIGN STUDY BY THE DESIGN INITIATIVE

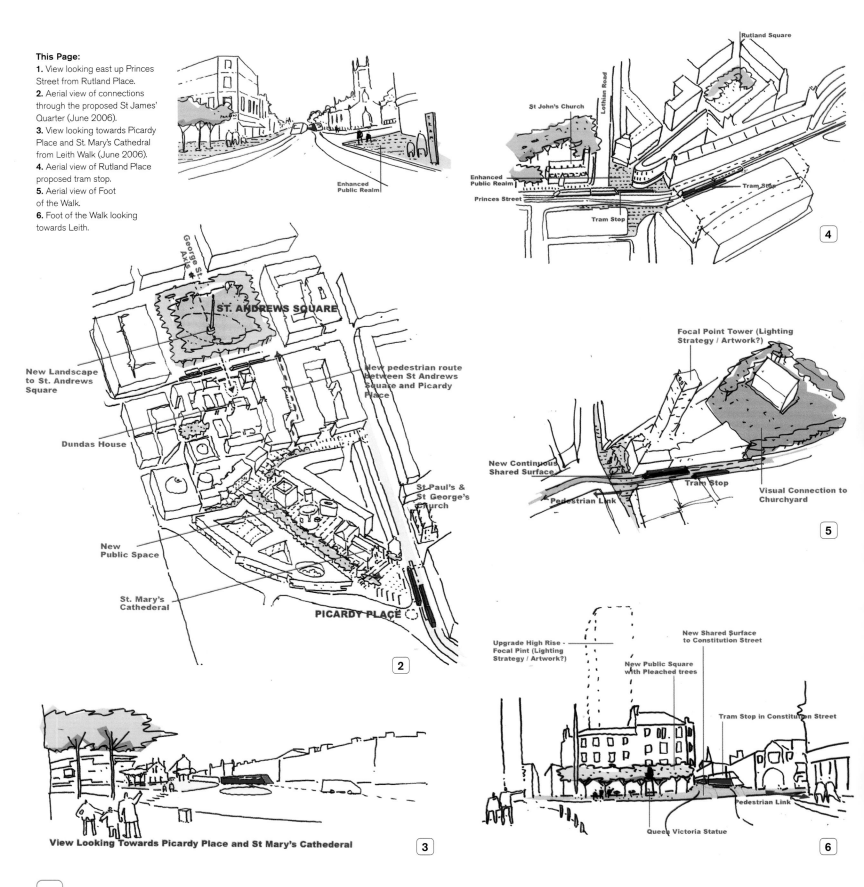

This Page:

1. View looking east up Princes Street from Rutland Place.
2. Aerial view of connections through the proposed St James' Quarter (June 2006).
3. View looking towards Picardy Place and St. Mary's Cathedral from Leith Walk (June 2006).
4. Aerial view of Rutland Place proposed tram stop.
5. Aerial view of Foot of the Walk.
6. Foot of the Walk looking towards Leith.

Enhanced Public Realm

Rutland Square

St John's Church

Lothian Road

Enhanced Public Realm

Princes Street

Tram Stop

Tram Stop

4

George St. Axis

ST. ANDREWS SQUARE

New Landscape to St. Andrews Square

New pedestrian route between St Andrews Square and Picardy Place

Dundas House

St Paul's & St George's Church

New Public Space

St. Mary's Cathederal

PICARDY PLACE

2

Focal Point Tower (Lighting Strategy / Artwork?)

New Continuous Shared Surface

Pedestrian Link

Tram Stop

Visual Connection to Churchyard

5

Upgrade High Rise - Focal Pint (Lighting Strategy / Artwork?)

New Public Square with Pleached trees

New Shared Surface to Constitution Street

Tram Stop in Constitution Street

Pedestrian Link

Queen Victoria Statue

6

View Looking Towards Picardy Place and St Mary's Cathederal

3

WAVERLEY STATION – DESIGN STUDY BY THE DESIGN INITIATIVE

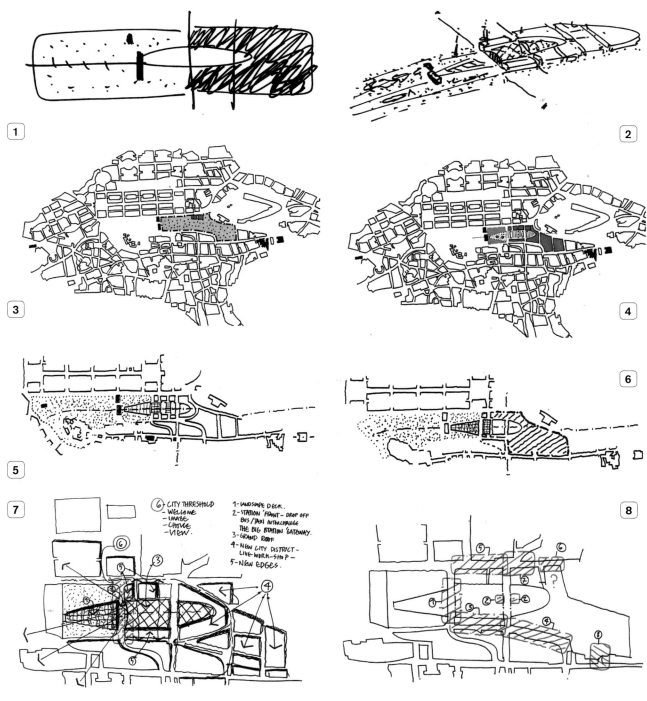

1 **2** **3** **4** **5** **6** **7** **8**

This Page:
1. Concept sketch.
2. Site plan sketch.
3. Waverley occupies a considerable acreage of central Edinburgh.
4. Continuity and connectivity north-south.
5. A new quarter of the city.
6. A great new station roof is possible with perimeter redevelopment and street connections to north and south, yet all low-rise sitting within the valley.
7. The largest central Edinburgh regeneration site.
8. Eight edge development projects.

Bottom left: The existing Waverley has an undistinguished, ad hoc roof sitting sunken in the valley.

Bottom right: The concourse effectively limits the ability of the station to achieve its full capacity by blocking potential east-west connections.

OCEAN POINT

Situated in the business quarter at the Port of Leith, Edinburgh's historic dockland, Ocean Point is a 70,000 sq. ft., eight-storey office block. It is set within Terence Conran's masterplan which incorporates Ocean Terminal, a key component of the area's retail offer, designed to increase the port's berth capacity and be the permanent site for the former Royal Yacht *Britannia*. The building contributes towards the balance of residential and commercial developments both underway and anticipated in future phases.

The office structure relates firmly to the geometries set out in the masterplan suggested by the proportions of the site, and has clean profiles relating to its nautical context. Carefully detailed coloured glass and metal panels reflect the sea, sky and panorama of the city in bright clarity, providing unique, iconic views in all directions.

The building's edges have been sculpted into distinct silhouettes to act as a foil to the purity of the sweep of the principal façades, each of which faces a point of the compass, allowing light to penetrate and reflect to differing degrees. Depending on the time and season, this gives a dynamic, ever-changing appearance which resonates with the dramatic coastal landscape.

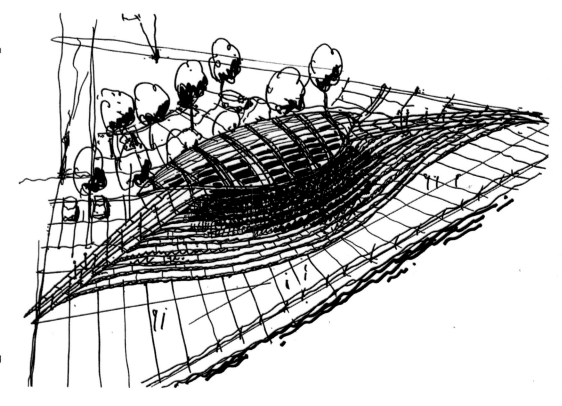

Clockwise from top:
1. Landscape structure sketch. As well as accommodating seating, shelter is provided with an elevated view of the port.
2. Responding to the linear blocks of Ocean Terminal, the building is a vertical landmark in the Port of Leith, allowing sea views and permeability.
3. Masterplan: the landscape treatment in the spaces between helps to connect the individual elements with a sculptural landform consisting of a sheltered bleacher structure.
4. The Ocean Point development is set within a colossal redevelopment initiative encompassing the entire water's edge of the Port of Leith, involving massive new infrastructure and land reclamation.

Opposite page:
With unique views in all directions, the building's horizontal layering echoes nautical themes.

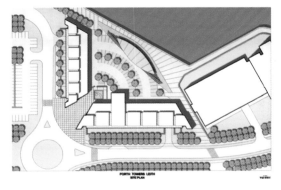

FORTH TOWERS LEITH
SITE PLAN

INVERNESS & DUNDEE

N. E. SCOTLAND

WHITENESS

INVERNESS
HOUSING

HIGHLAND
HOUSING
FAIR

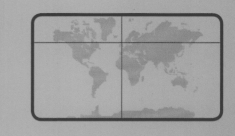

NORTH SEA

DUNDEE
UNIVERSITY

INVERNESS & DUNDEE

Design in the very north of the country emphasised the significance of landscape, climate and context and how a project could be shaped by the physical and cultural milieu of its setting.

Inverness enjoys a particularly rich natural setting, poised between the dramatic fault of the Great Glen – cutting straight across Scotland with Loch Ness nestled in its depths – and the Moray Firth, with its extraordinary north-western summer sunsets and teeming wildlife. Whiteness was the introductory project for the practice in this region. Its natural heritage was to form the entire ethos of

the design approach to 'letting nature back in' to create a new settlement that was in harmony with its natural landscape. We encouraged a holistic approach to living among a variety of habitats, as well as celebrating the architectural traditions of the area, themselves having been shaped by the elements. These in turn developed ways of respectively celebrating and avoiding the plentiful sun and wind prevalent in this region.

The analysis and understanding of indigenous forms, climate and landscape were applied at the Highland Housing fair – a masterplan, expo and

housing design competition that has now been built out, representing an approach to housing that recognises context in a sustainable way.

Further afield and further south-east – but still away from the central belt – lies the city of Dundee, with its industrial and natural heritage, and its well-established university. The masterplan commissioned here by the university was influenced by the internal programme for the rearrangement of faculties and the need for the university to establish a hierarchy of routes and spaces. A new central

green was required, and the influence of the city's geomorphology and history of land use was considered, looking to ancient field patterns to inform the relationship between built form and its setting. The campus was arranged by thematic quarters, each having a new focal space acknowledging its academic, urban and natural context, and each linked to the organising central green and its tributary routes. These were able to provide routes into the campus from the corresponding city quarters, and acted as ordering armatures around which new development

opportunities for teaching and residential facilities could be nurtured.

Working with the artist David Mach, who holds a professorship at the university, themes of cultural continuity and subliminal landscape were able to be explored.

Even the projects that were already commissioned prior to the completion of the masterplan were able to enjoy its influence, and to accommodate parts of the overall vision to ensure that the campus was able to look toward a unified future in the execution of its components.

Opposite page, left:
Aerial views of Whiteness Head looking out onto the Moray Firth. The remnants of its industrial heritage can still be seen.

Opposite page, right:
Model photograph of the new settlement at Whiteness.

Above: The proposed central green at Dundee University, around which a newly defined public realm is organised as part of the Farrells masterplan.

WHITENESS

In Inverness the Whiteness Head is an extraordinary and stunning landscape, jutting out into the Moray Firth. To the south lies the spectacular view down the Great Glen, with the mountains in the background and, to the north, an open vista of the Moray Firth. Closer to the site are a lagoon, dunes and salt marshes. These attract a rich variety of wildlife, including dolphins and seals in the Firth, and a host of migratory birds in the salt marsh and the lagoon. Terns nest on the spit and the forest nearby is home to the red squirrel. Erosion and sedimentation have created an intriguing coastal pattern, but it is more than just the natural landscape that makes Whiteness Head unique.

In the midst of all the natural beauty is a former brownfield industrial site. Reclaimed from the coast in the early 1970s to make an oil platform fabrication yard, Whiteness Head consists of a table-like form. Around 300 acres of land, now about two metres above the surrounding landscape, have been reclaimed from the marshland.

Four main influences helped shape the design for the masterplan. Firstly, enormously rich natural landscapes and ecological habitats surround the site. The aim of the masterplan was to enable nature to recolonise the site. The four principal landscapes have influenced the four residential neighbourhoods. The forest neighbourhood, the dunes neighbourhood, the salt marsh neighbourhood and the seafront neighbourhood all enlarge and extend the existing natural landscape into the abandoned industrial land. Secondly, the internal brief for a village has been developed from asking what is needed to make a community, to make a sustainable village. Thirdly, it was considered essential to work with the microclimate. The site enjoys the beneficial effects of the Gulf Stream (hence the dolphins in the Moray Firth), sunshine is high and the average rainfall is well below the UK average. However, the site is positioned in such a way that the strong winds are on occasion particularly fierce. The streets, public spaces and buildings were carefully aligned to minimise the impact of the wind and maximise sunlight. Lastly, the use and reinterpretation of industrial remnants such as the assembly hall and the crane rails has brought a subtle yet important dimension to the design. These are integrated into the landscape and artworks on the site.

Main image: Artist's impression of the development.

Inset: Movement diagrams illustrating strategies: walks, by car, by bicycle.

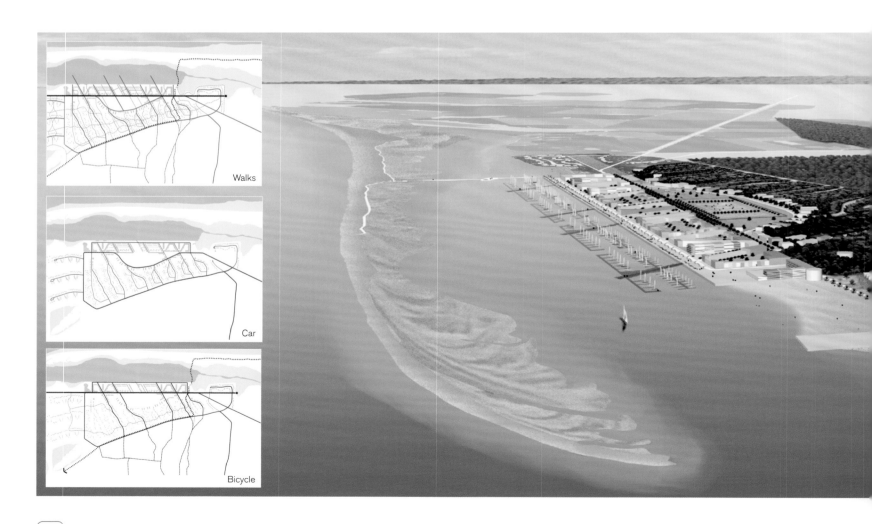

Walks

Car

Bicycle

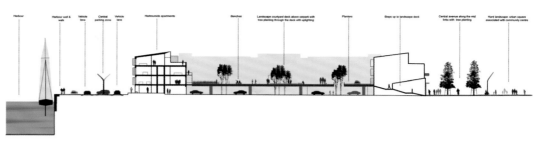

Far left: Aerial photo above Nairm.

Above: Seafront section through townhouses.

Left: Illustrative masterplan. The development of more detailed designs for the buildings and landscape indicates the importance of ensuring that the interconnecting fabric of the masterplan allowed the natural context to run through and inform the overall character of the new place.

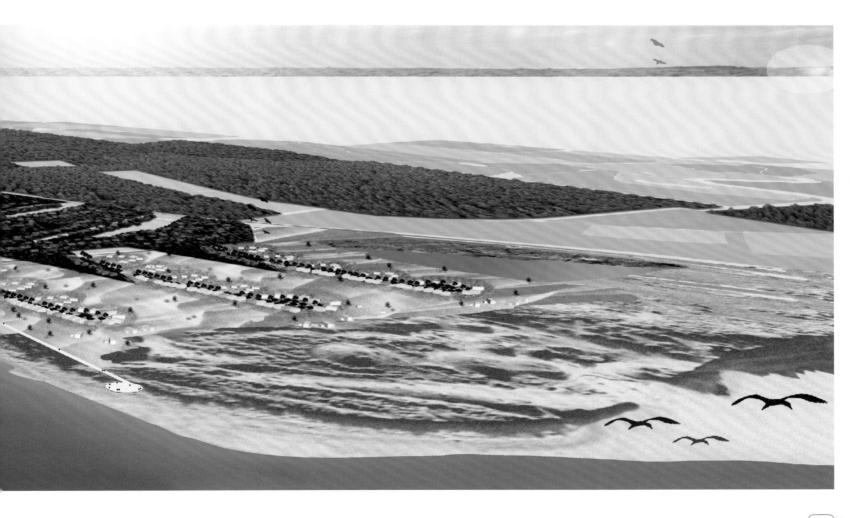

NEW ZEALAND & AUSTRALIA

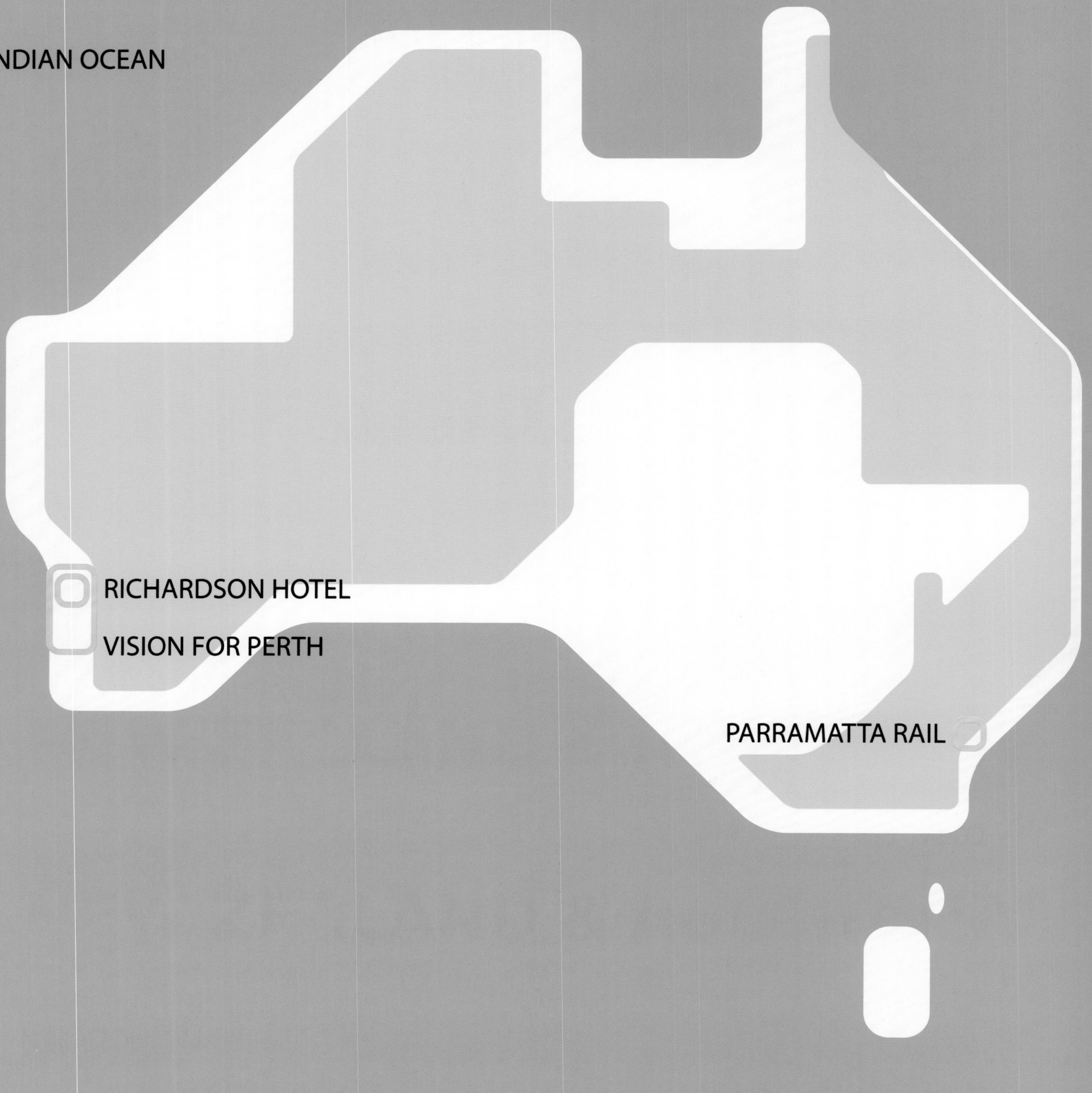

INDIAN OCEAN

RICHARDSON HOTEL

VISION FOR PERTH

PARRAMATTA RAIL

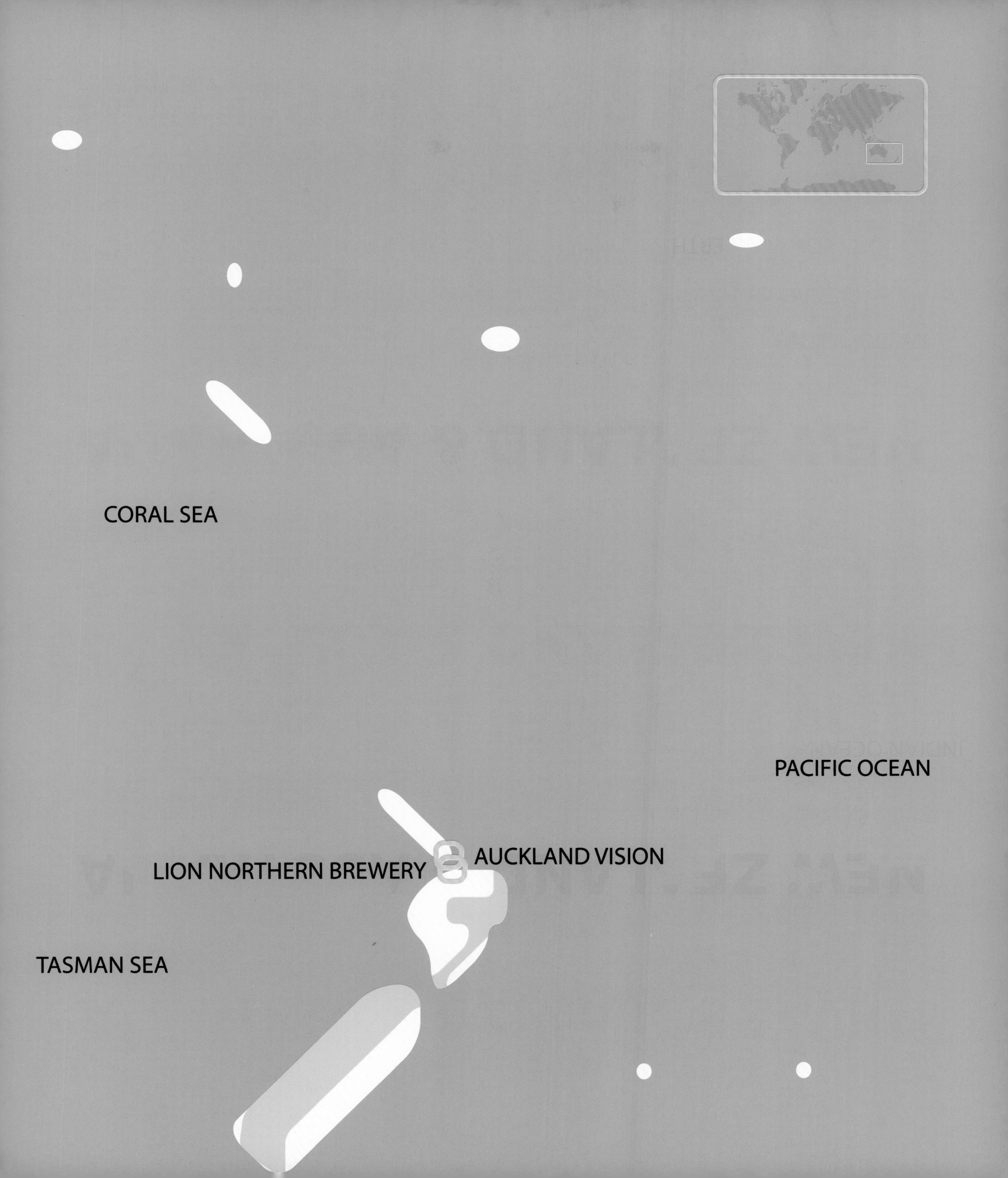

CORAL SEA

PACIFIC OCEAN

LION NORTHERN BREWERY 🍺 AUCKLAND VISION

TASMAN SEA

NEW ZEALAND & AUSTRALIA

Traditionally inhabited by a mix of ethno-cultures, colonisation of Australasia did not begin until the 18th century so large-scale urbanism is a relatively recent phenomenon. The early growth of settlements by Europeans responded to the same geographic influences as the preceding ethno-cultures – avoiding mountainous or inhospitable landscapes – whilst an abundance of deep natural harbours provided refuge for trading and fishing vessels. That pattern is evident today as the bulk of the population clings to the coastal fringes in cities that grew in the 18th and early 19th centuries.

Early settlements show rich and interesting communities arranged around burgeoning ports, but the demands of rapid population growth took its toll and urban sprawl has been the mode of development since the mid-20th century. Places were undermined by a move to US-style zonal planning and car transport with associated highway building. There is often a conflict between closed harbour freight areas and the urban motorways which feed them, leaving city centres and waterfronts isolated from each other and from residential neighbourhoods. Put simply, the focus on healthy outdoor lifestyles of this region has not always been matched by the quality of the urban environments. Today there is a growing desire for good urbanism to address these negative influences and increasing demand for vibrant city centre living. The most successful cities are wrestling with their isolation and looking to develop their relationship with Asia to be truly defined as world cities of trade, culture and quality of place.

Top left: Waterfront Perth in the 1940s.

Top right: Historic view of Auckland waterfront.

Bottom left: Waterfront Perth in 2010 following land reclamation.

Bottom right: Auckland waterfront in 2008.

A VISION FOR PERTH

In early 2009, Sir Terry Farrell was invited by the city of Perth to visit and to advise them on the issues facing the future of the city, as it seeks to deal with the issues of growth derived from a strong economy.

Perth is the capital and largest city in Western Australia – a region rich in natural resources which cushions it from the worst effects of the world-wide economic downturn – and with a population of approaching 1.7m, it is already the fourth most populous city in the whole of Australia.

Sitting alongside the Swan River, the heart of Perth enjoys one of the most beautiful settings of any city in the world; the riverside location of the core of the city has one of the great and most memorable skylines anywhere. Perth has vast areas along the waterfront devoted to parkland, along with clean beaches and a moderate climate, and it is no surprise that in 2010 Perth was listed in the top 10 of the 'World's Most Liveable Cities' by *The Economist* magazine.

However, more recent growth and relative prosperity has not always reinforced Perth's development as a place, especially since the mid-1960s when the motor vehicle began to dominate the thinking of the town planners. Perth today suffers from a lack of coherence that reflects the lack of an overall plan for future growth and development. The foreshore has been reclaimed from the water, but in the process it has become filled with motorways that divide and separate, and Perth's close relationship with the river has been lost. Furthermore, the city's road and rail transport infrastructure has divided the city core from the expanding neighbourhoods to the north and the west. The mental map has lost its focus and clarity.

Farrells' proposals to repair and restore the coherence of the city's heart are embodied in a 10-point 'Vision' document, which was offered back to the city as the basis for a plan for the city's future development. The proposals are simple and practical,

and aim to build upon the assets that once made Perth a great and connected place. They include the creation of great new boulevards to connect the heart of the city with west Perth and north Perth, to connect the two great public spaces of Kings Park and the Waterfront, and to re-establish the grandeur of the riverside – the genius loci of this great city.

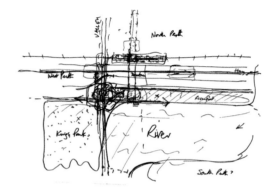

Above: Aerial photograph of the centre of Perth and its relationship with the Swan River.

Top: Terry Farrell's masterplan concept sketch for Perth.

Top left: A defined and developed 'green' agenda for Perth.

Top right: Making a virtue of Perth's dispersed multi-centred character.

Bottom left: Create a new great City Cross Route.

Bottom right: The water edge, regarded as an added parkland.

RICHARDSON HOTEL

As a high-end all-suite hotel, the Richardson includes serviced apartments, a business centre, a sumptuous day spa, and fine cuisine at the elegant Opus restaurant. The design creates a landmark destination for exclusive business travellers to Perth, with luxurious apartments and every amenity to ensure a comfortable and memorable five-star experience. This unique boutique hotel was designed with a holistic approach – grand and outstanding, yet conservative and pragmatic. Designed with the modern traveller in mind, the Richardson hosts 74 guestrooms and suites over eight floors, with private balconies and panoramic views of Perth city, Kings Park and surrounding areas.

The design incorporated environmental solutions to minimise natural heat load and glare. The development is orientated so that the north and west façades are not perpendicular to the setting western sun. All living rooms and bedrooms are angled so that the views are facing north-east or south-west. Additional architectural treatment through vertical louvres and double glazing was implemented to further reduce solar impact. The design maximises open space and 'breathing' space between adjacent buildings, allowing a flow of natural light into the development, increasing view corridors and minimising intrusion to neighbouring buildings. The project was designed in conjunction with local Perth architects Cameron Chisholm Nicol.

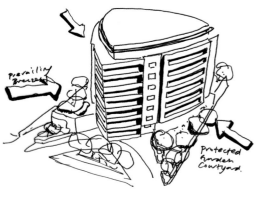

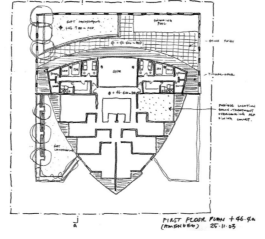

Top: The building is carefully orientated so that all living rooms and bathrooms enjoy views north-east and south-west.

Above left: Concept sketch.

Middle: Sketch of first floor plan.

Above right: The reception lobby.

PARRAMATTA RAIL LINK

Farrells, in conjunction with Sydney-based Conbeare Morrison & Partners, submitted an urban design strategy for Parramatta Rail Link which was shortlisted in competition. The core of the £100 million contract covers 27 kilometres of commuter railway running west of Sydney from Parramatta to Chatswood. The project involves the implementation of a new railway link and the design of 12 railway stations, both above and below ground. Each station is envisaged as a 'place-maker', enhancing and responding to its context, as well as redefining the character of the urban fabric. Iconic entrances to each station will create a unified identity for the line.

As part of its submission, Farrells designed the Parramatta Station Transit Interchange – a point of arrival in the town and a new civic focus. The new interchange offered an opportunity to reconfigure the heart of Parramatta's central business district and put right its current deficiencies. Farrells' design removes the barrier effect of the present station and railway line, opening up a large-scale plaza and transit mall at ground level that improves north-south pedestrian and vehicle connections. The design consists of an open station, naturally ventilated and admitting sunlight through an apparently floating glass-and-metal roof structure.

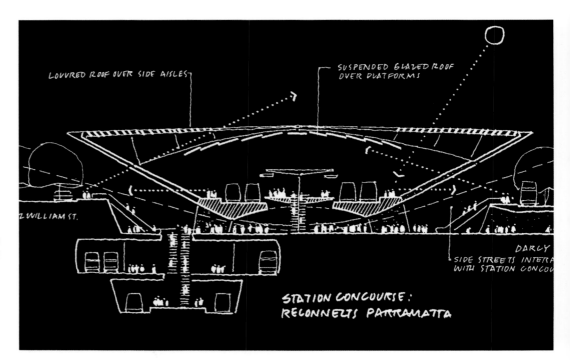

Left: Initial studies for the Parramatta town centre plan, which gave more development for the air-rights above and around the station.

Top: Concept sketch of the station roof. The roof visually unifies the ground floor plane of the station, which, like a town square, is the heart of the community.

Above: Model of the skeleton structure from the new concourse level.

AUCKLAND VISION

Like many cities today, Auckland is grappling with rapidly increasing population demographics and environmental concerns whilst looking to intensify and densify in a positive and sustainable way. Intensification of the city has to be the answer, rather than urban sprawl continuing to consume more and more of the surrounding natural environment.

In this context, it is possible to understand the significance of the Lion Brewery site. People are choosing to re-inhabit the city centre, and the challenge for this development is to begin to resolve its contrasts and create an urban environment of high quality – a connected place with a 24-hour life cycle, a legible, liveable, walkable, healthy place with easy access to public transport, social infrastructure and green space – in other words, a place to live, work and play. Aucklanders need to reach a position where they respect their urban environment as much as they respect their natural environment.

This approach has been at the core of our work in developing a concept masterplan for the former Lion Brewery works in Auckland. Auckland is a fascinating city at the meeting point of many seemingly divergent influences: a city on the physical and economic frontier between Australasia and the Pacific, a city with a unique, rich and varied multicultural society, strong cultural and economic links to both the west and to the east, by far the largest city in New Zealand yet with very low population density, a vast urban centre yet located within close proximity to one of the most beautiful landscapes in the world, a very European city yet planned on a North American car-based model.

Our work has been aimed at resolving these dilemmas, in producing a concept masterplan which responds to the strategic brief and the commercial and economic imperatives set by the client. At the same time we have created inherent flexibility in plot size and location to respond naturally and organically to changing market demands over the period of time that the masterplan is realised.

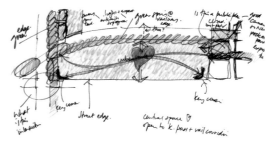

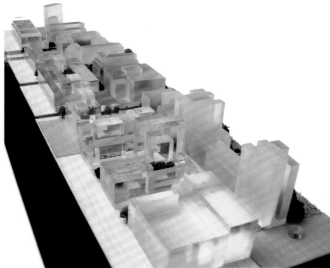

Above: Auckland today. Natural versus urban environment. With the arrival of zonal place-making and motorways, coherence was lost and the city sprawled.

Top right: Concept sketch – place-making in Newmarket.

Bottom right: Concept model.

Yet more than this, we have conceived a new kind of 'place' where urban living becomes a much more attractive proposition, where greater reliance on public transport is encouraged, where urban landscape meets green landscape, resulting in a blend of uses where opportunities to live and work and relax are integrated together.

The concept masterplan sets out height and massing strategies to create an urban form that can develop and support Newmarket as a strategic centre for intensification and increased density. At public transport nodes, streets open to create positive public spaces and building height and mass lift to mark these city nodal points. This experience of spatial variety contributes to the reading and understanding of the place and how it integrates with the existing spatial qualities of Newmarket.

Two character zones are defined by a green and natural identity along the new Green Way and an urban and mannered identity along Khyber Pass Road. These two 'characters' meet along the 'arrow shot' of the new east-west urban route, Newmarket Place.

The natural topography and underlying geology of the area are to be expressed in the public realm landform and levels. These elements also influence the choice and detailing of materials.

Water is used expressively to strengthen the above concepts and act as a memory of the underground spring on the site that drew the brewery to Newmarket. All streets of the development are designed as shared surfaces between pedestrian and vehicular traffic with priority given to pedestrians.

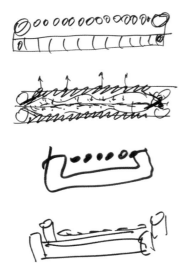

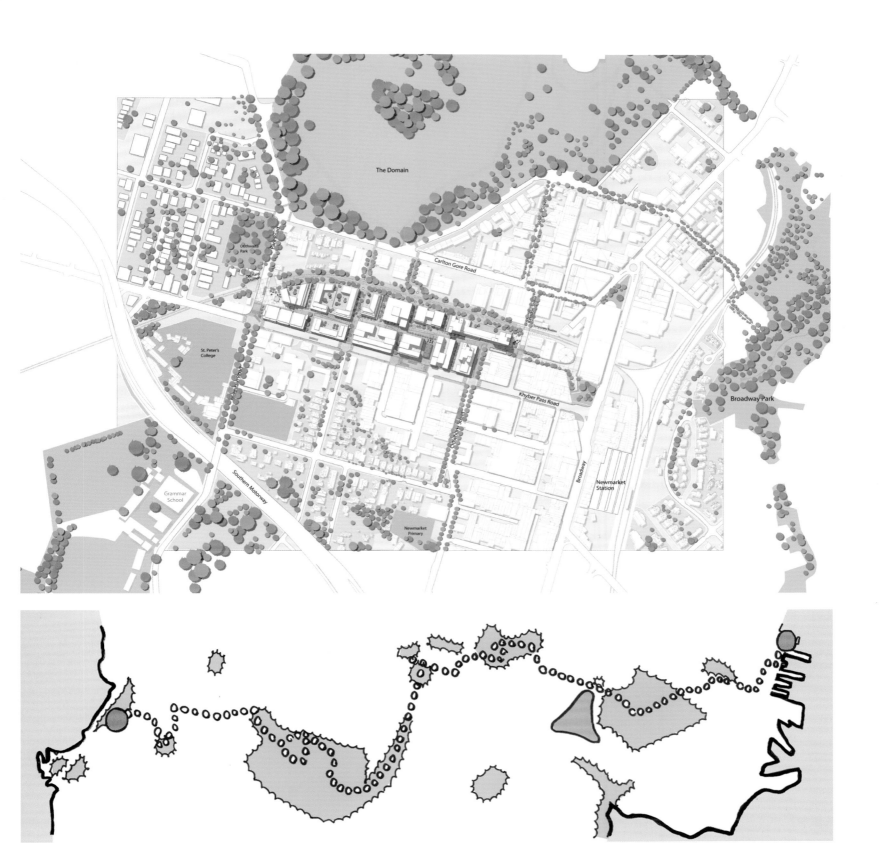

Opposite page:
3D view of concept masterplan massing with the domain behind.

Opposite page, far left:
Terry Farrell's concept sketches of the Lion Brewery site.

Top: The Lion Brewery site proposals in their wider context.

Above: There is an exceptional local landscape. The sketch shows the coast-to-coast walkway.

SEOUL

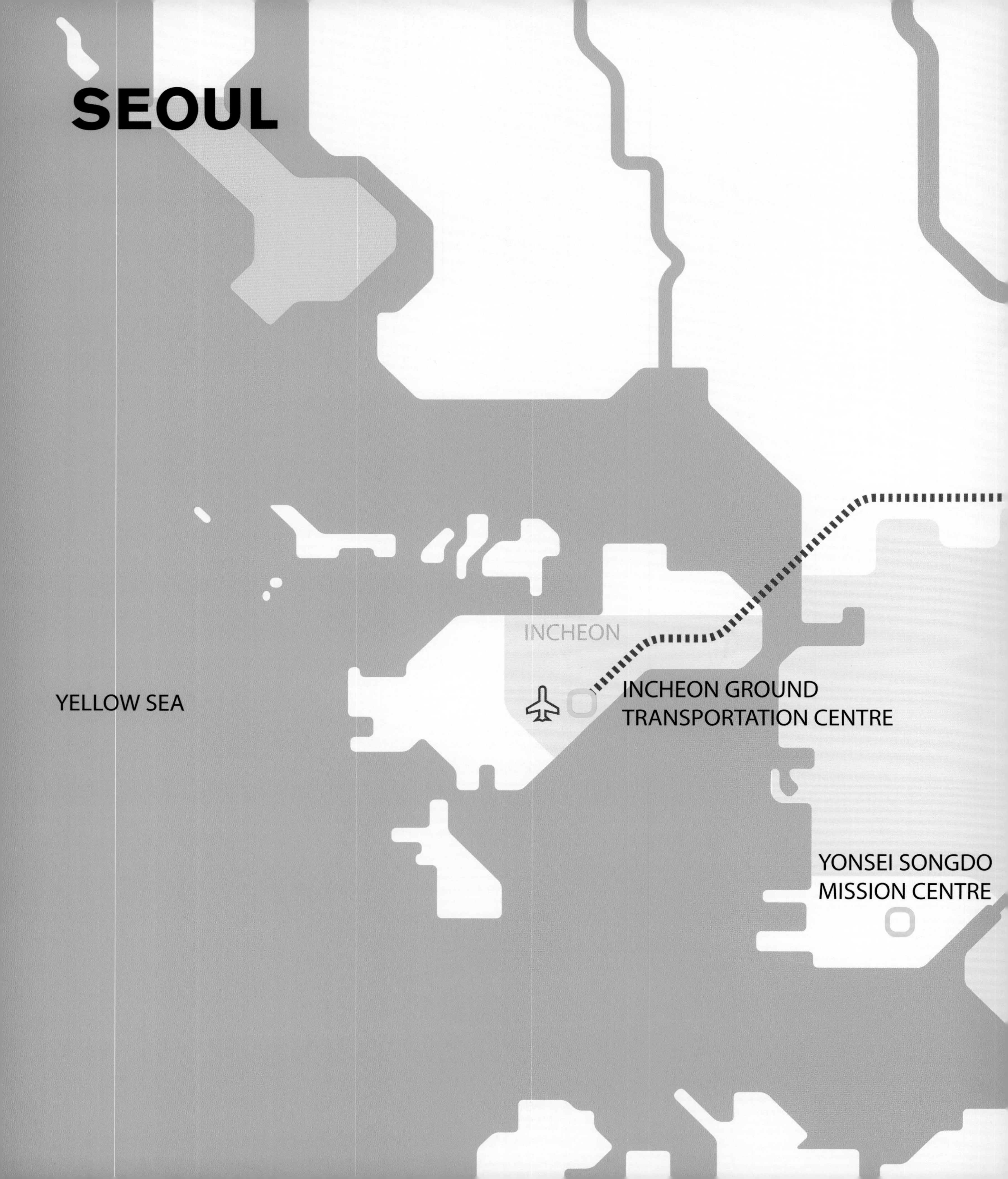

YELLOW SEA

INCHEON

INCHEON GROUND
TRANSPORTATION CENTRE

YONSEI SONGDO
MISSION CENTRE

HAN RIVER

Y BUILDING

SEWOON URBAN
REDEVELOPMENT

SEC DIGITAL MULTI - MEDIA
UNIVERSITY
& PRC

C BUILDING

SEOUL

GWACHEON NATIONAL SCIENCE &
TECHNOLOGY MUSEUM

SEOUL

The largest city in South Korea, Seoul has a population of over 10.5 million and a density of 17,288 people per km². Due to its geographical location Seoul has been the capital of Korea and now South Korea for over 2,000 years. Situated in a natural basin and surrounded by mountainous peaks, it has provided fortress-like protection and thrived as a global trade centre. Today it is recognised as an international centre for commerce and finance, benefitting from some of the most advanced technology and hosting innovative companies such as Samsung and KIA.

Seoul sits between China and Japan, only 2–3 hours away by plane, providing it with easy and convenient access to the rest of north-east Asia's economic hubs. Increasing urbanisation and transportation links have made Seoul and the neighbouring Incheon (70km west of the city) into one large urban region, and the site of the new international airport which opened in 2001.

Incheon International Airport has won major awards as the World's Best Airport by IATA and Skytrax since 2002. The Ground Transportation Centre was part of the project's first phase, designed to assist with the future development of transportation links to the city.

Seoul is renowned for embracing digital industries and technology parks, and in the past 10 years the government has funded educational, creative and heritage projects. In 2003 the city removed the Cheonggyecheon Highway that covered an existing river as part of an urban renewal project. A masterplan for this area was drawn up to celebrate the outdoors and encourage urban activities.

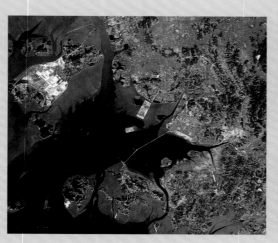

Opposite page
Top left: The Y-Building
– model of scheme.

Top right: The C-Building
– model of competition entry.

Centre: The River Ham flows
through the centre of Seoul.

Bottom left: Satellite image
showing Seoul, and Incheon
International Airport, which can
be seen top left.

Bottom right: The area
surrounding Seoul's Great
South Gate.

Below: View of the oculus
and platform enclosure of the
elevated light-rail system.

INCHEON GROUND TRANSPORTATION CENTRE

Reflecting the dynamic changes within Asia, air-traffic demand in the region has increased at double the rate of the rest of the world. When Seoul's existing airport could no longer cope with the vast numbers requiring its services, Incheon International Airport was built to cater for a projected 50 million passengers a year. It is currently the ninth largest passenger airport terminal in the world.

Won in an international competition, the Ground Transportation Centre (GTC) for Incheon Airport was designed in collaboration with DMJM and Samoo Architects. A freestanding structure between two passenger terminals, this six-storey GTC is the airport's primary transport interchange facility. It houses five rail systems, including: intercity, airport express and light-rail networks serving nearby towns, cities and remote airport hubs, a bus and coach station as well as taxi bays and car parks. The airport express (AREX) takes 43 minutes to reach the centre of Seoul. The Transport Centre design is primarily passenger-centered and all the components are strategically positioned to allow the seamless transition from one mode of transport to another.

The GTC was planned to ensure that the facilities and interchange support the smooth running of the airport as well as creating a strong physical and psychological gateway in and out of the country. The landmark quality of the scheme called for a dramatic and metaphorical design that celebrated South Korea as well as evoking the concept of flight.

The layout of the building is extremely simple. A great hall with a spectacular glazed concourse roof and clear spans of 190 metres forms the heart of the project and is the central space through which all passengers pass. Its large, naturally lit spaces are visible from all arrival points, ensuring clarity of organisation that helps passengers to find their way around.

Early designs were inspired by the idea of a bird in flight. On the roof there sits a jewel-like aerofoil, constructed from stainless-steel panels and glass, which hovers over the great hall and gives it natural ventilation.

The combination of the aesthetic with the functional continues through other areas of the project, such as the underground car park, which frees up space around the great hall to facilitate the creation of landscaped gardens. A 200-metre glazed pedestrian gallery, which draws on the Korean tradition of fortified walls, visually and physically links the car park with the great hall

while at the same time introduces a powerful new element into the landscape.

Positioned symmetrically on the north-south axis of the site, the Great Hall is the gateway pavilion between the ground transportation modes and the terminal buildings, which fan out to the north and south of the hub structure. Its location and form respond to the major pedestrian arteries connecting the airport terminals to the Ground Transportation Centre.

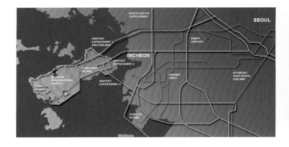

Above: Plan of Incheon Airport showing connections to Seoul and surrounding areas. **Below:** Original concept sketches by Terry Farrell.

Bottom left: Aerial view showing the complete airport city.

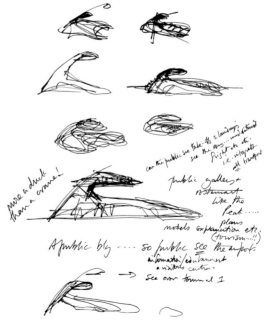

Top: Aerial perspective of the Ground Transportation Centre.

Bottom left and centre: The rooftop aerofoil symbolising a bird in flight, provides natural light and ventilation.

Bottom right: The Ground Transportation Centre's Great Hall and aerofoil illuminate the night sky.

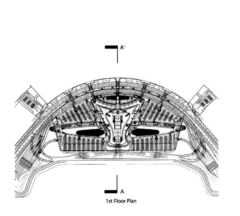

1st Floor Plan

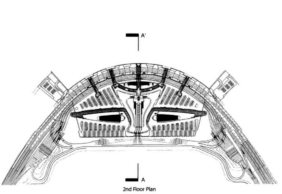

2nd Floor Plan

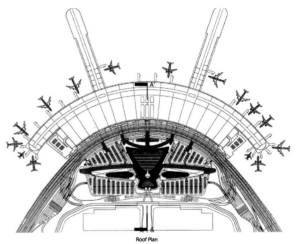

Roof Plan

0   20   50   100m

Top left: Stainless steel rainscreen panels.

Top centre: Solar shading is incorporated in the glazed walls.

Top right: The curved roof is formed of flat triangular

glass panes and stainless steel panels. Details of the exterior envelope.

Bottom row: Plans and sections of the airport.

Opposite: The Great Hall forms the heart of the building. Whether arriving or departing, by road or rail, all passengers pass through this spectacular space, topped by a glazed roof spanning 190m.

GWACHEON NATIONAL SCIENCE MUSEUM

The Gwacheon National Science Museum offers a full-scale immersion into science and technology, with interactive exhibits including earthquake, aeroplane and typhoon simulators, space camp and a 3D theatre. The design concept for the museum was inspired by the phenomenon of a nebula, a cloud of gas and dust, which leads to the formation of stars.

The main building houses science, technology and natural history exhibits, six interactive exhibition halls for special exhibits, and performance and conference halls, arranged over two levels. These major spaces are located in wings around a central distribution concourse, with a corridor leading to the planetarium. The museum is set in a scientific park complete with insectarium and an ecology learning pavilion.

As part of a team with Samoo Architects and Samsung Engineering Corporation, the museum was designed and built for the Korean Ministry of Science & Technology.

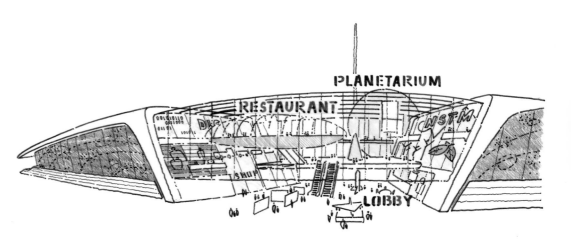

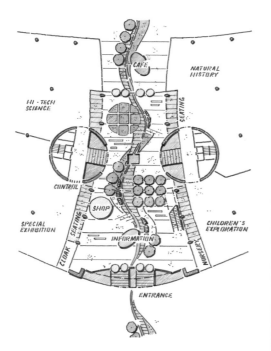

Above: Perspective sketch of the central hall entrance.

Far left: Conceptual plan of the lobby with the landscaped spine extending throughout the interior.

Bottom left: Conceptual section study of the lobby's interior elevation.

Left: The glazed foyer provides a central gathering area and exhibition space.

Bottom: Aerial view of the Museum and Science Park.

SEWOON URBAN REDEVELOPMENT

In the centre of Seoul lies the Cheonggyecheon Stream, a 10-kilometre waterway, which has been concreted over for the past 40 years. Once a river that ran through Seoul, it is now a stream. The restoration and urban redevelopment of this area was called for and Korean officials requested plans to be submitted for the Sewoon District 4 Redevelopment Area.

The proposed masterplan and building development is an architectural model of urban regeneration, embracing ecology and Korean culture. It forms a tightly woven community with a rich cultural context.

Although simple and contemporary, its design integrates traditional Korean components. The redevelopment site is bisected by two perpendicular axis which form a cross, with centralised landscaped courtyards overlooking the restored Cheonggyecheon Stream. Through the north-south axis is the new Cultural District, whilst west-east is the route along the stream.

The buildings were designed with large voids carved out of the typical solid block, which add visual interest and allow for the inclusion of sky gardens.

The proposal included further developments consisting of residential, office, retail, and public facilities including art, museum, library and auditorium space, aimed at reinforcing Seoul's cultural and historical heritage.

Below left: The strong axial scheme connects and integrates with the urban planning of Cheonggyecheong Stream's restoration to form a tightly woven community with rich cultural content.

Bottom: As part of Seoul's urban renewal, a masterplan was drawn up for the tourist areas along Cheonggyecheong Stream.

Below: Grand Cross showing how the cultural axis and water axis intersect in the masterplan.

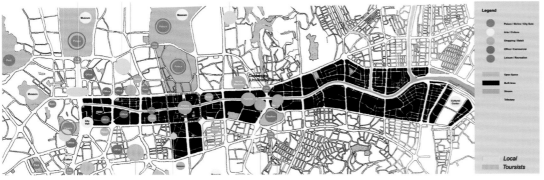

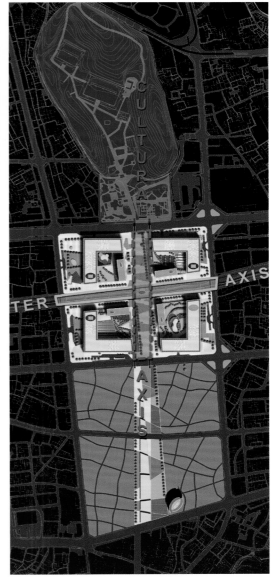

YONGIN DONGCHEON MASTERPLAN

Designed in collaboration with Samoo Architects this large-scale eco-city town masterplan is being instigated. Located 40km south of downtown Seoul and Incheon International Airport, Yongin is a serene retreat for city dwellers and vacationers needing a relaxing escape. In an area that has become popular for golfing and skiing resorts and events, the development provides eco-accommodation facilities. This 219,930m² masterplan was the winning design entry for a multi-residential complex that incorporates sustainability within an ecological parkland.

Framed naturally by the southern hills the site is accessed by an existing main road that connects to the nearby metropolis. Once there, visitors can meander along the eco-trail that flows through the development or dine beside the canalside; each creates a natural link between the different residential communities.

The heights of the buildings are arranged to complement the valley formation and allow for optimal views, creating greater openess. Villas in the woods are four-storey units with private gardens, using complementary natural elements of timber and stone; along the clifftop and canalside are high-rise, luxury apartments with roof top and sky gardens; the Landmark Towers act as gateways to create orientation and axis through the development.

Celebrating the outdoors, the masterplan promotes recreation and relaxation in the natural environment, embrassing eco-living by harnessing the area's assets.

Above: Masterplan concept sketches: (top row) landmarks, axis, community; (second row) topography, permeability, connectivity

Top: Masterplan sketch.

Right: Masterplan model, showing landscaping, canal, villas and Landmark Towers.

YONSEI SONGDO MISSION CENTRE

Located at the south-west corner of the new Yonsei University Campus, Farrells proposed Mission Centre connects people from the commercial and residential districts in the west and the cultural district to the east. South Korea has the largest Christian population in east Asia, with current statistics at 26% Christian, 23% Buddhist, 1% other and 50% non-religious.

One of the key concepts of the Mission Centre is that of the universe – its solid rectangular base represents the earth we stand on, with the light from the heavens above penetrating the ground below. A modern version of a cathedral space, the form of the building is deliberately designed as a simple box which symbolises Christianity as a modest and stoic religion. The grand atrium space sweeps to the top of the box in the shape of a crucifix. Like a canyon, it cuts a coherent vertical void that connects all spaces within the building volume. This incision opens up a north-south axis passage from the adjacent church to the Centre. The east-west incision relates directly to the green axis of the masterplan's landscaping, creating a visual and physical sensory experience.

The space-defining and screening functions of the internal walls were part of the development of the architectural concept of a layered series of walls. The Mission Centre's programmes require a flexibility of space so that walls open, tilt and close according to functional requirements.

The Mission Centre sits directly on a calm reflective pool of water, water having been closely associated in Christianity as a cleansing and self-exploring medium. Community members who arrive at the building on foot descend directly into the basement atrium space, embracing the sense of arrival both architecturally and spiritually.

Left: Perspective of a simple box form floating on a reflective pool.

Below: Concept sketch; masterplan of site showing Mission Centre in red; internal crucifix atrium.

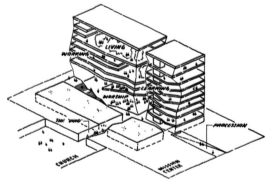

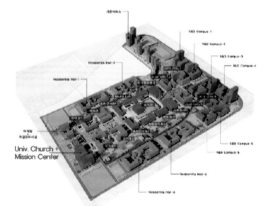

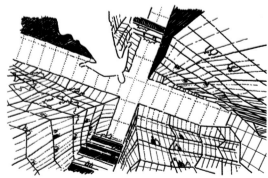

SEC DIGITAL MULTI-UNIVERSITY & PR CENTRE

In 2005, as the growth of the Suwon area engulfed the Samsung University Park complex and changed its environment from a suburban to an urban one in a short space of time, the pressure to redevelop and rethink the site was immense. By implementing this project the aim was to transform the urban fabric into an exciting and invigorating environment. The design of the masterplan had been developed to enhance the natural profile of the land form and promote the definition of space around the buildings and in a wider urban context.

Farrells and Samoo Architects were commissioned by Samsung to develop designs for a digital multi-university (DMU) and public relations centre (PRC), as part of a greater masterplan to transform the company's campus in Suwon from a manufacturing to a research-and-development-oriented environment.

The DMU is a dedicated facility for the education and training of company staff. The design seeks to offer an interactive environment and an immersive spatial experience, where social interaction is encouraged and cross-fertilisation of ideas and creativity can flourish. With more of an academic environment than the PRC, the DMU chiefly comprises an assembly of four portions. An auditorium, a central space, a dining area and a residential tower with other functional spaces are organised along the spine of an internal street that runs through the building. Two other principal elements are incorporated into the composition of the DMU: the Accommodation Tower and the Dining Pebble.

The public relations centre is a simple cube shape representing a 'magic box' that primarily displays large-scale digital images and is an exhibition building. The intention is to educate and stimulate visitors with various digital and media displays. The building uses technology to form a flexible and dynamic architecture, and is a blank canvas that will have the ability to evolve over time and be different things to different people.

The cube has seven storeys of exhibition space, divided into five components: the plinth, the sensory gardens, the digital valley, the galleries and the roof garden.

Bottom left: Sensory gardens lead up to the public relations centre.

Bottom: Images can be projected at large scale onto curved interior walls.

Below: Night view shows integrated digital images on the building's façade.

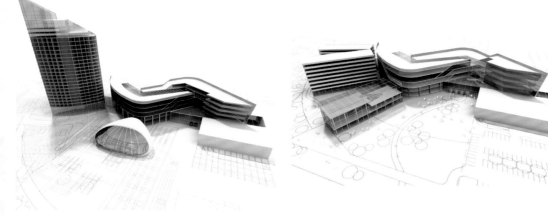

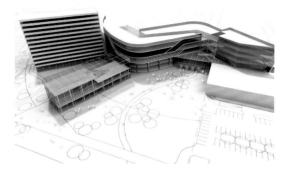

Top: The closest concept to the final scheme.

Above: Design concepts: a curved interlocking building with several low-rise blocks as 'fingers' branching off (right and middle), the Dining Pebble (shown left picture), as well as a single high-rise (left).

PHNOM PENH

MEKONG RIVER

VATTANAC
CAPITAL
TOWER

VATTANAC
GOLF RESORT

VIETNAM

GULF OF THAILAND

SOUTH CHINA SEA

PHNOM PENH

The capital of Cambodia, Phnom Penh is the country's pivotal commercial centre currently undergoing an economic revival in business and expansion. The turmoil of war over the past century has taken a heavy toll on its infrastructure and economy but today Cambodia is experiencing a resurgence in investment and development.

Founded in 1434, Phnom Penh first took shape in the 1870s when French colonialists contributed to the blueprint of the city. The city went through a regeneration during the 1950s-60s with the introduction of New Khmer Architecture, incorporating a modern vocabulary to Cambodia's culture, climate, and its vernacular and ancient architectural traditions. Today's Phnom Penh is a mix of traditional and new Khmer architecture, French Colonial and modern buildings.

Its current dense population of 2.25 million, over the city's 678.46km² area, creates an emergent need to establish new residential, commercial and recreational projects. The municipality of Phnom Penh in October 2002 began developing the masterplanning of the capital for 2020, assisted by the French Republic. In June 2011, the Phnom Penh government released the Capital Development Plan *Livre Blanc du Développement et de l'Aménagement de Phnom Penh*, a 330-page document on the characteristics of the city and a strategic masterplan for 2020.

The city streets are predominantly dense, low-rise structures designed to accomodate the tropical climate and monsoon season which can cause flooding from the river banks. New projects such as Vattanac Golf Resort and Bassac River development incorporate flood zone strategies into the overall masterplan and surrounding areas, to assist in excess water management.

Phnom Penh is built on soft foundations which necessitate expensive pilings for high-rise buildings. The first tall building, OCIC Tower, opened in 2010, the same year Vattanac Capital Tower started construction. The Tower will not only be the tallest building in Cambodia, it will also be the first LEED-certified construction. Designed as a centrepiece to modern Phnom Penh, it epitomises the progress and investment in the country.

Top left and centre: Phnom Penh is a city of diverse architecture, from French Colonial to traditional Khmer and modern blocks.

Top right: View of the marshland at the proposed Vattanac Golf Resort.

Bottom: View towards the Mekong River from central Phnom Penh.

VATTANAC CAPITAL TOWER

Cambodia's first high-rise utilises the extensive knowledge and experience of 'place-making' to create a visionary project and an internationally unique cultural presence for Phnom Penh. Designed as an iconic landmark with a strong Cambodian identity, Vattanac Capital Tower is bringing innovation to the city.

This 39-storey, 183.8m tower will be the tallest building in the city and positions the new Vattanac Capital headquarters solidly in the heart of an emerging new business and financial district. Situated on the busy Monivong Boulevard, a major north-south route through the capital and east-west via Praeh Mohaksat Treiyani Kossamak, the development is centrally placed with excellent transport connections.

As the country's economy continues to grow under the re-elected leadership of the Cambodian People's Party, this building is leading the way in setting the highest possible standards for design and construction.

Designed to incorporate a banking headquarters, trading floors, offices, high-end retail and luxury serviced apartments, it will be the first high-rise and international Grade-A, LEED-certified development in Cambodia. The iconic shape of the tower evokes images of a dragon's back — symbolising good luck and wealth. The southern elevation is recessed to allow a generous drop-off area immediately outside the bank and the high-end retail area where leading designer stores will be showcased under the expansive curve of the roof. The northern elevation

forms the reception for the luxury serviced apartments and high-end living options for executives.

The geometry of the tower is chamfered towards the east to allow occupants panoramic river views. As the building covers most of the site, the set-back allows for a small plaza area at its base. The tower will house VIP dining and entertainment areas, a cantilevered entertainment pod with a viewing deck and executive trading floors with views of the Tonle Sap and Mekong Rivers.

The curving west elevation of the tower symbolises the back of the great 'Dragon King'. According to ancient mythology Dragon Kings live in 'crystal palaces'. The towering glass façade of Vattanac Capital and banking hall will provide a suitable resting place.

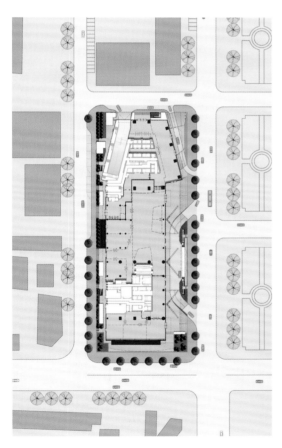

Above left: Ground floor plan in context.

Above right: Vattanac Capital Tower is centred in the heart of Phnom Penh.

The Retail Hall is located prominently at the heart of the podium on three levels, offering a unique shopping experience. The south elevation with its glazed façade and high ceilings maximises the visual connection between the shops and the landscaped green spine.

Designed as part of the floating low-rise structure that sits upon the podium, the high-efficiency office block was created for financial trading floors with maximum layout flexibility and an open floorplate that provides unobstructed views and abundant daylight. The rooms around the edge can be utilised as meeting rooms or data centres. Plant and air handling units have been located on the level below to maximise free space.

The cantilevered roof is designed to let light filter through the 'Dragon's Scales' or glass spandrels and underlying structure. Shading is provided under the roof structure to avoid overheating. The distinctive decorative screen on the elevations acts as a solar shade and takes reference from the carvings on ancient Khmer buildings.

The tower, hosting the bank headquarters and executive offices, stands to the east overlooking the stock exchange in the west; it utilises feng shui positioning so that the west loses money to the east.

Left: Detail cladding mock-up.

Top: Vattanac Capital Tower construction shot, July 2011.

Above: Retail area entrance level model study.

Opposite: Aerial perspective from Monivong Boulevard facing south-east towards the Mekong River.

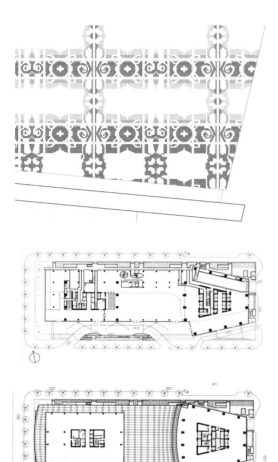

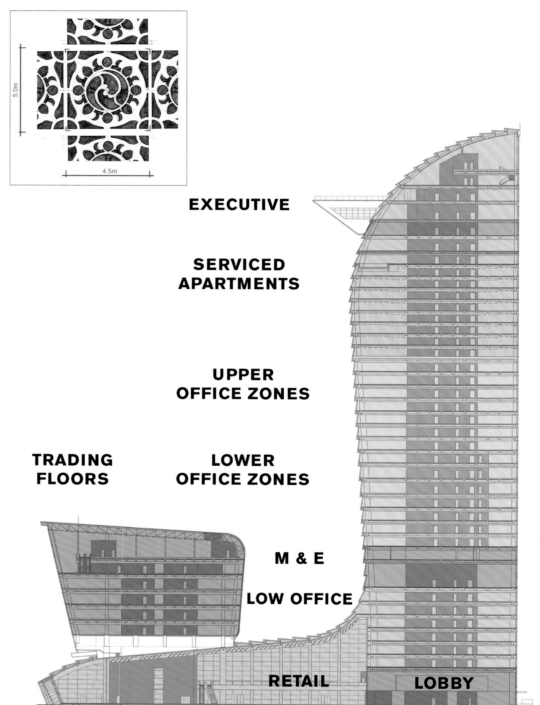

EXECUTIVE

SERVICED
APARTMENTS

UPPER
OFFICE ZONES

TRADING   LOWER
FLOORS   OFFICE ZONES

M & E

LOW OFFICE

RETAIL   LOBBY

5.0m

4.5m

0 1 5   20m   Section
   2   10   1 : 600

Right: Cross-section through
the main atrium, showing
function areas.

Top: Elevation and detail of
decorative screen.

Middle: Ground floor plan.

Bottom: Typical office
floor plan.

VATTANAC GOLF RESORT

Located in the Mekong River Delta between the Mekong and Bassac Rivers, the site is 12km south-east of the city of Phnom Penh. This 528-hectare masterplan presents a luxury residential community in conjunction with two 18-hole world-class golf courses.

The urban planning of the project is based on the Khmer tradition of 'hydraulic cities' settlements that are arranged on and around water. Neighbourhoods are created for the 1,580 villas located on islands within a framework of canals, parks and bicycle trails linking the communities. The golf courses are separated from the residential areas by an extensive canal network established across the site which provides a public ferry network and gives villas full waterfront access. The masterplan allows for an organic, incremental growth and flexible layout, around the public East Course and private West Course, which have been rigorously designed to championship-level standard by Nick Faldo Design.

Across the resort, buildings are a maximum of two-storey, including the 10,000m² clubhouse, a 25,000m² resort hotel designed in clusters of low-rise private bungalows, and a retail centre.

Four different types of villa are distributed across the resort, enriching the community with diversity. Set within courtyards and terraces, the one- or two-storey villa and condominium styles feature pavilions, infinity pools and private jettys. The design of the villas takes full-advantage of contemporary architectural ingenuity and embraces traditional Cambodian concepts.

This once barren site is set to become a sustainable community that will contribute to the local economy and create a luxurious destination for international and national visitors.

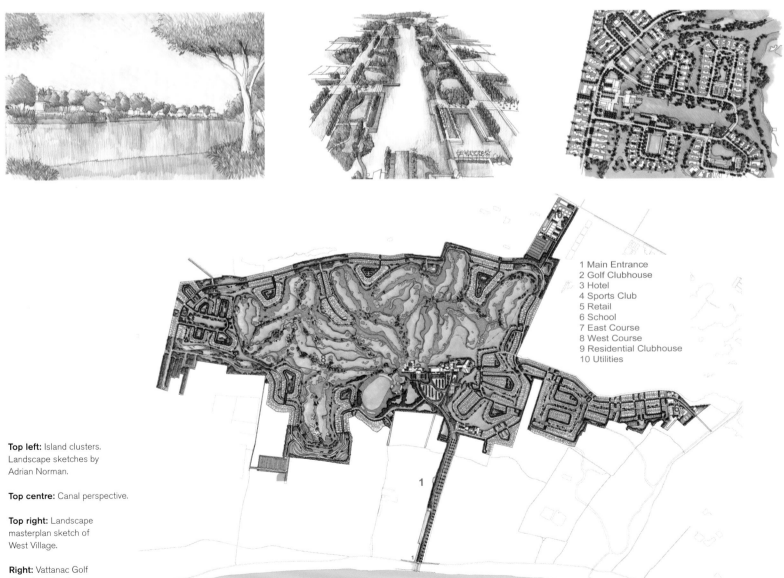

1 Main Entrance
2 Golf Clubhouse
3 Hotel
4 Sports Club
5 Retail
6 School
7 East Course
8 West Course
9 Residential Clubhouse
10 Utilities

Top left: Island clusters. Landscape sketches by Adrian Norman.

Top centre: Canal perspective.

Top right: Landscape masterplan sketch of West Village.

Right: Vattanac Golf Resort masterplan.

SINGAPORE

JOHOR STRAIT

MAIN STRAIT

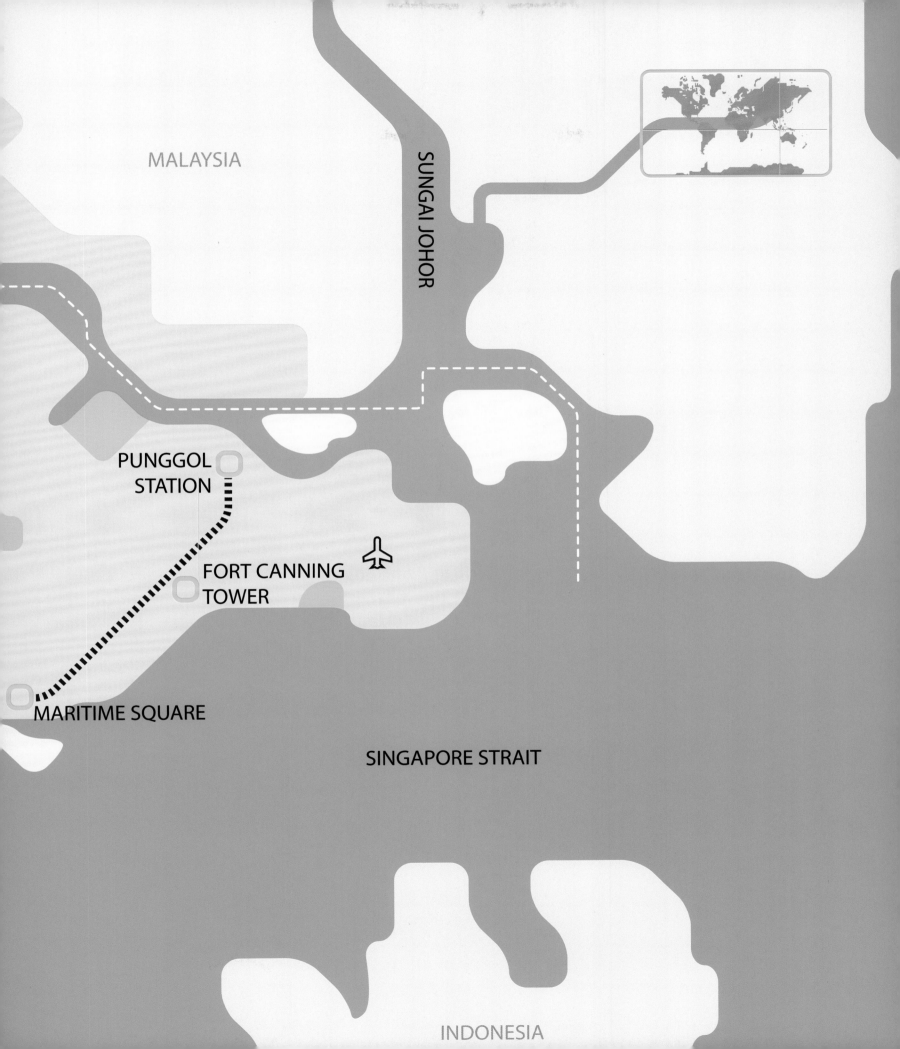

SINGAPORE

Singapore is a vibrant island off the tip of the Malay Peninsula. Covering a land area of 649km², it has a population of five million and a density of 7,315km². It consists of the main island and 63 smaller outlying islands, which in recent years have experienced additional reclamation to cojoin some islands.

The masterplan for Singapore was first formulated between 1952 and 1955 and has since undergone eight governmental reviews. In the current planning system, the Concept Plan maps out the long-term land use strategies for different planning areas and the masterplan translates the vision of the Concept Plan into detailed guidelines.

Singapore's Concept Plan is a strategic guide to meet anticipated population and economic growth, designed as an integrated approach and reviewed every 10 years, whereas the masterplan shapes Singapore's physical development in the medium term and is reviewed every five years.

The 1991 Concept Plan divided Singapore into five regions (north, north-east, east, central and west) and proposed the development of four new regional centres outside the central region to reduce congestion in the city centre. Priority was also given to the upgrading of the public transportation system, with new railway lines and stations connecting regional areas. The current Mass Rapid Transit (MRT) network consists of four main lines, covering a total of 138km in length, with 88 stations.

Punggol Town, located in the north-east region, was one of the new residential towns developed and built by this governmental plan. In 1996 the Land Transport Authority commissioned Punggol Station, a passenger interchange incorporating three of these rail networks. Under the Housing Development Board's Punggol 21 initiative, the creation of housing and transportation facilities in this area has made it a thriving community of over 60,000 people and one of the most sought-after residential areas in Singapore.

Farrells' first proposal in Singapore was for Maritime Square in 1995, followed by a design for the Fort Canning Radio Tower in 1999. More recently they have worked on design studies for the new Thomson Line, a mass transit rail network with 19 stations running from the northern part of the island to downtown Singapore.

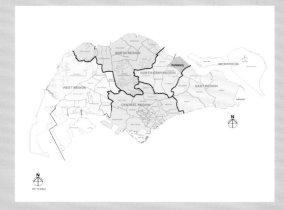

Top: Masterplan map of Singapore's five regional areas, with Punggol highlighted in green.

Centre: Proposal for Maritime Square.

Above: Fort Canning Radio Tower.

Left: Singapore's Central Area CBD and high-rises.

PUNGGOL STATION

Planned as a model housing estate for the 21st century, Punggol's transportation facilities were the first steps in creating a fully connected New Town away from the density of city life. Sitting dramatically in its surrounding landscape, the station serves as a spectacular gateway to Singapore's growing satellite city. This former sleepy fishing village has undergone a green makeover that has transformed it into Singapore's first 'eco-town'.

The Punggol interchange serves the Light Rapid Transit system (LRT) domestic line, the Mass Rapid Transit (MRT) and the North-East Line (NEL). This is a fully-automated, driverless rail system, running underground from Singapore's harbourfront to Punggol. The North Shore Line (NSL) tunnel box was also built below the station to incorporate future expansion links, including an express rail line to the Malay mainland.

A streamlined modern design with a curved aluminium and stainless-steel cladding, this 320m-long futuristic landmark is the longest station along the line and only one of two above-ground stations. Constructed over three levels with four entrances, the station has a split concourse, which sits directly above the platforms. Punggol's main road drives through the centre of the station

at ground level, providing a stunning singular gateway to the satellite city. This idea is visually reinforced when viewing the station from the north or south. As the vent shafts and cooling towers rise up and are contained within curved metallic enclosures, the LRT platform separates from the adjoining viaduct structure.

Pedestrian access to the station is located below the architectural facia, forming a continuous covered route around the concourse perimeter. The transport enclosure allows passengers to see directly into the concourse from any point on this route. The concourse ceiling is a continuation of the architectural facia unifying the inside and the outside of the station.

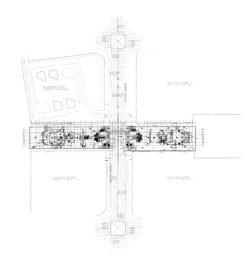

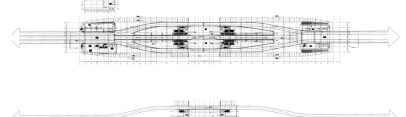

Above: Ground floor plan.

Left: Platform level plan.

Below left: Concourse level plan.

Below: Aerial perspective, early concept design.

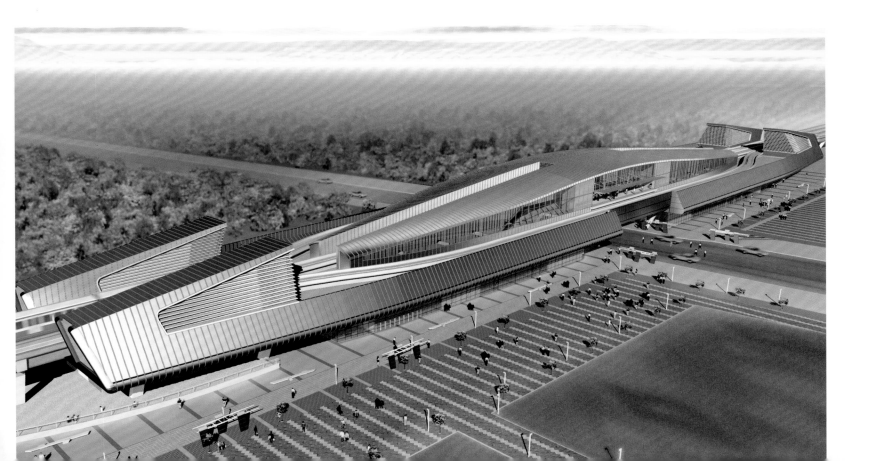

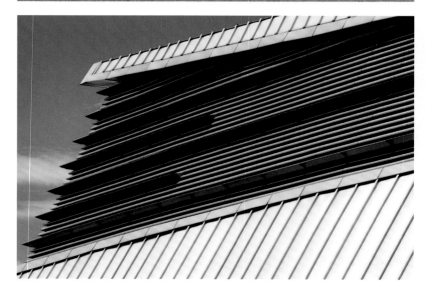

Left column: The streamlined modern design with curved aluminium and stainless steel.

Right column: The interiors are contemporary and incorporate artwork to enhance the passenger experience.

Opposite: The Punggol interchange links three different railway lines.

This page: The state-of-the-art Punggol Station sits dramatically in its surrounding landscape and is a spectacular gateway to Singapore's future satellite city – Punggol New Town.

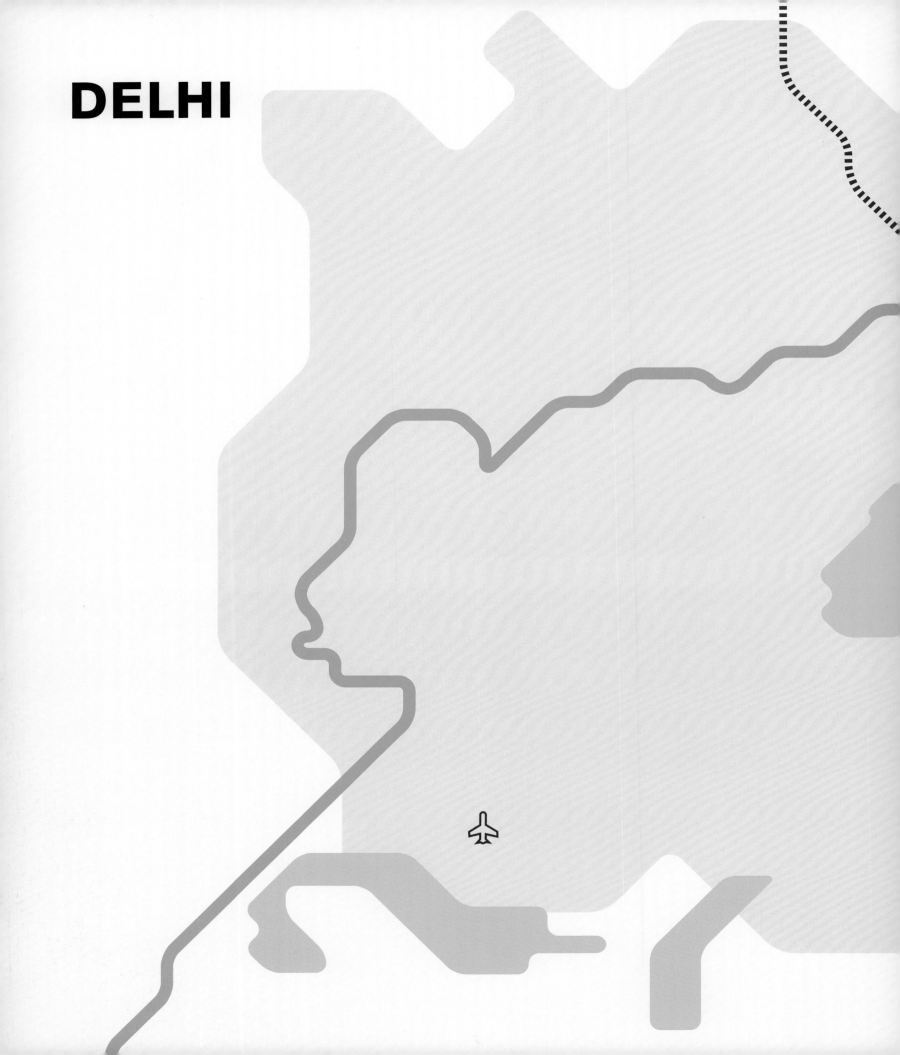

DELHI

NEW DELHI STATION

YAMUNA RIVER

DELHI

Located on the banks of the River Yamuna, Delhi has been continuously occupied for 3,000 years by an immense variety of cultures and religions. In the early 20th century Delhi became the capital of the British Empire, and Lutyens' famous capital city – New Delhi, with its monumental roundabouts and building complexes – was built as an addition rather than instead of what was already in existence. New Delhi became the capital of India upon independence in 1947.

The National Capital Territory of Delhi is the largest metropolis by area and the second-largest metropolis by population in India. It is the eighth largest metropolitan area in the world by population, with 16,753,235 inhabitants as of the 2011 Census. There are nearly 22.2 million residents in the greater Delhi urban area (which also includes Noida, Greater Noida, Ghaziabad, Gurgaon and Faridabad).

India has experienced enormous growth, requiring a more complex and modern transportation model that reflects its international status and the increasing demand for travel. The Indian rail network serves over 18 million people a day at 6,853 stations, on 63,974km of track. Rail travel is the country's arterial link and the importance of safe, well planned transportation infrastructures has dramatically increased.

As part of an invited team, Farrells produced a study on ways to improve and upgrade existing stations in Mumbai by assessing seven of the city's stations, to assist in relieving congestion, facilitate in-passenger and vehicular flow, and to provide faster inter-modal transfers. This in-depth study led to India's Ministry of Rail addressing the redevelopment of major rail stations.

The first station in the government's initiative was for the masterplan of New Delhi Station. As architects and technical consultants for this project, a comprehensive masterplan of the area and railway station was developed to transport New Delhi Station into a contemporary, sustainable and integrated infrastructure.

Above: Map of India showing Delhi and Mumbai.

Left, bottom left and right: Photographs of Delhi taken by Terry Farrell in the 1960s.

NEW DELHI STATION

Above: To get to other platforms passengers cross live tracks, New Delhi Station.

The second busiest station in India, New Delhi Railway Station is also a major railhead for the country's Northern Railways. Built in the 1950s to relieve pressure on Delhi Main Station, it initially comprised the station building and forecourt areas on the Paharganj side of the station that fronts Chelmsford Road. Over the past 60 years the station has outgrown itself in terms of facilities and accessibility. It currently handles a quarter of a million passengers per day; 245 trains including 78 suburban trains arrive/depart from its 16 platforms, plus the new airport express line metro that opened in June 2011. The existing infrastructure and utilities are over-extended and incapable of handling any expansion or regeneration. The intention is that a new multi-modal transport interchange will be created to service 272 trains and 500,000 passengers per day, with the potential for a peak capacity of 700,000 passengers per day.

New Delhi Station is the first station within the Ministry of Railways' World-class Station Programme, as identified in the government's 11th five-year plan for infrastructure improvement on India's railways. The design for a contemporary, landmark, New Delhi Railway Station will be the first of 26 stations in India to be redeveloped into benchmark, international-standard stations. The development covers 86

hectares in the very heart of Delhi. Its prominent location straddles the old walled city, the walled city's extension and the New Delhi masterplan by Edwin Lutyens to the south, and is only 2km from Connaught Place.

The masterplan and design for a first-rate transportation hub accommodates the projected growth of Delhi, reconnects the neighbourhoods and incorporates sustainability ideas and functions to reduce waste and lower utility costs and usage. The scheme is a vision of modern efficiency. Along with improved passenger services and train operation and maintenance facilities, it links the east and west of the city, which the old station had effectively divided. It illustrates how Old Delhi can be regenerated with minimal intervention and establishes an urban focal point in the north. It also follows the Hong Kong model of associated property development whereby real estate is used as a generator of funds for the railway.

It embodies the philosophy of place-making: that of uniting old and new, finding ways to reconnect and rejuvenate a city and providing opportunities for development potential in the air-rights above and the land around a station to generate revenue and revive public interest in the area.

The design approach focuses on the retention of the urban historical development. The masterplan

acknowledges the diverse areas around its perimeter by providing a series of nodes along its length. These nodes respond to the existing areas which they bound onto. One of the most pleasant aspects of New Delhi is its lush greenery; this is in sharp contrast to the narrow and congested alleys of the walled city and its extension. The masterplan creates a great urban park at the heart of Delhi to sensitively integrate the organic unplanned areas of the walled city and its extension. A series of parks, gardens and open urban plazas, which form a green lung reaching the entire length of the site, extend the green of the Lutyens' masterplan further north to provide a link to the fertile forest and parkland at Kamlu Nehru Ridge.

One of the main design solutions of the masterplan was to carefully plan a clear and convenient road traffic circulation network, taking into consideration city-wide connectivity and future projections to service this major transportation hub and neighbourhood. The masterplan is made up of three main components: commercial, operational, and community, and is intended to carefully integrate these areas through new connections and facilities, turning the site from a 'void' that divides these areas into a new integrated heart. This project is a unique opportunity to unify the historic centres of one of the world's great cities and maximise its potential.

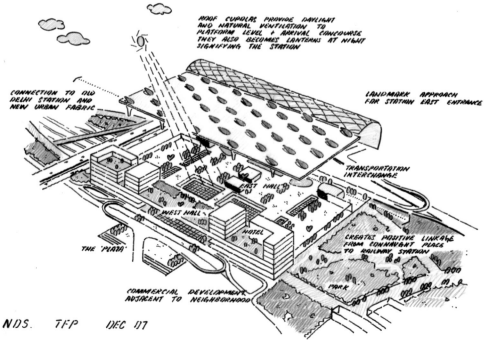

ROOF CUPOLAS PROVIDE DAYLIGHT AND NATURAL VENTILATION TO PLATFORM LEVEL + ARRIVAL CONCOURSE THEY ALSO BECOMES LANTERNS AT NIGHT SIGNIFYING THE STATION

CONNECTION TO OLD DELHI STATION AND NEW URBAN FABRIC

LANDMARK APPROACH FOR STATION EAST ENTRANCE

TRANSPORTATION INTERCHANGE

EAST HALL

WEST HALL

HOTEL

THE 'PLAZA'

CREATES POSITIVE LINKAGE FROM CONNAUGHT PLACE TO RAILWAY STATION

COMMERCIAL DEVELOPMENT ADJACENT TO NEIGHBORHOOD

PARK

NDS. TFP DEC 07

Above: Striking funnel-like columns diffuse the natural light.

Left: Exploded sketch illustrating how halls and landscaping are all under one roof.

Opposite top: Aerial perspective of New Delhi Station at night, showing the peacock-inspired roof.

Opposite bottom: Long section.

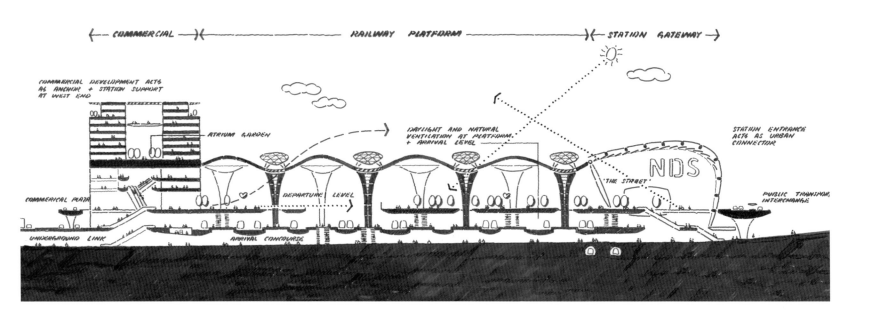

The segregation of arriving and departing passengers is the primary circulation principle. This dictates the planning within the station as well as outside in order to handle station-related traffic with optimum efficiency. Pedestrian routes are clearly segregated from streets to ensure seamless movements to and from the station.

The overall station design will incorporate sustainable technology to achieve optimum comfort levels whilst using minimal energy and relatively low cooling loads to reduce energy consumption and costs. The design of the roof and its large conical funnels serve a dual environmental purpose: ventilating and providing natural daylight to the platforms as well as being the primary support for the roof. The funnels allow light to penetrate vertically, deep into the building volume. The undulating roof form assists rainwater collection as well as promoting air movement across its surface.

The station design utilises the natural climate and facilitates ventilation by contouring the roof and its support columns to scoop the flow of air, working on the principle of suction and stack effect that allows hot air from higher levels to leave the building. To enhance this passive climate control a relatively high sectional building volume is necessary to allow the heat to rise above the personal comfort level, which increases air-flow and creates a natural buffer to keep cooler air on the lower inhabited levels. At the same time cooler air will stream from shaded areas creating a cool ambient environment with temperatures below that of outdoors. External shading to the station roof is provided by solar panels that will simultaneously generate energy whilst contributing to a cooler building envelope.

The structural steel construction combined with glazing and openings along the station's vertical elevation creates an image of columns of light holding up the roof. Effectively the natural lighting, via the hollow columns, follows the old principle of a heliostat, which offers a cheap and efficient means of providing lighting to either horizontally or vertically deep buildings. At night these columns will come alive with artificial light.

The station will become a significant landmark, representing contemporary India and embracing both historic and modern Indian culture. Its iconic architectural expression reflects its position as one of the world's largest and most progressive stations.

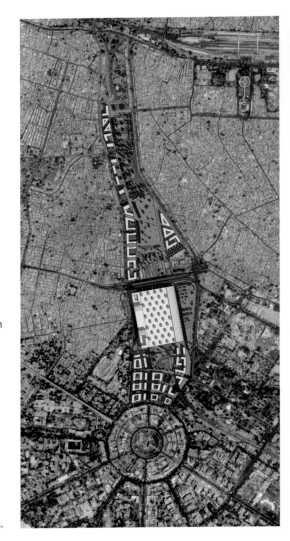

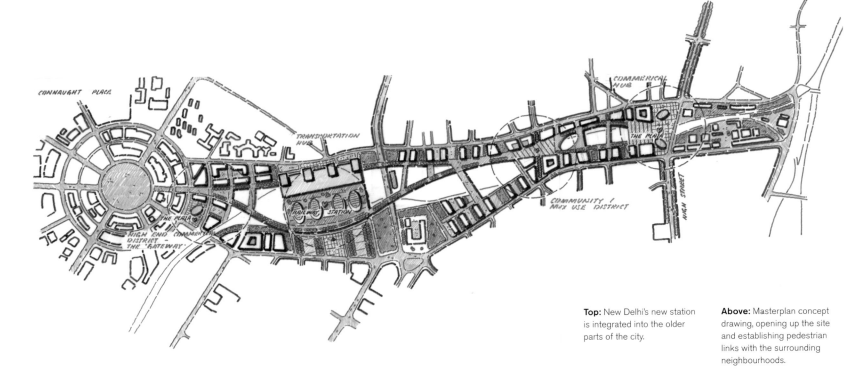

Top: New Delhi's new station is integrated into the older parts of the city.

Above: Masterplan concept drawing, opening up the site and establishing pedestrian links with the surrounding neighbourhoods.

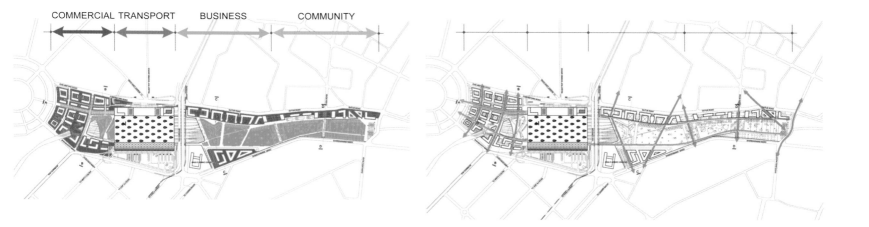

Top left: Plan showing green spaces.

Top right: Plan showing connectivity.

Middle left: Drawing of 'tree structure' detail.

Middle right: Environmental structure integrated system.

Bottom right: Photovoltaic panel roof sketch.

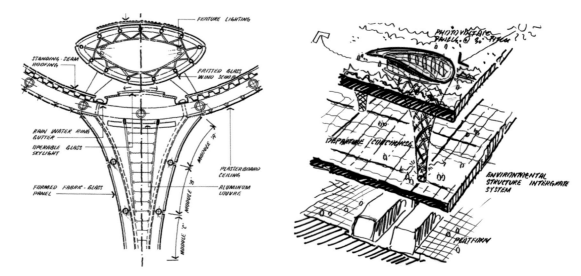

Above: Figure ground diagram of the existing site shows the relationship between buildings and the urban fabric.

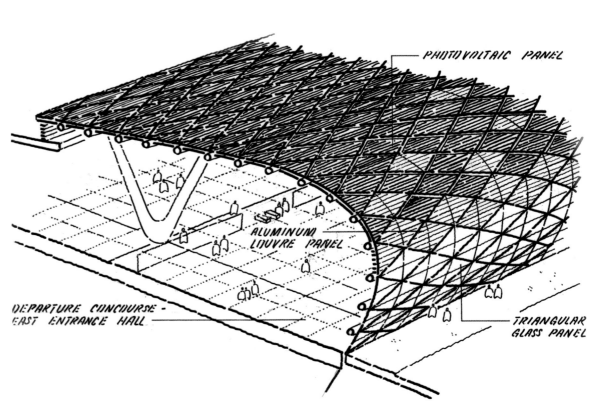

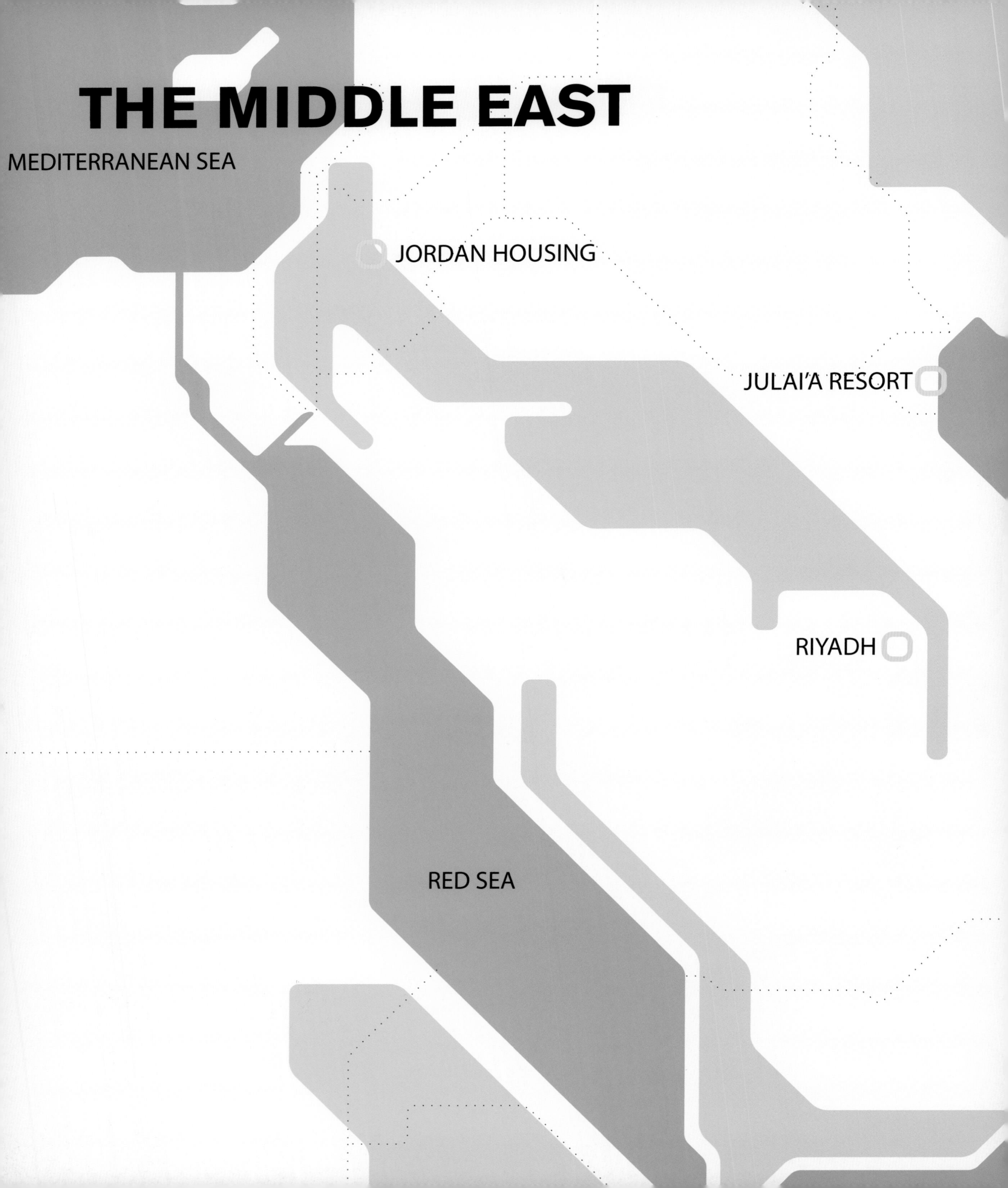

THE MIDDLE EAST

MEDITERRANEAN SEA

JORDAN HOUSING

JULAI'A RESORT

RIYADH

RED SEA

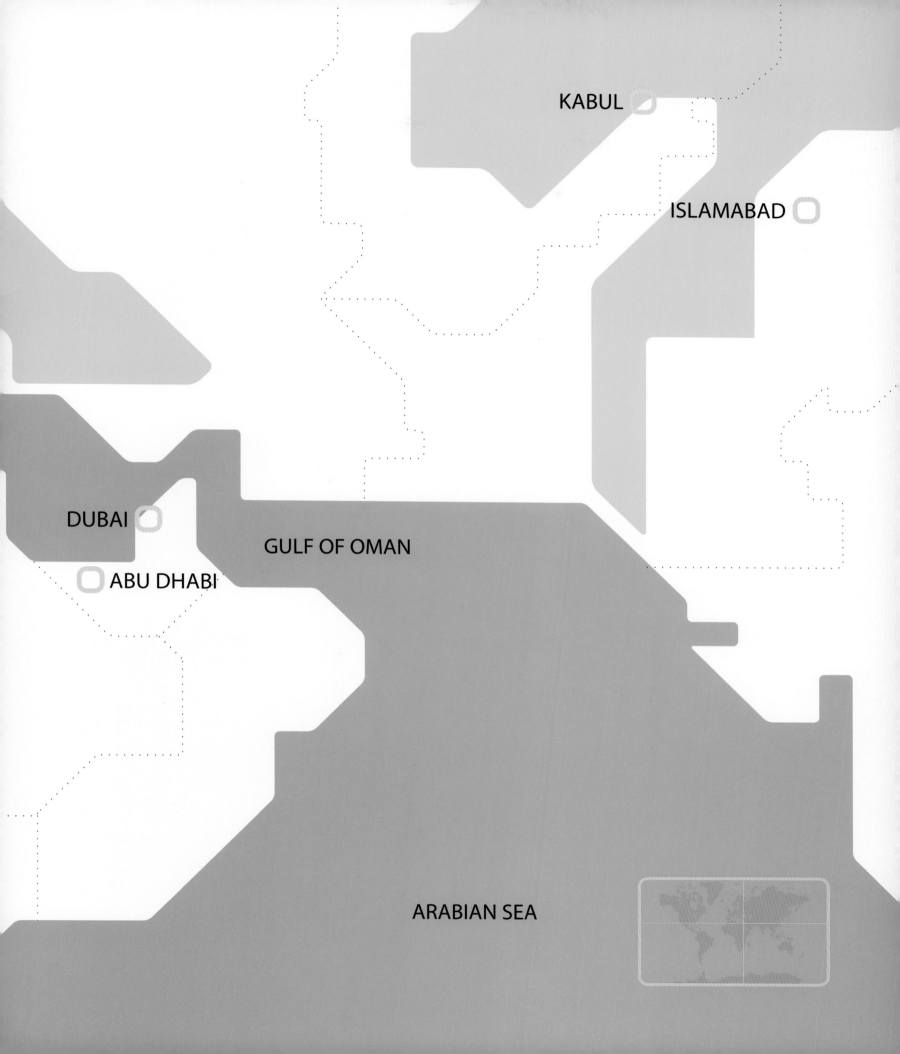

THE MIDDLE EAST

Farrells' work in the Middle East began in 1999 with success in an international competition to design a centre for Culture and Heritage in Dubai. The private founder of the centre wished to provide an inspiring environment for the collection of the heritage of the Islamic and Arab world. The basic concept derived from the symbolic associations and duality of the centre's two main components – the cultural centre and library – arranged about a central axis which organised pedestrian access from the north and service access from the south. Each element is balanced about this axis and is given its own expression. Although the founder chose not to proceed with construction, this project provided a very educational and interesting introduction to the region.

Julai'a Resort was the next project, commencing in 2005. The masterplan for this five-star hotel offers a new type of resort for Kuwait. Lying on a 480-metre stretch of prime Arabian Gulf beachfront, the comprehensive leisure development is like a mini-town within a resort, offering everything from luxurious hotel and villa accommodation to restaurants, shops, cinemas, sports, spa and leisure facilities.

In the same year, 2005, Farrells were commissioned to provide a masterplan for Park Square in Dubai, the proposed future home of the metro's Park Square Station.

Left: Axial view towards the library across courtyard of the Cultural Centre, and aerial view of the complete project.

Top: Competition model for the Centre for Culture and Heritage in Dubai.

Above: Julai'a Resort, a comprehensive leisure development masterplanned like a mini-town.

The following year Farrells were engaged to design a new mixed-use development on two adjacent sites in Business Bay, Dubai. The 20-storey development includes an office tower, retail, a 250-key, five-star business hotel and 100 serviced apartments. Local contemporary art is a strong feature of the architecture and interior design.

Saadiyat Island, Abu Dhabi, will house many museums and galleries in the Cultural District of this major new development. Experience gained in other countries and projects led to Farrells being commissioned to design the many ancillary buildings required to house the mechanical, electrical and ventilation equipment needed to maintain the correct environments in the museums and galleries and the internationally important collections they hold.

In Jordan, Farrells have designed a new urban area at Al Jeeza. The site is 30km south-west of Amman. The site area is a 4 million m² zone of vacant desert with very little existing infrastructure; 35,000 units are planned for some 200,000 inhabitants. Farrells have also provided masterplans and designs for housing developments in Riyadh, Saudi Arabia and also Islamabad, Pakistan and Kabul, Afghanistan.

Top: Local contemporary art inspired the response for the mixed-use development at Business Bay, Dubai.

Above left: Family housing for white-collar workers in Riyadh's industrial city.

Above right: Park Square masterplan, a mixed-use proposal in the heart of Dubai.

JORDAN HOUSING

Set within the metropolitan city of Amman, 30km south of the city centre, the concept masterplan proposed a new satellite city. Amman, the capital, is the largest city in Jordan, and one of the oldest continuously inhabited cities in the world.

The brief required a mix of affordable apartments, mid-price apartments and villas; the city would also need to house commercial buildings and public facilities including the creation of a new metropolitan landscape. The site area measured 4 million m² and consisted of desert with very little existing infrastructure; 35,000 units were proposed for some 200,000 inhabitants.

An important element was to connect the existing metropolitan highway to a new rural highway. This ensured the area would become a destination as well as enhancing key connections into central Amman. East-west and north-south road connections allowed accessible circulation for transport links. This had the added benefit of removing most vehicle traffic from the proposed residential areas.

The Concept Masterplan was based on the three key principles of infrastructure, grid and green routes, with the inclusion of green spaces key to the growth

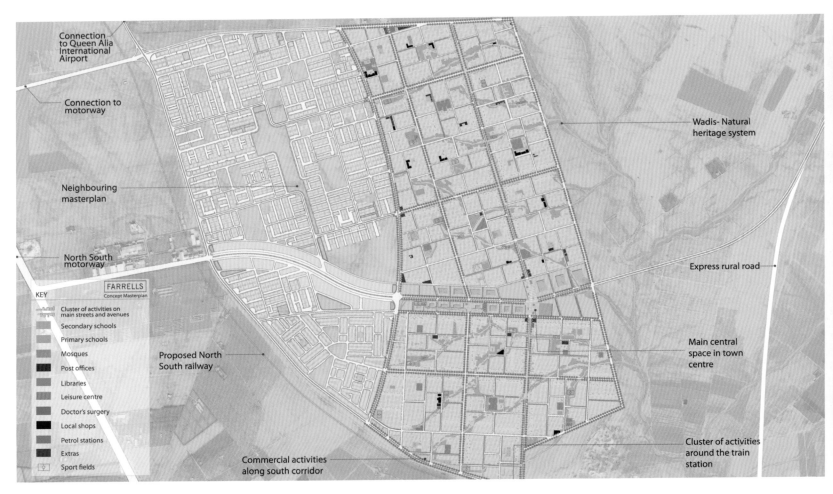

Connection to Queen Alia International Airport

Connection to motorway

Neighbouring masterplan

North South motorway

KEY

FARRELLS
Concept Masterplan

Cluster of activities on main streets and avenues
Secondary schools
Primary schools
Mosques
Post offices
Libraries
Leisure centre
Doctor's surgery
Local shops
Petrol stations
Extras
Sport fields

Proposed North South railway

Commercial activities along south corridor

Wadis- Natural heritage system

Express rural road

Main central space in town centre

Cluster of activities around the train station

Above: The proposed masterplan sought to integrate with neighbouring proposals but also responded to the subtleties of landscape and the organic Wadis network.

Right: Metropolitan corridor.

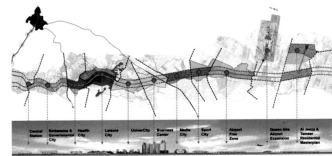

of the city. Working with the topography and the natural patterns of the site, defined by water courses, agricultural practices and ancient routes, a series of grids were used as a planning device. This allowed for the phased development of neighbourhoods containing their own amenities. While planning a grid, Farrells observed that the geometry in the grid had similarities with Islamic art and the basic foundations of Islamic patterns were incorporated in the masterplan.

An important factor in the initial design was that the scheme and its developments would be in harmony with the existing land and its challenging climate. Water preservation was essential along with grey water recycling to sustain the new green spaces.

Top: Typical section through the building.

Above: Aerial perspective of the proposed settlement with its central business, retail and leisure zone and neighbourhood facilities.

Right: The Amman plan produced by the Amman municipal authority shows the proposed growth of the city over the next 16 years. The Al Jeeza site is highlighted in red.

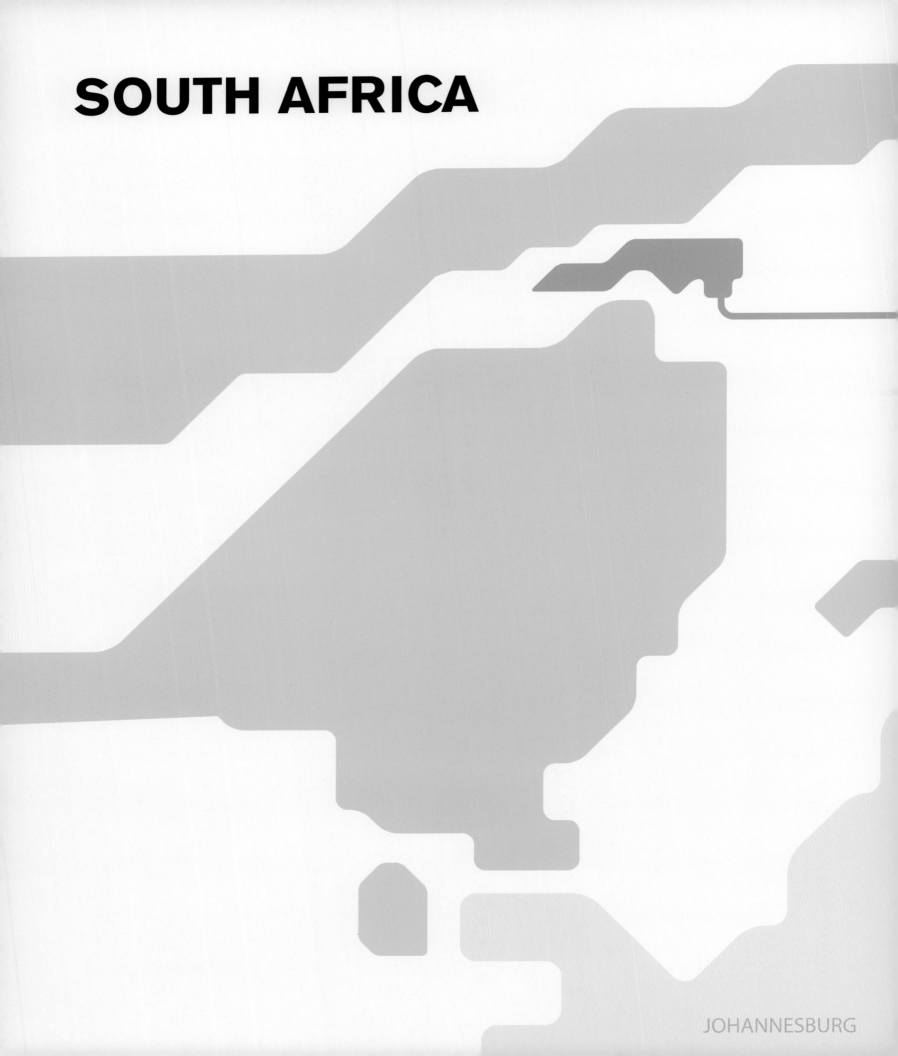

SOUTH AFRICA

JOHANNESBURG

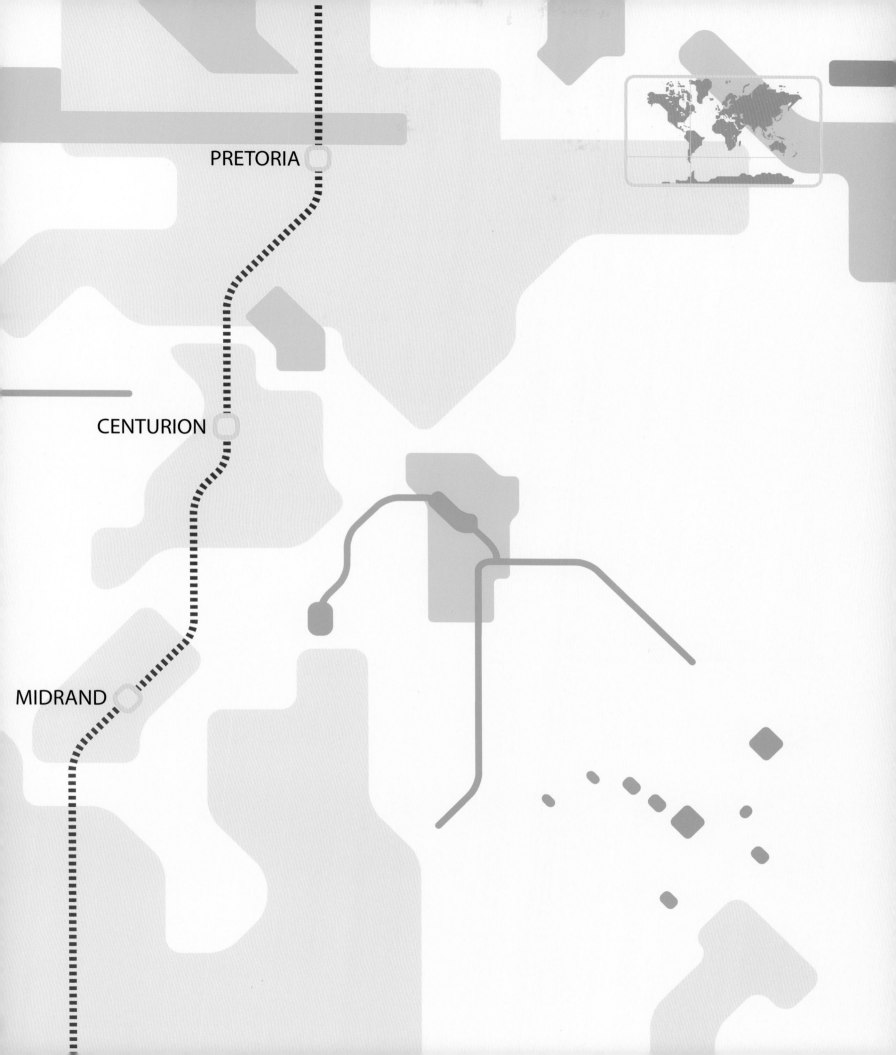

PRETORIA

CENTURION

MIDRAND

SOUTH AFRICA

Sitting at the base of Africa, South Africa is unique in the continent due to its climatic, ethnic and socio-economic diversity. In recent centuries, waves of migrants from central Africa, Europe and Asia displaced the indigenous peoples and led to a diverse ethnic mix. Initially its global importance lay in it being a refueling port for ships sailing between Europe and Asia, but the discovery of vast reserves of gold and diamonds in the country's interior in the late 19th century changed the country dramatically. The desire for these resources provided the context for over a century of fierce internal conflict and political isolation.

With the creation of a progressive constitutional democracy, South Africa has emerged as a primary beacon of political, social and economic assertiveness on the African continent. The FIFA World Cup in 2010 successfully showed South

Africa's ability to modernise and attract investment from overseas. One of the country's challenges is to provide strategic urban infrastructure that meets the burdening demands of population growth whilst containing urban sprawl. To this end, public and private stakeholders hope to stimulate sustainable economic growth and create better conditions for efficient, modern and liveable cities.

The Gautrain project is an initiative to implement a modern mass-transit railway network in the country's largest metropolitan area. The state-of-the-art infrastructure is the first of its kind in Africa and will replace an outdated railway system. Linking Johannesburg, the continent's primary financial and business hub, with Pretoria, the nation's political capital 80km to the north, the line is set to relieve the extreme road traffic congestion between these cities. There is also

a connection to OR Tambo International Airport, ensuring that the network serves as a backbone for the Gauteng megalopolis, integrating rail with bus, air and other modes of safe public transport.

Commissioned by the largest public-private venture in Africa, Farrells designed three successive stations along the northern part of the spur line: Midrand, Centurion and Pretoria. All three were sited in different urban contexts and provided different challenges. A system-wide architectural concept was inspired by the umbrella-like canopy of the acacia tree. The stations, held up by tree-like structures that cover its platforms, are open at the sides to provide natural ventilation. The tree has strong reference in African culture, serving as a place for meeting, relaxing and trading. These stations and this portion of the Gautrain Spur Line were opened in July 2011.

Left: Gautrain Spur Line - Launch Edition ticket 2010.

Below: Aerial view of Johannesburg and its railway station.

Opposite page:
Top left: Map showing the route of the Gautrain Spur Line.

Top right: Centurion Station, vertical circulation from the concourse level to platform level.

Bottom left: Alexandra Township in Johannesburg.

Bottom right: Aerial view of Johannesburg and its station.

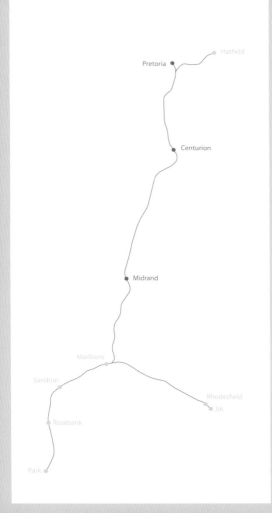

Platform B

MIDRAND STATION

An at-grade station constructed on a greenfield site, Midrand will gradually be encompassed by a new high-density mixed-use development. The site's framework has been designed to consolidate the station by linking the old and new areas through the extension of the Business District. Positioned midway between Johannesburg (the economic hub of Africa) and Pretoria (the capital of South Africa), the new connection will stimulate future growth and development in this area. The station is expected to attract 44,500 commuters daily by 2017.

Located adjacent to the primary through-route of the Pretoria–Johannesburg Road (K101) east of the Midrand central area and next to the Grand Central Airport, the station sits on the site of the proposed Zonk' Izizwe (all nations) new town development that will have shopping, entertainment, office and residential developments and is envisaged to be one of the largest development nodes in South Africa. This rapidly growing residential and business development area will benefit from the improved accessibility of the area provided by Gautrain.

Typical of suburban stations, Midrand has a simple ground-level concourse and two side platforms, one of which is accessed through the concourse and the other via an underpass running beneath the track. The organisation of the station's layout and facilities, signage and open sight lines ensure that passengers can easily and effortlessly find their way around. The station is 175m in length and 20m wide, with a floor area of 6,755m^2.

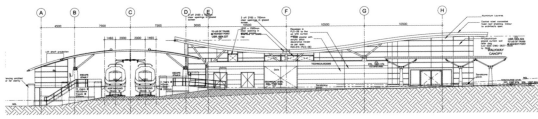

Top left: Gautrain at platform, July 2011.

Top right: Aerial view of station, October 2011.

Bottom left: Midrand Station from street level.

Bottom right: Cross-section. The station's design helps

compensate for the difference in level between the two sides of the track.

CENTURION STATION

Centurion Station is located in an area of 349,000 inhabitants, in Gauteng Province between Midrand and Pretoria. It was formerly an independent municipality, with its own town council, and it is now part of the new city of Tshwane Metropolitan Municipality.

Since 1995, it has welcomed rapid growth in economy and trade networks, bolstered by its close proximity to Pretoria. Property development has escalated, and with the influx of commuters the need for a fast, reliable transport connection

had become imperative. The station also offers one of the most extensive local bus feeder services on the line, as well as park-and-ride facilities for 1,800 cars.

Similar in scale to Midrand, the 6,099m² Centurion Station is the next stop on the Spur Line and the focal point of the town's Central Business District; it is designed for a projected hourly passenger flow of 4,530 people. The station also neighbours proposed new developments: an international Convention Centre, a five-star

hotel, a luxury lakefront lifestyle complex and a sports park.

The station is in the middle of one of the longest viaducts as it is built above unstable dolomitic rock. The railway line over this portion of the network is an elevated viaduct independent of localised ground conditions. The entrance to its concourse is at ground level, with the station platforms above.

Above: Entrance to the station.

Left: Aerial view of Centurion Station.

Middle: Elevation.

Bottom: Cross-sections.

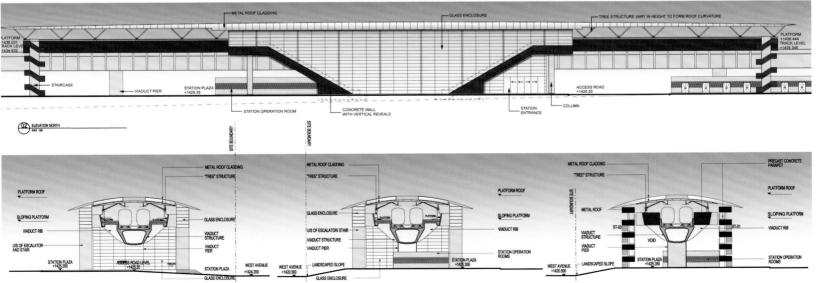

PRETORIA STATION

The capital city of South Africa, Pretoria is nestled in a sheltered, green valley in the Tshwane municipality. The area has been continuously inhabited by humans for several thousand years, but the city as it is today was established in 1855 by European settlers. The original Pretoria station was designed by British architect Sir Herbert Baker in 1910, terminating the southern axis from the city's historical centre – Church Square. The historical station is home to the luxury Blue Train, as well as various metro and intercity rail links. The new Gautrain lines lie directly adjacent to these.

One of the main anchor stations of the Gautrain Spur Line, Pretoria Station provides access to and from the Central Business District of Tshwane. With an anticipated daily passenger turnover of 55,000, the station offers multi-modal transport interchanges into the city and its surrounds. The station precinct is set to stimulate urban renewal and development in the inner city, catalysing growth in the area and also playing a valuable role in accessibility to the city's tourist attractions.

The challenge was how to sensitively integrate the new station into the existing and historical urban fabric. The station is discreetly tucked behind Baker's building between the original covered platform and the old washing shed – a unique structure in that it is constructed from modified railway tracks. Architecturally the new station unites all three structures into a cohesive whole. It is a light and airy modern reinterpretation of the shed, with a gently curving roof canopy above glazed curtain walling and a projecting overhang above the entrance. Contemporary and yet sensitive in scale and position to the prominence of Baker's building, the station opens into a new public plaza beside the old building's

Opposite page, top: Aerial photograph of Pretoria station (September 2010), with the watershed directly behind and the existing Herbert Baker station building (bottom right).

Top right: Detail of Pretoria Station canopy.

Bottom right: Entrance to Pretoria Station, May 2011.

Opposite page, bottom left: Gautrain at platform, March 2011.

Opposite page, bottom right: Front elevation of the station, May 2011.

PROJECT LIST: HONG KONG, 2001–2011

1992–2002: Kowloon Station Development, Hong Kong

1996–2004: Kowloon Station Landmark Tower Study, Hong Kong

1996–2002: Incheon Ground Transportation Centre, Seoul, South Korea

1996–2002: Punggol Station, Singapore

1997–2003: West Rail TS 300 Tsuen Wan West Development, Hong Kong

1997–2001: Shangdong International Conference and Exhibition Centre, Qingdao, China

1997–2003: DD300 Tsuen Wan West Station, Hong Kong

1998–2002: Guangzhou Daily Cultural Plaza, Guangzhou, China

2002–2004: Walton Plaza, Shanghai, China

2003–2005: Noble Tower, Shenzhen, China

2000: Daily News Swires, Guangzhou, China

2001: Shekou Logistic Centre, Shekou, China

2001–2006: Kowloon Southern Link, Hong Kong

2001: Lido Hill, Guangzhou, China

2002–2004: Mount Davis Villa, Hong Kong

2002–2003: Linyi Riverfront, Shangdong, China

2002–2004: Bailian Villas, Beijing, China

2002–2005: Mumbai Urban Transport Project, Mumbai, India

2002–2003: Wuxi Life Science Park, Wuxi, China

2003–2005: The Richardson Hotel, Perth, Australia

2003–2008: Beijing South Station, Beijing, China

2003–2010: Guangzhou South Railway Station, Guangzhou, China

2003–2004: Chilgok Campus of Yeungjin College, Daegu, South Korea

2003–2004: Chong Ming Island, Shanghai, China

2003–2004: SDC-600 Causeway Bay Station, Hong Kong

2003–2005: Yangpu University Avenue, Shanghai, China

2003: National Library of China, Beijing, China

2003: Shanghai Garden Hotel, Shanghai, China

2004–2008: China National Petroleum Headquarters, Beijing, China

2004: Sewoon Urban Redevelopment, Seoul, South Korea

2004–2009: BEA Financial Tower, Shanghai, China

2004–2007: Dameisha Resort and Hotel, Shenzhen, China

2004: Pudong International Airport (Phase Two), Shanghai

2004: Zhong Hai Plaza, Beijing, China

2004: Yangzhou International Leisure and Wellness Resort, China

2004–2005: Bao'An Masterplan, Shenzhen, China

2004–2005: SEC PR Centre and Digital Multi-University, South Korea

2004–2008: Gwacheon National Science Museum, Seoul, South Korea

2004: Shiji Avenue Lot 2–4, Shanghai, China

2004: Tongzhou Garden, Beijing, China

2004–2005: Suzhou Jingi Lake 'Island B', Suzhou, China

2004–2011: KK100 Tower and Development, Shenzhen, China

2004: Nanjing Road East, Shanghai, China

2005–2006: Dubai Park Square, Dubai, UAE

2005–2006: Mid-Levels Residential Tower, Hong Kong

2005: Yongin Dongcheon Masterplan, South Korea

2005: Changsha Tower, Hangzhou, China

2005: Hong Qiao Station, Shanghai

2005: Beijing National Art Gallery, Beijing, China

2005–ongoing: Le Papillon, Guangzhou, China

2005: Julai'a Resort and Hotel, Kuwait, UAE

2005: Samsung University Park, Seoul, South Korea

2005: Samsung Public Relations Centre, Seoul, South Korea

2006: Nanshan Business and Cultural District, Shenzhen

2006: Leatop Plaza, Guangzhou

2006–ongoing: Tamani Arts Office and Hotel, Dubai, UAE

2006: Huawei Science Park, Beijing, China

2006–2007: Tianjin Kerry Centre, Tianjin, China

2006–ongoing: Mount Kellett Villas, Hong Kong

2006–2011: Midrand Station, South Africa

2006–2011: Centurion Station, South Africa

2006–2011: Pretoria Station, Pretoria, South Africa

2006–ongoing: Express Rail Line (XRL), Hong Kong

2006–ongoing: Changsha Chun Hua New Town, Changsha, China

2006: Huizhou Exhibition Centre, China

2007–2009: New Delhi Station, Delhi, India

2007–2008: TCL Tower, Shekou, China

2007–2008: Jeddah KAEC Masterplan, Jeddah, Saudi Arabia

2007–2008: Jeddah Tamani Hotel, Jeddah, Saudi Arabia

2007–ongoing: Vattanac Capital Tower, Phnom Penh, Cambodia

2008–ongoing: Ningbo Eastern New Town, Shanghai

2008–2011: Saadiyat Island, Abu Dhabi, UAE

2008–2011: TCL High Tech Industrial Park (Phase One), Shenzhen

2008–ongoing: Sheung Wan and Kennedy Town MTR Stations, Hong Kong

2008: Bassac River Masterplan, Phnom Penh, Cambodia

2008–2011: Kennedy Town Swimming Pool (Phase One), Hong Kong

2009: Wuxi TV Tower, Wuxi, China

2009–ongoing: West Kowloon Cultural District, Hong Kong

2009: Hong Qiao CBD Masterplan, Shanghai

2009: Financial Street, Beijing, China

2009: Hauxia Masterplan, Shanghai

2008: Yonsei Songdo Mission Centre, South Korea

2010–ongoing: SCL – SWT and LOM Stations, Hong Kong

2010–ongoing: Lion Rock Tunnel to Diamond Hill, Hong Kong

2010–ongoing: Vattanac Golf Resort, Phnom Penh, Cambodia

2010: Datong Art Museum, Beijing, China

2010–ongoing: TCL Masterplan, Er Hai, Yunnan, Dali, China

2010–ongoing: Shangri-la Mixed-use Development, Ulaanbaatar, Mongolia

2010–2011: Olympic Cultural District Masterplan, Beijing, China

2010–ongoing: Kaiter Plaza, Beijing, China

2011–ongoing: The Springs, Shanghai, China

2011–ongoing: Z15 Tower, Beijing, China

2011–ongoing: Chaoyang CBD Masterplan, Beijing, China

2011–ongoing: Shougang Steelworks Masterplan, Beijing, China

2011–ongoing: Shijiazhuang Masterplan, Beijing, China

2011–ongoing: Central Market Development, Hong Kong

2011–ongoing: Hong Kong Macau Bridge, Hong Kong

Right: Detail of roof and main drop-off, Beijing South Station.

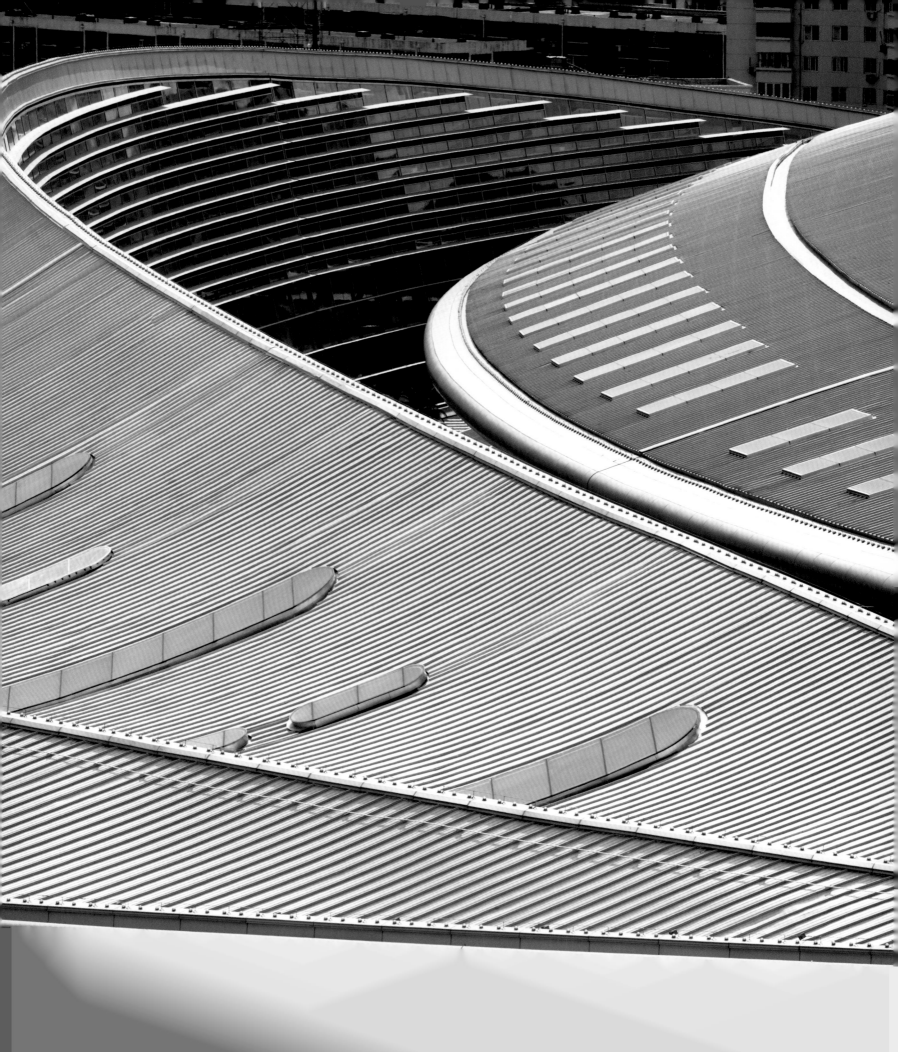

PROJECT LIST: LONDON, 2001–2011

1996–2005: Paddington Basin Masterplan, London
1997–2000: Pacific Northwest Aquarium, Seattle
1997–ongoing: Lots Road Power Station, London
1998–2005: Home Office Headquarters, London
1998–2002: Business Centre, Hull
1998–2002: The Deep Aquarium, Hull
1999–2008: The Royal Institution of Great Britain, London
2000: Margate Waterfront Masterplan, Margate
2000: Manchester Southern Gateway, Manchester
2000–2003: Preston Town Centre, Preston
2000–2003: The Point, Paddington Basin, London
2000–2005: Parramatta Rail Link, Sydney, Australia
2000–ongoing: Greenwich Peninsula Masterplan, London
2001: Manchester University Masterplan, Manchester
2001: Bristol Brewery
2001: London Clinic Masterplan, London
2001–2008: Cambourne Eco Town, Cambridgeshire
2001–ongoing: Isle of Dogs Landscape Strategy, London
2002: London Business School
2002: Biota! National Aquarium, London
2002: Keele University Masterplan, Keele
2002: Founder's Place Masterplan, London
2002–2004: Macintosh Village Masterplan, Manchester
2002–2004: Swiss Cottage Leisure Centre, London
2002–2006: The Green Building, Manchester
2002–ongoing: Newcastle Cultural Quarter Masterplan, Newcastle
2003: Friargate Masterplan, Coventry
2003: Lower Lea Valley, London
2003: St. Barts Hospital, London
2003: Oncology Unit, London Clinic, London
2003–2008: The Great North Museum, Newcastle
2003–2010: Regent's Place Masterplan, London
2004: Dundee University Masterplan, Dundee
2004: Eagle House, Islington, London
2004: Paddington Health Campus, London
2004: Isle of Wight Vision
2004: Northfleet Masterplan
2004: White City Masterplan, London
2004: Whiteness Masterplan, Inverness
2004–2006: Petersham Courtyard Housing, London
2004–2006: Sheraton Hotel Edinburgh
2004–2006: The Home Office Headquarters, London
2004–2007: Ocean Point, Edinburgh
2004–2008: Design Champion for Edinburgh
2004–ongoing: 'Nash Ramblas', London

2005: Bloomsbury Urban Realm Study, London
2005: Pilgrim Street, Newcastle
2005–2005: Eastgate Masterplan, Leeds
2005–2007: Newcastle Quayside Housing, Newcastle
2005–ongoing: Newcastle University Masterplan, Newcastle
2005–ongoing: Thames Estuary Parklands Vision
2005–ongoing: Oxford University Masterplan, Oxford
2006: Brent Cross Cricklewood
2006: East End of Oxford Street Public Realm Study, London
2006: Prescott Lock, London
2006–2009: 6 Mitre Passage, Greenwich Peninsula, London
2006–2009: 14 Pier Walk, Greenwich Peninsula, London
2007–2010: 10 Triton Street, Regent's Place, London
2007–2010: 20 Triton Street, Regent's Place, London
2007–2010: 1 Osnaburgh Street, Regent's Place, London
2007–ongoing: Aire Valley Masterplan, Leeds
2007–ongoing: Bishopsgate Goods Yard Masterplan, London
2007–ongoing: St. Giles Circus Masterplan, London
2008: Marble Arch Initiative, London
2008: Medway: Five Towns Make a City, Kent
2008: Thames Estuary Parklands Core Strategy, HCA
2008: Hoo Peninsula, Medway
2008: Kent County Vision
2008: Littlehampton Seafront Masterplan, Littlehampton
2008–2012: Jordan Housing Amman, Jordan
2008–ongoing: Auckland Vision Auckland, New Zealand
2008–ongoing: North Wharf Gardens, London
2008–ongoing: Residential Building, Islamabad, Pakistan
2008–ongoing: Marylebone Euston Road Study, London
2008–ongoing: Project Skylines London
2009: Wallingford Vision, Wallingford
2009: British Library Strategic Vision, London
2009–2011: Bicester Exemplar Eco Housing, Bicester
2009: Ebury Street Housing
2009–2011: Embassy Gardens Masterplan, Nine Elms, London
2009–ongoing: Folkestone Seafront Masterplan, Folkestone
2009–ongoing: Mount Pleasant Masterplan, London
2009–ongoing: Newcastle Civic Boulevard, Newcastle
2009–ongoing: Bicester Eco Town Masterplan, Bicester
2009–ongoing: Euston Circus Study, London

2009–ongoing: Vision for Peabody Trust, London
2010: Great Maytham Stables, Kent
2010: Tenterden Strategic Vision, Kent
2010: Ebury Bridge Centre
2010: House in the Provence, France
2010: Ashford Design Champion, Ashford
2010: NE Essex Coastal Strategy, UK
2010: Seagrave Road Masterplan, Earl's Court, London
2010: Southend Core Vision, Southend
2010–2011: St Ermin's Hotel, London
2010–ongoing: Laing Art Gallery, Newcastle
2010–ongoing: Amberley Road Centre, London
2010–ongoing: Earl's Court Masterplan, London
2010–ongoing: Gorleston Street Key Worker Housing, London
2010–ongoing: Inmidtown Business District Masterplan, Holborn, London
2010–ongoing: Royal Docks Vision, London
2010–ongoing: St. Ermin's Hotel, London
2011: Wujin Zero Carbon Eco Town, China
2011–ongoing: Heuston Station Masterplan, Dublin, Ireland
2011–ongoing: Leicester University Masterplan, Leicester
2011–ongoing: Nausicaa Aquarium, Boulogne-Sur-Mer, France
2011–ongoing: Newcastle Gateshead Spaces and Places, Newcastle
2011–ongoing: Old Oak Common Transport Superhub, London
2011–ongoing: Ouseburn Housing, Newcastle

Right: Detail of residential and doctor's surgery, Swiss Cottage.

STAFF LIST: HONG KONG, 2001–2011

Amy Au; Heidi Au Yeung, Kevin Begg; Catriona Bertoli; Kira Bester; Erik Brasse; Shawn Bruins; Amanda Byrne; Paul Byrne; John Campbell; Darren Cartlidge; Hilda Chak; Florence Chan; Helen Chan; John Chan; Simon Chan; Alan Chan; Carrie Chan; Dominic Chan; Eric Chan; Margaret Chan; Brian Chantler; Gigi Chao; Kevin Chao; Irene Chong; Erica Choi; Angie Choi; Vincent Choi; Lina Chong; Felix Chow; Sonia Chow; Wendy Chu; George Clarke; Alan Cook; Simon Corbett; Toby Denham; Eugene Dreyer; Kate Edwards; Gavin Erasmus; Jo Farrell; Terry Farrell; Theresa Farrol Goosen; Nicholas Foo; Felix Fung; Fred Fung; Teresa Gonzalez Aguilera; Jonathan Greasby; Rami Hageali; Tolga Han Ozbilen; Herrick Ho; Charles Ho; Voon Hoong Lay; Serge Horta; Vera Hung; Ray Ip; Win Kaaka; Atul Kansara; Rakesh Kapur; Raminder Kaur; Michael Kloihofer; Stefan Krummeck; Eric Kurtzman; Polly Kwai; Xiaohung Lai; Crystal Lam; Katty Lam; Tanni Lam; Winnie Lam; Karen Lau; Victor Lau; Benjamin Lau; Cherie Lau; Jacky Lau; Louis Lau; Molly Law; Roy Law; Jane Lee; Winna Lee; Becky Lee; Elllen Lee; Sharen Lee; Anthony Lee; Belle Lee; Pablo Leppe; Sandy Leung; Felix Li; Wilson Ling; Nicholas Lo; Jacky Lok; Julia Lou; Gary Lui; Connie Luk; Danny Ma; Jessica Ma; Keith Ma; Julie Mackenzie; Richard Mah; Joyce Mak; Arnd Manzewski; Darren Maryon; Anca Matyiku; Laura Mazzeo; Alastair Mehl; Paul Merrick; Ross Milne; Devan Mistry; Simon Moles; Mel Mong; Eve Murzyn; Timothy Narey; Patrick Ng; Terence Ng; Patrick O'Rourke; Daniel Patzold; Ian Perrins; Mel Ping; Elaine Radcliffe; Rabbi Rehman; Melanie Riach; Stephanie Roland; Peter Ross; Malcolm Sage; Wing Sai Tsui; Andrew Shields; Kenton Sin; Joshua Sin; Benny Siu; Bosco So; Cedric Tang; Shiu Tang; Francois Thibaudeau; Davina Thomas; Pearly Tsang; Amy Tsang; Mandy Tsang; Vivien Tsang; Winnie Tsang; Carmen Tse; Sing Tung Li; Dirk U Moench; Markus Vilsmaler; Daniel Voelker; Stella Wan; Connie Wan; Melissa Williams; Matthias Wolff; Carrie Wong; Cathy Wong; Eiffel Wong; Wendy Wong; Carey Wong; Dennis Wong; Enid Wong; Janice Wong; Joey Wong; Larry Wong; Rodney Wong; Sheree Wong; Steve Wong; Jason Woo; Chen Wu; Christopher Yee; Francesca Yeung; Celia Ying; Corris Yip; Jacqueline Yip; Samuel Yip; Patrick Yue; Canny Yuen; John Zastera; YiLun Zhang; Gregoire Zundel.

STAFF LIST: LONDON, 2001–2011

David Abdo; Zoe Adeline; Vil Alexander; Jacob Alsop; Sherin Aminossehe; Craig Appleyard; Celina Auterio Gordo; Florian Baeumler; Simon Baker; Peter Barbalov; Chris Barber; Jessie Barrell; Keith Barrell; Michael Barry; Christopher Bell; Neil Bennett; Nigel Bidwell; Laura Binns; Martin Birgel; Hannah Blunstone; Jeremy Boole; Fatima Bouabdillah; Michele Brackx; Toby Bridge; Jackee Brown; John Campbell; Denise Cannon; Darren Cartlidge; Rui Carvalheiro; Alejandra Celedon; Brian Chantler; Hiten Chavda; Barrie Cheng; James Cheung; Kam Chung; Abigail Clancey-Low; David Cole; Garry Colligan; James Cregan; Jess Crook; Andrew Culpeck; Liliana Dalla Piana; Gennaro D'Alo; Emma Davies; David Davies; Jana De Voss; Tamara Deetman; Guilio Dellatorre; Toby Denham; Gregory Desjardins; Gennaro Di Dato; Dennis Dornan; Eugene Dreyer; David Drummond; Amy Dunn; Chris Dyson; Godfrey Edwards; Jo Evans; Simon Evans; Fang Fang; Max Farrell; Bee Farrell; Terry Farrell; Camilla Finlay; Libertad Fonseca; Steve Foster; Emily French; Marta Garriz; Tom Gent; Michael Gil; Shevaughn Gill; Teresa Gonzales Aguilera; Michal Goras; Dee Graham; Jo Greenoak; Andrew Grethe; Oliver Grimaldi; Russ Hamilton; Anna Hanson; Rory Harmer; Jo Harrop; Matt Holder; Rebecca Holmes; Jonathon Holt; Wayne Hosford; Stuart Houghton; Moz Hussain; Cos Ioannou; Ben James; Karl James; Maggie Jones; Erica Jong; Simon Kaufmann; Sangsoo Kim; Myoungjae Kim; Tom Kimbell; Sandra Kopatz; Doris Lam; Oliver Leech; Malcolm Lerner; John Letherland; James Lewis; Rob Lewis; Natalie Lunt; Layla Majothi; Elizabeth Makinson; Mike Makki; Benoit Marchant; Laura Mark; Giles Martin; Laura Mazzeo; Edel McAleer; Laura McCudden; Brendan McCullough; Tracey-Ann McKoy; Matteo Meliolli; Paulo Mendes; Tiago Mendes; Magnus Menzefricke-Koitz; Jane Merrell; Steve Middleton; Stacey Milburn; Pamela Millar; So Jung Min; Davan Mistry; Graciela Moreno; Michael Morgan; Andres Moroni; Lorraine Mulraney; Gemma Murphy; James Murphy; Catherine Murphy; Eileen Nicholl; Suzanne O'Donovan; Mary Ogden; Dawn Osterbauer; Mark Owen; Sharon Palmer-Dell; Jessica Parsley; Kalpesh Patel; James Patterson; Thierry Ploum; Aidan Potter; Gareth Pywell; Elaine Radcliffe; Nicola Rains; Chris Ravenscroft; Liz Reilly; Duarte Reino; Donna Riddington; Ross Robertson; Madeleine Rohan; Raj Rooprai; Daniel Ross; Jessica Rostron; Brigitte Rothfuss; Michaela Ruffatti; Stefan Rust; Stefania Salvetti; Lauren Sandy; Pablo Sanz Claramunt; Eric Schatz; Margarete Schmid; Michal Scieszka; Akshay Sethi; Mariam Shaham; Damien Sharkey; Natasha Shea; Cherry Sherlock-Tanner; Mark Shirburne-Davies; Roger Simmons; Russell Skelton; Victoria Small; Hannah Smart; Carrie Smith; Steve Smith; Philip Smithies; Jason Speechly-Dick; Stefanos Spyrakis; Sean Stanley; Anna Stefano; Mike Stowell; Doug Streeter; Kristine Sulca; Ida Tam; Joanna Tancrel; Yukiko Tani; Andrei Tarnavcik; Elinor Taylor; Sarah Thomas; Catriona Thompson; Derek Timms; Jane Tobin; Julian Tollast; Timor Tzur; Shaharazad Ujam; Honore Van Rijswijk; Benjamin Viale; David Viljoen; Chris Wade; Duncan Whatmore; Michael Whitwell; Barbara Wilkinson; Rachael Williams; Mark Williams-Jones; Simon Wing; Daniel Woolfson; Jim Yang; Herve Yoo Foo; Bea Young; Gary Young

PICTURE CREDITS

The authors and publisher would like to thank the following for providing images for use in this book. In all cases, every effort has been made to credit the copyright holders, but should there be any omissions or errors the publisher would be pleased to insert the appropriate acknowledgment in any subsequent edition of this book.

FRONT COVER
Zhou Ruogu Architecture Photography

INTRODUCTION
2	Andy Haslam
4	Richard Bryant / Arcaidimages.com
7	John Campbell
8	Top: Zhou Ruogu Architecture Photography; inset: Park Young Chea
9	Kim Jaen Youn
10	Top: Paul Rogers
11	Andy Haslam
13	Andy Haslam
14	Nigel Young
15	Nick Hufton
16	Top: Peter Cook; bottom left: Peter Cook
17	Barry Hermann

BEIJING
24	Top: Jo Farrell; bottom: Hayes Davidson
28–29	Top: Zhou Ruogu Architecture Photography; bottom: Fu Xing Studio
30–31	Top: Fu Xing Studio; bottom left: Fu Xing Studio; bottom right: Zhou Ruogu Architecture Photography
31	Bottom: Zhou Ruogu Architecture Photography
32	Bottom right: Jo Farrell
33	Top: Fu Xing Studio
35	Fu Xing Studio
36	All photos: Fu Xing Studio
37	Top: Charlie Fong; bottom left and right: Fu Xing Studio

SHANGHAI
52	Bottom: Francois Thibaudeau
53	Paul Dingman
55	John Campbell
56	Top left: Paul Dingman; bottom left: Zhou Ruogu Architecture Photography; right: Paul Dingman
57	Paul Dingman
58	Carsten Schael
59	Top: Carsten Schael; bottom: Carsten Schael
62	Bottom row: Zhou Ruogu Architecture Photography

GUANGZHOU
73	Top: Nan Fang Doushi-Liu Photography; bottom: John Campbell
74	Nick Hufton
76	Bottom: Nick Hufton
77	Top: Nick Hufton;

---

	bottom left and right: Nick Hufton; bottom middle: John Campbell
78	Top: Nick Hufton; bottom left: Nick Hufton; bottom right: John Campbell

SHENZHEN
82	Top right: Stuart Woods; bottom: Getty Images
83	Main photo: John Campbell
85	All photos: Carsten Schael
86	All photos: Jo Farrell
87	Top: Peter Mealin; bottom left: Jo Farrell; bottom right: Carsten Schael
88	All photos: globalphotos.org
90	All photos: John Campbell
91	John Campbell
93	Left: Carsten Schael; top right: John Campbell; middle right: Jo Farrell; bottom right: John Campbell
94	Bottom: Bartlomiej / Magierowski
95	All photos: Carsten Schael

HONG KONG
100	Left: Colin Wade
101	Left: Peter Cook; middle: Getty Images
102	Top left: Geocarto International Centre; top right: Bonham Media Ltd; bottom: Aerial photo reproduced with permission of the Director of Lands, © The Government of Hong Kong SAR. License No. 18/20
103	Top: Daniel Wong; middle: MTRC
110	Bottom left: MTR; bottom right: John Campbell
113	All photos: Carsten Schael
116	Bottom: Ove Arup & Partners (HK) Ltd
117	Stuart Wood

LONDON
120–21	Top: Nigel Young; inset (120): Nigel Young
122	Bottom row: Richard Cowan M3 Consulting
124	Bottom row: Andy Haslam
125	Andy Haslam
126	Andy Haslam
127	Andy Haslam
128	Andy Haslam
129	Andy Haslam
130	Dennis Gilbert
131	Middle left: Andy Haslam; right: Dennis Gilbert
132	Bottom: Dennis Gilbert
133	Tim Soar
134	Bottom right: Sean Gallagher
135	Richard Bryant / Arcaidimages.com
137	Richard Bryant / Arcaidimages.com
138	Main photo: Marcus Robinson; two insets: Richard Bryant / Arcaidimages.com
140–41	Visualisation: Hayes Davidson
143	Richard Bryant / Arcaidimages.com
144	Richard Bryant / Arcaidimages.com
146	Top left: Andy Haslam; top right: Andy Haslam; middle left: Andy Haslam; middle right: Andy Haslam;

---

	bottom left: Sanders and Lund; bottom right: Andy Haslam
147	Sanders and Lund
153	Andrew Putler
154	Sean Gallagher
155	Barry Hermann
156	Barry Hermann

THAMES ESTUARY
160	Top: Pipers
161	Peter Young / Fotolibra
165	Right: Andrew Putler
170–71	Andy Haslam
172	Top: Andy Haslam; bottom: John Campbell
173	Andy Haslam
174	Andy Haslam
175	Andy Haslam

LONDON-ON-SEA
181	Bottom: Studio Weave
185	Bottom right: Heatherwick Sudio, photo: Andy Stagg; bottom middle: Studio Weave

MANCHESTER
190	Top and bottom left: Manchester Archives and Local Studies
191	Bottom left and middle: Manchester Archives and Local Studies; top: Peter Cook; bottom right: Peter Cook
198	Peter Cook
199	Daniel Hopkinson; inset: Daniel Hopkinson

HULL
202	Left top and bottom: Hull Maritime Museum
204–5	Richard Bryant / Arcaidimages.com
206	Richard Bryant / Arcaidimages.com
207	Richard Bryant / Arcaidimages.com
208	Richard Bryant / Arcaidimages.com
209	Richard Bryant / Arcaidimages.com
210	Top: Richard Bryant / Arcaidimages.com; bottom left: Tim Soar; bottom right: Richard Bryant / Arcaidimages.com
211	Richard Bryant / Arcaidimages.com

NEWCASTLE
221	Top left: Newcastle Tourist Board; top middle: David Churchill; bottom left: Graeme Peacock, courtesy of Wilkinson Eyre Architects; bottom middle: David Churchill
228	Top: Andy Haslam; bottom: Andy Haslam
229	Andy Haslam
230	Top left: Steve Mayes; top right: Andy Haslam; bottom left: Steve Mayes
231	Andy Haslam
232	Top: Andy Haslam; bottom: Andy Haslam

EDINBURGH
239	Top left: Graeme Duncan; Top right: Tim Soar;

---

	bottom: Nigel Young
244	Richard Bryant / Arcaidimages.com
245	Richard Bryant / Arcaidimages.com

NEW ZEALAND & AUSTRALIA
257	Top and bottom: Greg Hocking
258	Left: Andrew Putler; right: Andrew Putler

SEOUL
264	Bottom left: Spot Image / Science Photo Library; bottom right: Getty Images
265	Kim Jaen Youn
267	Bottom row: Kim Jaen Youn
268	Left: Park Young Chea; middle: Kim Jaen Youn; right: Park Young Chea
269	Park Young Chea
270	Park Young Chea

PHNOM PENH
278	Bottom: Jo Farrell
280	Top: Vattanac Capital; bottom: John Campbell
283	Drawings top row: Adrian L Norman Ltd

SINGAPORE
286	Bottom: Felix Li
288	All photos: Tim Nolan
289	Top: John Campbell; bottom: Tim Nolan

SOUTH AFRICA
308	Bottom: Alastiar Mehl
309	Top: Gautrain Image Gallery; bottom left: Getty Images; bottom right: Getty Images
310	All photos: Gautrain Image Gallery
311	Top left: Gautrain Image Gallery; top right: Gavin Erasmus
312	All photos: Gautrain Image Gallery
313	All photos: Gautrain Image Gallery

END MATTER
315	Zhou Ruogu Architecture Photography
317	Richard Bryant / Arcaidimages.com
319	Andy Haslam

BACK COVER
Richard Bryant / Arcaidimages.com